Building Arguments

DREW E. HINDERER
Saginaw Valley State University

WADSWORTH PUBLISHING COMPANY
Belmont, California
A Division of Wadsworth, Inc.

Philosophy Editor: Ken King
Editorial Assistant: Cynthia Campbell
Production Editor: Karen Garrison
Designer: Andrew H. Ogus
Print Buyer: Karen Hunt
Permissions Editor: Robert Kauser
Copy Editor: Margaret Moore
Cover: Andrew H. Ogus
Signing Representative: Thor McMillen
Compositor: T·H Typecast, Inc.
Printer: Malloy Lithographing, Inc.

This book is printed on acid-free paper that meets Environmental Protection
Agency standards for recycled paper.

12345678910 — 95 94 93 92 91

Library of Congress Cataloging in Publication Data
Hinderer, Drew E.,
      Building arguments / Drew E. Hinderer.
         p.   cm.
      Includes index.
      ISBN 0-534-16158-8
      1. English language — Rhetoric.   2. Persuasion (Rhetoric)
   I. Title.
   PE1431.H5   1991
      808'.042 — dc20   91-11301
   ISBN 0-534-16158-8

Contents

3

USE ARGUMENTS WHEN THEY ARE NEEDED   *30*

4

USE RELIABLE ARGUMENT FORMS   *43*

5

DEFINE KEY WORDS CAREFULLY 60

6

MAKE REASONS RELEVANT 73

7

MAKE RELIABLE ASSUMPTIONS *91*

8

MAKE YOUR POINT CLEAR *107*

9

PROVE YOUR POINT   126

10

WRITE ARGUMENTS PERSUASIVELY   142

13

CRITICIZE ARGUMENTS FAIRLY *188*

14

WRITE CRITICISMS EFFECTIVELY   207

15

MORE CONTROVERSIAL ARGUMENTS   226

Preface

Over the past fifteen years of teaching informal logic, I have become increasingly uncomfortable with the exclusively critical emphasis of the many texts I have used. Instead of leaving my courses more open minded, less rigid, and better able to argue persuasively for what they think is true, most of my students had learned what the books and I had taught them: how to spot and identify errors in reasoning and how to label them. At the same time, even as my university was seeking to implement writing across the curriculum requirements, many of my students remained unable to see the connection between reasoning and writing, and sought to avoid courses that would expose their writing deficiencies. Again, the informal logic texts I had used permitted them to do this.

Accordingly, I have written *Building Arguments,* which emphasizes developing the abilities involved in arguing for one's own point of view, as well as the abilities involved in critiquing the ideas of others. It also emphasizes the importance of integrating reasoning and writing, and includes writing assignments which, while not onerous either for students to write or for faculty to read, are useful for deepening students' linguistic and reasoning skills. Finally, I have tried to address the interests of the changing student audience that takes informal logic: a mix of traditional and nontraditional students whose academic preparation, motivation, and concerns vary widely.

The result, I hope, is a rigorous yet accessible philosophically based text that is sensitive to rhetorical issues and the importance of writing in reasoning. The chapters are simple and straightforward, especially in the beginning. They are written in a deliberately accessible style that becomes more sophisticated as the book progresses. Examples and exercises are intended to be appealing and relevant. Traditional philosophical material and other issues of increasing complexity are introduced gradually, as students' reasoning, reading, and writing skills mature.

Building Arguments is set up for one chapter per week for a fifteen-week semester, with more difficult or time-consuming assignments separated by less difficult and time-consuming ones. Instructors who wish to change the order of the chapters—especially those who think critical skills should be developed before persuasive skills—should feel free to do so. While there are references to earlier chapters in later ones, I have tried to keep the chapters fairly independent of each other. If a topic needs to be omitted to fit a different curricular pattern, I suggest consolidating Chapters 1 and 2. Another alternative, for those who do not think an informal logic course requires an introduction to symbolic logic or a discussion of valid and invalid argument forms, is to omit Chapter 4.

While *Building Arguments* is intended primarily for teachers of lower-division informal logic courses, it has also been used successfully by teachers of persuasive writing and English composition, especially when supplemented by prewriting work and more extended writing assignments.

I am deeply indebted to many people for their assistance as I have worked on this book. The following reviewers made helpful comments and suggestions: Dan Baker, Ocean County College; Phyllis Berger, Diablo Valley College; John Furlong, Transylvania University; James Gustafson, Northern Essex Community College; Marion Lanham, Harford Community College; and Craig Walton, University of Nevada, Las Vegas.

I hope *Building Arguments* proves to be useful for students and faculty. More than that, I hope it helps make what can sometimes be a difficult teaching and learning experience a more enjoyable one.

Drew Hinderer
Saginaw Valley State University

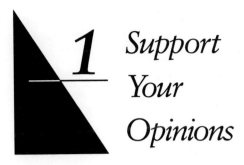

1 Support Your Opinions

To get started in logic, you need to understand why giving reasons for your opinions is important and how giving reasons for your opinions is different from explaining what your opinions are. This chapter is about giving and using reasons in your thinking and writing. We'll look at what reasons are, what they're used for, when they're needed, and how they work. Then we'll look at some things that may appear to be reasons, but aren't. And we'll see how reasoning can help you organize information and make sense of it.

OPINIONS, BELIEFS, AND REASONS

Different people have different **opinions,** especially when they're talking about their values and individual attitudes about things. Sometimes it's not too important to try to get people to agree. But sometimes it's very important, where tax money, the government, or society in general are concerned, for example. When it is important to get people to agree, we need to do more than just say what our ideas are. We need to give good reasons why other people should think our ideas are right and why they should agree with us. Learning how to do this well is one of the goals of this course.

Logic, the study and practice of reasoning, has other uses besides convincing people to agree with our opinions. Sometimes it's hard to figure out what to believe when we're given a lot of confusing information. One of the goals of logic is to help you organize information to see how it connects, or what it adds up to. And sometimes people want to know why we think what we do, meaning what reasons we have for our opinions. Another goal of logic is to help you explain why you think what you do in a way that people will respect. We'll work on all three of these goals of logic in this chapter.

First, what are reasons? **Reasons** are statements you give or think of in order to get people to believe something. They usually supply **evidence**—factual support or proof—to show that your opinion is worth taking seriously. **Reasoning** is seeing connections between evidence or information, so that if you believe the reasons are good ones, you should be willing to go along with what they point to. But it's often easier to understand about reasons and reasoning from examples. So here are some examples.

Imagine that Central College's student government is trying to decide whether to add $10 to the activities fee that all students have to pay along with their tuition. The $10 would go to support a day-care center for children of students at the college while the children's parents are in class. Arlene, who is a single mother with a three-year-old daughter and who's trying to put herself through school, thinks adding the $10 fee would be a good idea. Carlos, who is also working his way through school but hasn't any children, doesn't agree. They might say something like this:

> *Arlene:* **I think the $10 fee is a good idea. I can't afford to pay for day care for my daughter because books and tuition and everything else just eat up all my money. If she could be at the college's daycare center, I wouldn't have to worry about**

her while I'm in class and I could focus on my work better. Let's go for it.

Carlos: Hey, not so fast. You might want free day care, but other students have money problems too. Why should they have to chip in $10 so people with kids won't have to pay for their own day care? Ten dollars doesn't sound like much, but sometimes it's more than I've got. I don't think we should add on the fee.

In this situation, Arlene and Carlos have different **beliefs** — opinions based on some kind of support — about whether or not the $10 fee should be added to support the college daycare center. Arlene's belief is expressed in the first sentence when she says, "I think the $10 fee is a good idea." The rest of what she says are reasons for adding the fee. That is, when Arlene says that she doesn't have the money to pay for day care herself and that she could focus on her work better if her daughter were in day care, she's trying to get Carlos and the rest of the student government to agree with her that adding the fee is a good idea. And it's the fact that she has these reasons to support her viewpoint that makes it a belief, not just a personal feeling or opinion.

Carlos's belief, stated in his last sentence, is that the $10 fee should not be added to the bill for student activities. He too gives reasons for his belief. But Carlos's reasons are not stated as clearly as Arlene's. That is, to understand what Carlos is really saying, you'll have to think about what's happening in the situation, rather than reading his words literally. First, he's saying that other students besides Arlene have money problems and implying that Arlene's problem about day care might not be all that important compared to the problems other students have. Then he's saying that students who don't have kids shouldn't have to pay $10 toward day care for students who do have kids. (He's doing that in the question "Why should they have to chip in $10 so people with kids won't have to pay for their own day care?") And finally, he's saying that even though $10 doesn't seem like much, it's sometimes more than he can afford.

Now, you might agree with Arlene, or you might agree with Carlos. That's not what we need to worry about right now. The point is, if you're **rational,** who you agree with should be influenced by what their reasons are. If you agree with Arlene's reasons, you should be more likely to agree with her belief that adding the fee would be a good idea. But if you agree more with Carlos's reasons, you should be more likely to agree with his belief that adding the fee would not be a good idea. Also, if you're rational, the stronger the reasons are the more strongly you should agree with the belief they support.

One thing that might make Arlene's reasons seem somewhat weak is that it looks as if she's thinking only of herself and her daughter. This is probably the point Carlos is trying to make when he says that other people besides Arlene have money problems and why should students who don't have children pay for day care for those who do. By understanding where Carlos is coming from, Arlene can give reasons that will be more convincing to people like Carlos. So the reasons she might give in reply to Carlos might involve explaining why day care isn't just her problem—that it's a problem every student should care about and get involved in solving.

But suppose Arlene feels hurt and replies to Carlos this way:

> **You're only saying that because you're totally selfish. You don't have kids yourself, so you don't care about people who do. You don't understand how hard it is to deal with a job and school and kids all at the same time. I'm saying we need this fee because we need free day care. The problem here is that you just don't understand.**

It's easy to see why Arlene might feel this way. But you can tell that what she's saying here is not going to convince Carlos she's right. That's because instead of giving him reasons why adding the fee would be a good idea, she's attacking him personally by saying that he's "totally selfish" and that he doesn't care about anything that doesn't affect him directly. She's also saying that he doesn't understand how much she needs free day care. But that's not why Carlos doesn't agree with her. Carlos might understand very well how much Arlene needs free day care for her daughter and still think that he shouldn't have to pay $10 to make sure she gets it.

ARGUING VERSUS EXPRESSING AND EXPLAINING OPINIONS

The moral of this story is that support for our beliefs is more successful when it is made up of good evidence and reasons than when it is only personal opinions and feelings. This, and other factors that make reasons effective, will be discussed further in later chapters of this book. For now, let's suppose Arlene asked Carlos, "Why do you think people without children shouldn't help support daycare services for people who do have children?" That is, suppose she asked Carlos to give reasons for his belief. He might reply in any of several ways.

Carlos might say:

I just don't think they should have to.

Notice, though, that this is not a reason *why* other students shouldn't help support daycare services. Rather, it just expresses Carlos's opinion in a slightly different way. Or he might say:

It's wrong to ask students who don't use daycare services to help pay for them.

But, again, this sentence doesn't supply any new evidence or reason that students who don't have children shouldn't help pay for day care. By saying "it's wrong," Carlos is once again expressing his opinion in a slightly different way. The same thing goes for all of the following replies he might make.

It wouldn't be fair to ask students who don't have children to help pay for day care.

Daycare services should be paid for by the people who use them.

There's no free lunch. Nobody should get services they don't pay for.

There's no reason I should have to pay for someone else's kids.

That is, every one of these replies only expresses Carlos's point of view in slightly different ways. None of them provides Arlene with a reason why she should agree with Carlos.

Sometimes even a long and complicated reply turns out not to offer much in the way of reasons either. If Arlene asked Carlos why he thinks the fee is a bad idea, he might say this:

Well, Arlene, I'm not sure you really understand what I'm saying. When I say that other people have money problems too, I mean that the cost of tuition, books, transportation — you name it — keeps going up. We all have money problems, and we just have to face them. I'm not saying you don't need day care. I'm

just saying we shouldn't tack on another $10 to the student activities fee.

But if you look carefully at this reply, you'll see that Carlos is explaining what he means, explaining what his opinion is, but still not giving any reasons to support it. Instead of giving reasons why people with children should pay for the full cost of day care, or proving that most students can't afford to pay $10 toward day care, Carlos is just repeating what he said in the first place but doing it in a more thorough way. The problem is not that Arlene doesn't understand what Carlos is saying. Rather, the problem is that she thinks what Carlos is saying is wrong.

This is a very important point. There's a difference between explaining and giving reasons. When you explain something, your purpose is to help people understand your point. When you give reasons for your belief, your purpose is to get people to accept your point. You sometimes hear people say, "I don't think you are really hearing what I'm saying" or "I'm not sure you really understand," when they mean "You should agree with me." But understanding what someone is saying and believing that person is right are two different things.

Sometimes, the better you understand what someone is saying, the more likely you are to agree with him. But sometimes, the better you understand the less likely you are to agree. For example, the better you understand what Hitler was saying the less likely you are to think he was right. It is important to make sure people understand what you think—this is the function of a good explanation. But it's also important to make sure they have reasons to agree with what you think. And this is the function of giving reasons. They are two different jobs.

Sometimes on exams you will run into a situation like the one where Arlene is asking Carlos to give her some reasons. You will see that the professor asks you not only to answer a question but also to "discuss" or "justify" or "defend" or "argue for" your answer. All of these terms mean basically the same thing on a test. What the professor is asking you to do is to give reasons for your answer. He's not just asking you to tell him what your answer is in a more complicated or complete way. And he's not asking you to tell him how you came to think what you do. He's asking you to tell him why he should agree with your answer.

Suppose that you are writing a paper on the topic "Why people should prefer living in a free society." And suppose the assignment says to "argue for your point of view." You might think of a society in which there is a lot of freedom, such as the United States or Canada, and compare it with another kind of society—China, for example. You might then list a lot of ways in which American or Canadian life is better than life in China—you have less fear, more opportunity, a higher standard of living, and so on. Giving a list like this is part of what the professor will want, but only part. Next, you'll need to give reasons why these advantages are important and why they outweigh any advantages of living in China. The reasons you give should provide evidence or proof.

Here are some answers that would do fine as reasons.

1. Life in free societies offers people far more opportunities than people in more repressive societies have. For example, in China, people do not have the right to leave the country without special permission, and they do not have the right to worship as they please. And they are sometimes subject to brutal personal attacks, such as the ones in Tienanmen Square. Rights and personal security are very important to people because without them, they do not feel they are in control of their own lives. So free societies are preferable in these ways.

2. In spite of what the Chinese are trying to do by opening up their market, their standard of living is not as high as the standard of living is for most citizens of free societies. Where business is not free, the supply of food, housing, and other goods is much less than what is available in most free market economies. Because a good supply of food, shelter, and other goods is important to most people, and freedom seems to promote this, free societies are preferable.

But the next three answers would *not* count as reasons to support your belief:

3. I think freedom is better than life in China because I was raised here. If I had been born in China, I'd probably think living there is better.

4. Everything I've ever heard about China is bad.

5. I, personally, would not want to give up my freedom, because I like being able to do what I want.

What makes the first two answers good ones is that they include reasons and point out how the reasons support the main idea. The problem with the next three replies is that they tell us something about the speaker—where she has lived, what she has heard, how she feels—but they don't tell us why her beliefs are reasonable. The third answer tells us how the speaker came to think freedom is better, but it doesn't give any reason why it actually is. That is, it doesn't give any reason why freedom is important. The fourth answer tells us something about what the speaker has heard, but it doesn't show that what she has heard about China is true. And the last answer expresses her personal opinion, but it doesn't give reasons to think her opinion has anything to support it.

The problem with these three bad answers is that they're just like Carlos's response to Arlene in the earlier example. That is, they just restate or explain what his belief is rather than offering support for his belief. When someone asks you to "discuss" or "defend" or "justify" or "argue for" your answer, then, be sure you give reasons. And more generally, if you want to do well on exams or assignments, it's very important to understand the question and do exactly what it asks you to do. If you don't understand the question or you're not sure how to answer it, ask the professor to explain it to you.

So far, we've covered three important points about reasons. One is that reasons provide evidence or other support for a belief. The second is that repeating what you think or explaining your ideas further is not the same thing as giving reasons. And the third is that when you're asked to "defend" your answer or belief, you're being asked to give reasons why people ought to agree with you, rather than to give an explanation of how you acquired the opinions you have. Remember, the purpose of giving reasons is to try to get someone to agree with you or accept your point. But the purpose of explaining or restating something is to get people to understand what you think. Both are important, but they're not the same.

REASONING AS SEEING CONNECTIONS AMONG IDEAS

Although there's a lot more to say about reasons, we'll save most of it until later. Right now, let's turn to the other purpose of reasoning: seeing connections among pieces of information. Let's go back to Arlene's need for day care for her daughter and the question of whether or not the student government should add $10 to the activities fee to support a daycare center. To make a good case for her point of view, Arlene will have to come up with convincing reasons. To do that, she not only will need to understand what a reason is and how it works. She will also need to see how the information interrelates so she can decide what to say. Here are ten pieces of information.

1. Arlene's daughter's name is Felicia.

2. If Felicia is left alone for more than about five minutes, she often gets into trouble.

3. Arlene is depressed and angry that people like Carlos can't seem to understand how difficult her problems with Felicia are to deal with.

4. Felicia's favorite activity is having someone read to her.

5. Felicia's favorite color is blue.

6. Twenty-three percent of Central College students have children between the ages of three and five.

7. Children who get into day care do much better in school later on than children who are cared for at home by a parent.

8. Almost all of the Central College students who have children cannot afford private day care, and most feel they cannot do their best schoolwork having to care for their children full time as well.

9. The student government funds only programs that benefit at least 10 percent of Central College's students.

10. Although only 5 percent of students with children used the gym, the student government recently added a $10 recreational activities fee for all students to keep the gym open more hours.

Now, as a first step in deciding what information to bring up to support her beliefs, Arlene will need to organize all of this information and see how it interrelates. Because she's interested in showing that the student government ought to add a $10 fee, the connections she'll need to look for have to relate to the fee. So the fact that the first five pieces of information all mention Felicia by name is probably not a connection that will matter much. Arlene should be looking for connections that add up to funding day care.

Probably the best way to begin is for Arlene to see that there's probably a connection between her situation with Felicia and the situation of other students. Carlos, remember, implied that Arlene is thinking only about herself. But information mentioned in #6—that 23 percent of the other students also have children—and #8—that they can't afford private day care either—shows it's not just Arlene's problem. Number 8 also says that, like Arlene, other students don't feel they can do their best schoolwork without being able to put their children in day care. Now, when she sees these connections, Arlene will realize that her problem is not unique—it's shared by 23 percent of the other students. So Arlene's concerns probably will be shared by the other 23 percent of students with children too.

Once she's seen this connection, Arlene might go on to another one. That is, because (#2) Felicia gets into trouble when left alone and (#4) she enjoys having people read to her, it's likely that other children like Felicia might get into trouble when left alone and might enjoy being read to. Besides, (#7) if other children who have been in day care do better in school later on, then it's likely that Felicia will too. The connection Arlene has seen is that Felicia is like other children in these respects and that other children are like Felicia. So what's good for Felicia should be good for the other children too.

Now, what's the connection between these ideas and getting the student government to add on the fee? Well, #9 says that at least 10 percent of students have to benefit from something before it will be funded. But now we know that 23 percent of students and their children, including Arlene and Felicia, would benefit from funding day care. So we know that there is more than the minimum number of students needed for funding. But does that mean the student government should add on the fee? Number 9 doesn't say that if 10 percent of students benefit, the program will definitely be funded. It says only that the program *won't* be funded if less than 10 percent benefit.

But #10 says the student government has put a $10 fee into place to support the gym, even though only 5 percent of students with children use it. That means very few students with children benefit from the $10 gym fee. Wouldn't it be fair to fund some services that students with children would benefit from? What Arlene needs to see is the connection between funding for programs that benefit students who don't have children and the idea of funding day care, a program that will benefit students who do have children. And once she's seen all of these connections, she's in a position to give some convincing reasons for adding on the $10 fee.

Here are Arlene's reasons: (1) At least 23 percent of Central College students and their children could benefit from the $10 day-care fee. This is because (2) the children will not get into trouble, (3) will enjoy being read to, and (4) will do better in school later on. Besides, (5) their parents, most of whom can't afford private day care, will be able to put more of their energy into their own academic work. (6) Because 23 percent can benefit, there is a large enough number of students involved to justify funding. (7) And because students with children don't benefit from some other programs they help pay for, it seems fair to ask for funds from all students to support a daycare program. And all that adds up to a pretty good group of reasons.

But several pieces of information were not included in this connected list of reasons. Among these are that Arlene's daughter's name is Felicia (#1), that Arlene is angry and depressed about not being understood (#3), and that Felicia's favorite color is blue (#5). They were not included because they don't provide evidence that day care should be funded by all students. Even if her name is Felicia, that doesn't mean the student government ought to OK the funding. And the fact that Felicia's favorite color is blue doesn't seem as important as that she enjoys being read to and that other children probably do too. This is because being read to probably helps children do better in school later on, whereas their ideas about color don't seem to matter.

Finally, the fact that Arlene is angry and depressed about how a lot of people don't seem to understand or care about her problems probably won't help persuade people to contribute their $10 for day care. It's too bad that she's angry and depressed. But she needs to show that there's a connection between how she feels and what the student government should do. And it's not obvious what connection there is. So she's probably better off showing that it would be fair for all students to fund day care for students with children than to rely on people feeling sorry about how she feels.

What we've seen in this section is an example of how important it is to see connections between pieces of information. Some of these connections will help you find reasons when you need them, and some will help you leave out things that won't help. Of course, we'll be looking at connections again, especially in Chapter 4. Meanwhile, remember that ideas usually don't just stand by themselves. Look for how they interrelate—you'll be off to a good start in logic.

SUMMARY

The most important ideas in this chapter involve reasons and reasoning. These are both different from expressing an opinion, which is telling people what you think or how you feel, or explaining something, which is helping people understand what you think through examples or illustrations. Reasoning is seeing connections between different pieces of information. Giving reasons is offering evidence or support to get someone to agree with your belief. Reasoning also means seeing connections among pieces of information. Putting information together in relations of evidence or support — and leaving out personal feelings and unrelated ideas — can help you convince others of your beliefs.

EXERCISE I

For each of the passages below, decide whether or not reasons are given for the ideas expressed. If so, identify them. If not, explain what's going on in the passage instead. (Is it an explanation? Does it just restate an opinion another way?)

1. Tuition at this school is too high.

2. Tuition at this school is too high, because over 85 percent of the students have to take out loans to pay it.

3. Tuition at this school is higher than at a lot of other schools. Besides, there's too little financial aid. (Hint: What is the relation between these two sentences?)

4. Tuition here is higher than at a lot of other schools. It's higher than at Delta College, Mott Community College, Grand Rapids Junior College, and at least eight other schools I can think of. (Hints: What's the conclusion here? What sort of evidence would be useful in proving it?)

5. Tuition here could be lowered if less money were spent on costly, low enrollment, academic programs. Too much money is wasted on some sports, too. (Hint: Does the second sentence help prove the first?)

6. Instead of raising tuition, the administration should get more support from other sources. The legislature, alumni, and grant

agencies are all possibilities. (Hint: Are the other sources mentioned in the second sentence examples, or do they show that
the administration should get money from them?)

7. Instead of raising tuition, the administration should get more
support from other sources. Many students have difficulty
financing their educations as it is, and those who have to take
jobs often don't do as well in their classes. (Hint: Does the
second sentence offer reasons why support should come from
sources other than students?)

8. The administration has an obligation to serve all of the students in this area, not just the ones who have a lot of money.
If tuition is increased, more and more students will not be
able to afford to continue attending college. That's why tuition shouldn't be raised again. (Hint: What's the conclusion
here?)

9. The administration thinks that just because a lot of students
have nice clothes, or drive good cars, they have a lot of extra
money to spend on tuition. But they're wrong. Just because
you have a nice car or some decent clothes doesn't mean
you've got extra cash. (Hint: Do the first and last sentences
really say different things?)

10. Students who have nice cars and decent clothes don't have a
lot of spare cash for tuition. They've already spent it on cars
and clothes!

EXERCISE II

Suppose you're trying to prove that the library isn't meeting students'
needs. Here are ten pieces of information. Tell which of them might
connect with that conclusion, and explain how they might be used to
help prove it.

1. The library is open only two nights each week.

2. The library was closed during the Christmas break while the
campus was closed.

3. Over the past five years, the college has added majors in criminal justice and information services.

4. Also over the past five years, the number of courses requiring research papers has increased by 40 percent.

5. Due to financial problems, only $600 has been spent on new library materials in each of the past five years.

6. All new programs require research papers.

7. About 33 percent of students take evening classes because they work during the day.

8. The library's collection is between 20 percent and 40 percent smaller than the collections at the other colleges in the same conference.

9. The head librarian has a reserved parking spot just outside the library's back door.

10. It costs about $500 to subscribe to the most important professional journals in information services and about $400 to subscribe to those in criminal justice.

EXERCISE III

Using the information you've worked on in Exercise II, write a one- or two-paragraph letter to the college president, giving reasons why the library budget should be increased.

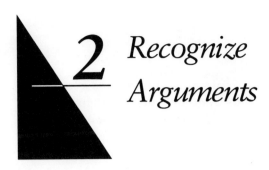

2 *Recognize Arguments*

As we've seen, logic concerns arguments, and the first step in developing the skills involved in logic is becoming able to identify arguments and distinguish them from other uses of language. We'll look at some examples of arguments and also at some ways of influencing people that don't involve arguments. Then we'll talk about how to decide in difficult cases whether or not to count something as an argument.

ARGUMENT DEFINED

The term *argument* has a special meaning in logic, and it has little to do with disagreements. In logic, the term **argument** means *at least one reason offered to influence a person's belief about something.* Some arguments are more convincing than others, depending on how well their reasons support their conclusions. Here are four examples of arguments:

1. If Anne watches "General Hospital" instead of going to her chemistry class, she will flunk chemistry. So if she doesn't want to flunk, she'd better not watch "General Hospital."

2. The last three guys from Phi Tau Nu I went out with were losers. So I have no interest in going out with guys from that fraternity.

3. No one has ever proved that the people who see alien space-craft are wrong. So aliens have probably visited the earth.

4. For something to be a truly worthwhile goal in life it must be good for its own sake and possible to achieve on your own. Money isn't good for its own sake, and fame depends on the attitudes of other people. So neither money nor fame is a worthwhile goal.

In the first argument, the goal is to support the idea that if Anne doesn't want to flunk chemistry, she'd better not watch a soap instead of going to class. "If she doesn't want to flunk, she'd better not watch 'General Hospital'" is the argument's **conclusion.** The other sentence is a **reason** (also called a **premise**), which offers evidence or support to influence your belief. If we assume that the information given in the reason is **true**—that it corresponds with the facts—it should increase the likelihood that you will believe the conclusion.[1] This is because the reason is relevant to the conclusion and sufficient to prove it (always assuming it's true). So the first argument is also a good argument, in the sense that it ought to persuade a rational person.

In the second argument, the conclusion is "I have no interest in going out with guys from that fraternity [Phi Tau Nu]." The reason is

---

1. Some teachers of logic prefer to describe reasons as "cogent" rather than "true" because it's the statement or proposition a reason expresses that is true or false.

that the last three guys the speaker went out with were losers. In this case, the speaker is reasoning that her experience with other fraternity guys will be the same as that with the last three. She's offering evidence — her past experience — to support her conclusion. But this might not be enough to prove her conclusion. After all, Phi Tau Nu might include some winners as members. So there's room for some doubt.

In the third argument, there is even more room for doubt. The conclusion, that "aliens have probably visited the earth," is not proved by the reason, "No one has ever proved that people who see alien spacecraft are wrong," even if we assume that the reason is true. That is because it's their job to prove that they actually have seen alien spacecraft. Even if no one has proved alien spacecraft reports are all untrue, that may mean only that the evidence is so doubtful we can't prove anything one way or another. So this argument should not convince a reasonable person. But that doesn't mean it's not an argument. It's just not a good argument.

But in the fourth argument, "Neither money nor fame is a worthwhile goal" should be convincing, assuming that the reasons are true. Of course, everything depends on whether or not these reasons are true, especially the first one, "For something to be a truly worthwhile goal in life it must be good for its own sake and possible to achieve on your own." (Money is useful only to the extent that it lets you get something else that you want, and fame does depend on others, so neither of those reasons seems especially controversial.) So deciding whether or not this fourth argument is reasonably convincing boils down to understanding the reasons and determining whether you think they're true.

VALIDITY, INVALIDITY, AND SOUNDNESS

Whenever an argument is like this fourth one in that how convincing it is depends only on whether or not the reasons are true, the argument is called **valid**. Valid arguments cannot have true reasons and a false conclusion.[2] So if you want to object to the conclusion of a valid argument, you'll need to show that the reasons are not trustworthy. **Invalid** arguments, like the alien spacecraft example, don't

---

2. This definition refers to valid *deductive* arguments, a form of argument that will be discussed in Chapter 4.

prove their conclusions even if their reasons are true. That is, they can have true reasons and a false conclusion. So if you want to object to an invalid argument, you can do it by pointing out how the conclusion isn't proved by the reasons, regardless of whether the reasons are true. Bear in mind, though, that invalid arguments are still arguments. Finally, arguments that are both valid and have only true reasons are called **sound**. If an argument is sound, a rational person will believe its conclusion. If you object to a sound argument's conclusion, and you know the argument is sound, you're being irrational!

When an argument is like the dating example in providing some evidence — but not necessarily completely convincing evidence — to support a conclusion, it is usual to talk about its being relatively strong or weak, rather than valid or invalid. The more relevant, reliable evidence there is for a conclusion the stronger the argument is. But if there is good evidence to support the other side, or if the evidence offered is unreliable, the argument is weak.

So arguments differ from other uses of language — expressing an opinion, informing people, explaining — in that they are offered in order to influence someone's belief, whether or not they actually succeed. The essential difference between arguments and other uses of language, then, is their purpose. In Chapter 3, we will talk about some other uses of language that differ from argument.

However, arguments are not the only ways to influence someone's beliefs. For example, I might hypnotize you and plant the belief that aliens have infiltrated the Pentagon. I might get you to believe you're fat and ugly by just repeating it often enough. Or, by threatening to harm your children, I might get you to believe you'd better pay off your gambling debts. But these are not arguments. The first two are forms of **manipulation** — using psychological tricks to induce belief. The last is an example of **coercion** — using force or pressure to induce people to believe or do something.

DISTINGUISHING BETWEEN ARGUMENTS AND OTHER PERSUASIVE STRATEGIES

The difference between arguments and other persuasive strategies is that in the case of arguments, the persuasion is accomplished, at least in part, by offering reasons. How does reasoning work? **Reasoning** is the experience of seeing supporting or evidential connections between ideas and adjusting one's beliefs on the basis of those connections. Sometimes this "understanding" or "seeing connections" is described in terms borrowed from motion, as in "moving" or "passing" from one idea to another. Sometimes it's described in terms of building, as in one idea being the "support for" or "foundation of" another. What is important is that in arguments more than one idea is involved, and there must be a connection between them so that one of them, the reason, if it's true, makes the other one, the conclusion, more worth believing.

Here is another example.

In 1989, the Detroit Pistons had the best regular season record in the NBA.

This sentence, though true, is not an argument, because no reason is given to prove it. On the other hand, the following is an argument:

Dennis Rodman was the most valuable player on the '89 Detroit Pistons because of his great defensive performances.

The conclusion is the first part of the sentence, and the reason is the clause beginning with "because." Of course, the conclusion expresses someone's belief, which is often true of the conclusions of arguments. But it's not just a personal opinion or feeling, because he's giving reasons. The speaker is relying on the connection between the value of a basketball player and defensive performance to influence people's belief in favor of Rodman.

Here are two examples you might find in an economics class:

1. Trade and budget deficits continue to dominate the economic news. In spite of the weak dollar against the Japanese yen, the trade deficit between the United States and Japan remains high. Continuing deficits have proved troublesome to U.S. policy makers. Many in Congress have called for heavy tariffs or other sanctions against Japan.

2. While trade and budget deficits continue to plague the American economy, the imposition of tariffs is unwise in the long run. Tariffs generate economic inefficiencies and slower long-term growth, while threatening serious political problems.

The first example does not contain reasoning; the second does. In #1, although much information is presented, each main idea is stated

Figure 2.1

without any support and without showing any supporting connection among the ideas. In the second example, however, the judgment that "the imposition of tariffs is unwise in the long run" depends on the reasons that "tariffs generate economic inefficiencies and slower long-term growth" and also "threaten serious political problems." Pointing out the bad effects of tariffs gives us a reason to believe that imposing them would be unwise.

The Blackhurst Realtors ad in Figure 2.1 is another example of argument. In fact, it gives a whole series of reasons for the conclusion that people interested in a "home in [their] future" (that is, in buying or renting a home) should contact Blackhurst. Starting at the top and going clockwise, the reasons cited by this ad include that Blackhurst can help potential buyers find mortages, can match home builders with customers interested in new houses, can help renters and landlords rent their properties, can assist customers moving to a distant

BEAUTIFUL REMODELED HOME on a large
lot out of the city. Features a new bath, new
paint, newer roof, all kitchen appliances,
wood stove, and a garage. $42,900.   **Figure 2.2**

state to find realtors there, are experienced working with people
transferring to this area, and can show any home on the market. In
addition, the ad assures customers that "personal service is our spe-
cialty" and that Blackhurst is committed to equal housing opportunities. Of course, it is possible that other realtors in the area can do
these things too. But this ad does effectively present reasons to choose
Blackhurst, offering arguments instead of empty slogans.

INTERPRETING ARGUMENTS IN CONTEXT

Not all arguments are as clear as this Blackhurst Realtors ad. Here
are some more difficult examples, also concerning real estate, taken
from a brochure called "Real Estate Today."

Consider the ad in Figure 2.2. As it stands, it appears to be nothing more than a description, which by itself is not an argument. But
if you remember that it appears in a brochure listing real estate for
sale, it is a reasonable assumption that those likely to read "Real
Estate Today" are potential buyers, so that the purpose of the ad is to
offer reasons to buy this house.

This brings up two important points about arguments. The first is
that context is very important in deciding whether or not a passage
should be treated as an argument. The second is that although arguments generally require a reason that is actually stated, a passage in
which the conclusion is strongly implied but not stated may still
function as an argument. (In fact, the Blackhurst Realtors example
we considered earlier was like this, in that the conclusion—that people interested in a "home in [their] future" should contact Blackhurst
—was not fully stated.) These complications require you to exercise
careful judgment about what the main purpose of a passage really is.

The example in Figure 2.3, however, requires that the reader bring
too much information to the ad for it to constitute an argument. No

Figure 2.3   **PACKED WITH POTENTIAL —**
Take a look and make an offer.

information is supplied to persuade anyone to "take a look and make an offer," except, possibly, the claim that whatever the property is, it is "packed with potential." Of course, everything is packed with potential in some way or other. So even bearing in mind the context, that would not be enough to qualify this ad as an argument, because nothing is given here that could count as a reason.

The context is part of what is called **background information,** or the assumptions on which an argument depends. All arguments assume some background information; otherwise, the argument could never get off the ground. For example, all of the arguments given so far in this book assume that you understand the words in which they are expressed. The question is, "How much background information can you assume?" Problems arise when someone assumes everyone else has background information that they don't have. When that happens, people may not recognize the speaker's comments as an argument, or they may misunderstand the argument. We will come back to assumed background information again in Chapter 7.

When you're giving an argument, it's best not to assume that your **audience** — those to whom the argument is directed — has much background information, especially if it is technical or controversial. An example of too much controversy is this argument:

Abortion is murder only if fetuses are persons in the full, legal and social sense. Fetuses are not persons in these senses. So abortion is not murder.

The problem is not the topic nor even the conclusion. The problem is that the speaker is assuming some controversial background information, in this case that the only beings who can be murdered are persons in the full, legal, and social sense. Of course the reasons the speaker gives are also controversial. For example, those who think abortion is (at least sometimes) murder will not agree that fetuses are not persons. So this argument is not likely to be convincing.

In face-to-face discussion, the problem of unshared background information is less difficult to deal with than in written work. This is because in discussion, people can express their confusion, ask for more information, and indicate what they don't agree with. In written work, however, you must guess what your audience knows and agrees with. Again, the best rule is to avoid controversial background information and controversial reasons as much as you can and to provide background information that is essential to your argument. And in interpreting the written work of others, the best rule is to give the author the benefit of the doubt as much as you can by looking up any background information you need to understand the argument.

In English composition classes, the point is often made that all writing is addressed to some audience and that effective writing requires the audience be kept in mind. This is also true in logic, as this section about background information indicates. As you formulate your own arguments, remember to think about what your audience can be expected to know, and use only background information they are likely to understand and accept.

Another point about the audience for logical argument is that this audience is assumed to be reasonable, unprejudiced, and moderately well informed. This is to say that the audience for logical argument is assumed not to have overwhelmingly strong prejudices that will influence their decisions about what to believe. Whether this is actually true of people in general may be doubtful, but it tends to be true of people who are sincerely interested in the truth, which is what logic cares about.

PERSUASION WITHOUT ARGUMENTS

Many advertisers do not share the preceding impression of their audience, which is why so few ads seem to offer much in the way of arguments to their audiences. In general, it is reasonable to assume that most advertisements are efforts to **persuade** people — to influence their opinions and beliefs — so the only question in identifying arguments in ads is whether or not any reasoning is being offered. It is reasonable to assume that much of what goes on during political speeches, in law courts, and in articles on controversial topics is also an attempt to persuade, so, again, you should look for reasons in order to decide whether something should be considered an argument. There are no hard-and-fast rules on this; you will just have to develop judgment by examining many examples.

Association

Finally, we should recognize that many ads do not involve arguments. You are probably familiar with Chevrolet's "Heartbeat of America" ads, which feature many different scenes of Americans in various "down home" situations — going on picnics, taking children to scout meetings and athletic events, and so on. These ads rely on a psychological mechanism called **association,** which is our tendency to identify ourselves in all respects with people who are like us in some respects. Most people who might consider buying family-sized Chevrolets and Chevy trucks can probably identify with these family scenes because they too go on picnics and drive their children to a lot of events. The ad works because people who do feel this association with the characters in the ads may also come to believe they ought to buy Chevrolet vehicles. Note, however, that none of this is explained in the ad. If it were, people might wonder whether other car and truck manufacturers might produce vehicles that better meet their particular needs, get better gas mileage, have better repair records, or cost less. So here, instead of reasons, the image and the psychological mechanism substitute for an argument.

Projection

In the Xi'a Xi'ang perfume ad (Figure 2.4), another psychological mechanism substitutes for argument in an effort to persuade. Here we are invited to project ourselves into a romantic scene, assigning ourselves appropriate roles in the implicit fantasy, believing and doing what the fantasy characters do. This mechanism, **projection,** persuades without reasoning because of our tendency to adopt all of the feelings and attitudes required by the roles we give ourselves in our imaginations. Actually, to introduce reasoning into this ad would be a disaster, because if you *think* about what the ad says or invites you to imagine, it makes no sense. How can you "travel forward to the past," for example? And how romantic would this cologne be on a becalmed, cramped, smelly sampan?

THE FRAGRANCE
OF THE IMAGINATION

Xi'a Xi'ang.
To travel forward to the past.
To allow what is forbidden.
To obtain that which is elusive.

Xi'a Xi'ang
(pronounced see-ah see-ahng)

Figure 2.4

SUMMARY

An argument is at least one reason offered to influence a person's belief about something. Not all arguments are good ones, but the best offer strong evidence or valid reasoning to support their conclusions. A valid argument is one that cannot have a false conclusion if the reasons are true. Invalid arguments can have true reasons and a false conclusion. Strong arguments offer adequate reliable evidence to support their conclusions without ignoring other possibilities. Arguments that offer less are weaker. All arguments appear in a context, so identifying arguments requires being sensitive to what's going on in the situation. And all arguments assume some background information. But in general, it's best not to assume too much background information, especially if it's information your audience is unlikely to agree with. Finally, there are ways besides arguments to influence beliefs. Two persuasive techniques are called association and projection.

EXERCISE I

Determine which of the following expressions are arguments by identifying reasons and conclusions. Explain what's missing from expressions that are not arguments. Be reasonably strict about interpreting these passages, and remember that not all arguments are good ones.

1. It was a dark and stormy night.

2. Suddenly, a shot rang out. Because only the killer had a gun, I knew he was near.

3. Inflation is a danger the American economy can't seem to overcome. Meanwhile, the average consumer pays the price, and it just keeps getting higher.

4. Steffi Graf is probably the greatest female tennis player who is currently on the Tour. She's won a higher percentage of matches than anyone else has.

5. Lots of snobs put down popular music, but I say it's just as valid as any other form of expression.

6. You can't afford a new car, and you don't want a junker. At World of Wheels, we've got affordable, quality cars. Come to World of Wheels and find the used car that's right for you.

7. Because whales are fish and fish are mammals, it follows that whales are mammals.

8. Most insects reproduce more rapidly than rabbits, and rabbits reproduce more rapidly than elephants. Therefore, insects reproduce more rapidly than elephants.

9. America's trade deficit with South Asia is getting larger. The deficit is harming the American economy. Deficits develop when we buy more imports than we sell exports. We need to design more goods with the South Asian market in mind.

10. No one should stay in an abusive relationship. Sheila's boyfriend constantly yells at her. So she should break up with him; after all, verbal abuse is abuse too.

EXERCISE II

What conclusions could reasonably be drawn from these reasons together with standard background information? (Assume the reasons are true.)

1. Comprehensive insurance on John's car costs $250 for six months from Farm Bureau and $300 from Allstate for the same coverage. John thinks the only important thing about picking an insurance company is low cost. He needs to get auto insurance.

2. Ann wants to get into a good law school. Among the criteria for admission to law schools are a broad liberal arts background and high scores on the LSAT. Philosophy majors, on average, scored 8.9 percent higher on the LSAT than did majors in any other field. Philosophy majors have broad liberal arts backgrounds.

3. Students who choose a lot of "basket-weaving" courses usually don't develop the discipline and ability to move into middle or upper management. Students who think of college as a series of meaningless requirements tend to choose the simplest courses they can find.

4. If the federal deficit continues to grow, interest rates will rise. If interest rates rise, gold increases in value and the return on money market investments gets better, while stocks and bonds both tend to fall in value. You own some bonds and stocks, but no gold, and you have little cash on hand or in money markets. You think the deficit will continue to grow and want to make some money.

5. The probability that a fair coin will come up heads is 50 percent, which is also the probability that it will come up tails. On

four of the past five tosses, one football official's coin has come up tails. He's about to toss that coin again.

6. During the years 1972–77, *Consumer Reports* rated many Chrysler automobiles below average in most respects, while from 1978 on they improved markedly. In 1971, Chrysler's management was reorganized, with many design decisions made by accountants rather than engineers. In 1977, engineers were again given control over many design decisions.

7. In the case of people, the only reason you have to think they have experiences much like yours is that their behavior resembles yours in similar situations. Animals exhibit behavior that resembles human behavior associated with such emotions as love, happiness, and fear. It is morally wrong to kill beings for sport that are capable of love, happiness, and fear.

EXERCISE III

Write out the best arguments you can for the following conclusions. Make use of the suggestions, but you don't have to limit yourself to them. Remember that you don't have to agree with the conclusion to come up with a good argument in favor of it.

1. Conclusion: Therefore, most Americans should eat less saturated fat. (Hints: What effect does saturated fat have on people's health? Why would this be bad?)

2. Conclusion: So baseball is one of the least exciting professional sports. (Hints: What makes a sport exciting? Does baseball have these features?)

3. Conclusion: Higher education will become increasingly necessary to get a good job. (Hints: What kinds of good jobs are there? What level of education do they require?)

4. Conclusion: To rely heavily on Third World countries for a large proportion of needed raw materials is risky. (Hints: How much control does the United States have over economic decisions in Third World countries? What are some risks the U.S. might face if its supply of raw materials were cut off?)

5. Conclusion: The next U.S. president will be a man. (Hints: Who are the most likely presidental candidates from the Democratic and Republican parties? Does anyone else have a reasonable chance to win?)

6. Conclusion: The next U.S. President should be a woman. (This one is tougher! Hints: What are the most important qualities that a U.S. president needs to perform well? Are any of these more likely to be found in a woman candidate than in a man candidate?)

7. Conclusion: The best way to deal with America's crime problem is to provide greater opportunities for all citizens. (Hint: Why do people turn to crime?)

8. Conclusion: The salaries of people in service professions such as teaching and nursing must be raised. (Hints: How do salaries in nursing and teaching compare with salaries in other professional fields? How important are salary considerations when choosing a profession? Are enough top students entering these fields to meet the need?)

9. Conclusion: Parents should be able to decide which high schools their children attend. (Hint: What advantages would there be if parents could choose?)

10. Conclusion: Parents should *not* be able to decide which high schools their children attend. (Hint: What disadvantages might occur if parents could choose?)

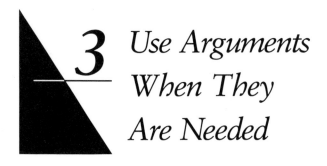

3 Use Arguments When They Are Needed

Once we know what an argument is, we need to know what to use arguments for. To understand the roles arguments play in thinking and writing, we need to understand a number of different language uses, as well as the differences between questions of fact, value, concept, and interpretation. In this chapter, we'll look at five ways people use language, and only one of them will involve arguments. Then we'll look at four kinds of issues people might disagree about and pick out the ones that are best resolved by argument. We can then refine our sense of what makes arguments good or bad.

THINGS PEOPLE DO WITH LANGUAGE

Arguments are tools people use to influence each other's beliefs about various topics. They always include at least one reason which is given to support a conclusion. But not everything people do or talk about involves arguments or persuasion. Consider these five important things people do with words:

- ▶ Stating and explaining things, the **informative** use of language; saying something is true, providing information, answering questions, instructing, commenting, clarifying, giving examples, telling a story, and so on.

- ▶ Asking about things, the **interrogative** use of language; for example, asking a question, seeking to find out information, inquiring.

- ▶ Telling people to do things, the **directive** use of language; giving commands or instructions, ordering, guiding actions, giving directions, and the like.

- ▶ Expressing things, the **expressive** use of language; for example, cheering and booing, cursing, reassuring, frightening, calming.

- ▶ Persuading people to believe things, the **persuasive** use of language; influencing, convincing, giving reasons, getting people to change their minds, and so on.

Informative Language Uses

Language is used informatively when a person says something that could be either true or false. That is, when you state an opinion, say something happened, report on something, advise others about something, describe something, or explain something, you're using language informatively. It doesn't matter whether the person you're talking to already knows what you're saying. As long as what you're doing is saying something that could be true or false, you're using language informatively.

As we said in Chapter 2, a sentence is true when what it says corresponds with the way things are, independent of our opinions. A sentence is false when what it says isn't the way things are. A sentence is neither true nor false when what it says doesn't report anything about the way things are. Of course, how we find out the way things are is a complicated business involving interpersonal observation, reasoning, and acting on our beliefs to see how they turn out. For the moment, though, let's get back to the kinds of sentences.

"There are three cars in the parking lot outside this building" is true if there is a parking lot outside this building and there are exactly three cars in it. "There are three 200-foot-tall grasshoppers in the parking lot outside this building" is false, since even if there is a parking lot outside this building, 200-foot-tall grasshoppers do not exist, so there can't be three of them in the parking lot. "Is there a parking lot outside this building?" is neither true nor false because it's a request for information, not a report of how the world is. Certainly, people might disagree about what they see in the parking lot. Also, there are some statements that are not easy to test. We'll come back to those possibilities when we talk about questions of fact later in the chapter.

The simplest example of an informative use of language is a declarative or assertive sentence such as "Oak is a hardwood." This sentence says that a certain kind of wood (oak) is (or falls under the category of) hardwood (a close-grained, heavy material taken from the trunks of trees). You probably already know that oak is a hardwood, but again, that doesn't mean the sentence is not informative because its content could be true or false. (In this case, it's true by definition.)

Here are several more examples of informative language uses:

Some lawns are green. (It's not news, but it is information.)

More than 45,000 abortions were performed at public expense in this state last year. (It doesn't matter whether the subject matter is controversial, only that it's information.)

There is a herd of unicorns on one of the moons of Jupiter. (This sentence doesn't seem very likely, but it hasn't been checked. Still, since what it says might be true or false, it's an informative sentence.)

The trickiest informative language uses are those stating beliefs. If someone says, "Most of the people you meet are really aliens in disguise," without giving any reasons, he's stating an opinion he probably thinks is true. But if someone says, "Abortion is always immoral," or "Most contemporary art is ugly," it's tempting to say that she's just *expressing* her own opinion rather than saying something true or false.

Of course, it's hard to know what would prove these sentences true or false. Besides, people are often uncomfortable telling someone her opinions about ethics or art are false. But if people can give reasons for their opinions, they are giving us the chance to take their beliefs seriously and to decide whether they should be considered justified or well supported or true. We need to recognize that when people state their beliefs about ethics, art, or whatever, they usually expect others to agree or disagree, to believe or not believe, or to accept their viewpoint or reject it. This is why stating opinions can be an informative use of language.

Informative language uses can be found everywhere: in magazines, textbooks, newspapers, radio announcements, road signs, conversations, talk shows — the list is endless. What makes informational language uses relevant to logic is that uncontroversial informative statements (the ones people agree on) can serve as reasons in arguments, whereas controversial statements (the ones people don't agree on) work well only as conclusions supported by reasons. Unless people believe your reasons, they won't believe your conclusions. And unless your informative statements are reliable, people usually will want some reasons to believe them. This is especially true when you state an opinion. So if you want people to believe your opinions without any reasons, say things that are either true or uncontroversial. But if you say something controversial, give some uncontroversial reasons for it.

Interrogative Language Uses

When you ask a question and you're sincerely interested in the answer, you're using language interrogatively. The simplest example of an interrogative sentence is one like "What time is it?" Any sentence that is used to get someone else to respond with information (e.g., "It's 3:30") is interrogative. Interrogative sentences don't play much of a role in logic because they don't seek to persuade people or influence their beliefs. Instead, they seek to get people to do something, namely, to answer your question. Notice how strange it would be if someone asked you "What time is it?" and you responded "False!" Since interrogative sentences direct actions rather than influence beliefs, they don't function as either reasons or conclusions.

The only exception to this rule is what are called **rhetorical questions**. A rhetorical question states an opinion in the grammatical form of a question. If someone says, "You're not going to waste your time watching football again, are you?" and he really means "You shouldn't watch football again," he's using a rhetorical question. So is a person who asks, "You don't really believe in astrology, do you?" or "You're not going out this weekend with that loser, are you?" People often use rhetorical questions to conceal the fact that they're expressing opinions for which they have no good reasons. You can check this by converting rhetorical questions into assertions. So, for example, when "You're not going out with that loser?" is translated into "You shouldn't go out with that loser," it's easier to ask "Why not?" or "Why call him (or her) a loser?"

Also, bear in mind that because rhetorical questions are really statements, they can appear as reasons or conclusions in arguments. Suppose Anne has been trying to quit smoking, but her friend Rosa sees her about to light up. Rosa might say, "Anne, what are you doing with that cigarette? Don't you know how bad those things are for you? Why don't you just get rid of it once and for all?" All of these sentences are rhetorical questions. And the last two amount to an argument, the conclusion being "Anne should get rid of her cigarettes once and for all" and the reason being "Cigarettes are bad for you." It is the fact that rhetorical questions can play a number of roles in reasoning and communication that makes it important to identify them.

Directive Language Uses

Directive language uses are like interrogative ones in that they don't try to influence people's beliefs; they try to influence people's actions. A simple example of a directive use is "Read the next chapter for Thursday," because the sentence is used to get you to do something (namely, to read the next chapter). Again, notice how strange it would be to respond, "Read the next chapter? False!" Of course, there is a sense in which a directive language use also informs, since "Read the next chapter" does inform you of what I want you to do. But if the main purpose is to get you to do something, rather than to describe what I think, the use is directive. (Notice the differences between "I feel you should read the next chapter" and "Read the next chapter!")

Directive language uses play a minimal role in logic, again because they don't involve beliefs. Of course you might ask for reasons why you ought to read the chapter. But then giving reasons is persuading, not directing, because I'm trying to influence your beliefs. If the main purpose is to get you to act, as opposed to influencing your beliefs, the use is directive.

Expressive Language Uses

Language is used expressively when it vents or evokes a feeling. The simplest expressive uses are spontaneous, as when you curse when you hit your thumb with a hammer or groan when you double-fault in tennis. But some expressive uses are more complicated, as when you soothe a restless child by repeating "It's all right, it's all right," during a thunderstorm. The characteristic all expressive language uses have in common is that their main point has more to do with how people feel than with what they think or believe. So, while some expressive uses may also have the effect of informing people, their main purpose is to vent feelings. This is why expressive language also has little connection with logic: where questions of belief or truth cannot arise, logic is irrelevant. (Be careful not to confuse informative uses of language, which *report* feelings, with expressive uses of language, which *vent* feelings!)

Sometimes, expressive language uses can have the effect of persuading people, even though they don't offer evidence or support for conclusions. Suppose you admire the New York skyline because "it's so dynamic and powerful," and I reply "What a crock!" My reply expresses my rejection of your reason, and you might feel embarrassed enough to back down on your belief about the skyline. But I haven't given you any evidence or support for my feeling; it's just an opinion expressed aggressively.

Persuasive Language Uses

Language is used persuasively when someone uses it to influence another person's beliefs or attitudes. Some (but not all) persuasive language uses are arguments. Others rely on psychological mechanisms besides reasoning. (Two examples, projection and association, were discussed in the previous chapter.) Needless to say, we will be focusing on persuasive language uses emphasizing reasoning.

COMMON TYPES OF ISSUES

Logic is a tool for deciding what to believe and for influencing the beliefs of others. It is useful in situations in which it's important to resolve disagreements by determining what is most likely to be true or reasonable to believe. So logic is most necessary and useful in situations in which it's difficult to know what's true and situations in which there are different opinions or disagreements. These situations tend to fall into three categories: questions of value, questions of concept, and questions of interpretation. And these in turn are distinguished from questions of fact.

Questions of Fact

An issue is a **question of fact** if it can be answered completely by finding out the right information, from either direct observation or reliable sources. While this may sometimes be difficult to do, as long as information will resolve a difference of belief or determine what is actually true, the issue is a question of fact. Here are several questions of fact:

How many people in this room own Chevrolets?

What is the most valuable export commodity from Argentina?

Do most classical music critics consider Beethoven to be the greatest composer?

Are there other life forms in our galaxy?

What color were Louis XIV's socks when he said "L'état, c'est moi"?

What makes all of these questions of fact is that we can decide what it's reasonable to believe by finding the right information—the right **facts.** In the first case, we can find out by counting. In the second, we'd have to rely on economic data from a good secondary source. The third question, too, can be resolved by counting the opinions of music critics. And even though the last two questions would be very hard or impossible to find out about, the fact that information would settle each question is what makes them questions of fact. The difference between questions of fact and questions of value, concept, and interpretation is that although these other three all involve knowing some facts, the facts alone will not resolve disagreements among people with different opinions.

Questions of Value

These are some questions of value:

Are Chevrolets basically good cars?

Should the Argentine economy be so dependent on exports of raw materials?

Is Beethoven actually the greatest classical composer?

If there are intelligent beings elsewhere in our galaxy, should they be granted the same rights as we have?

Is absolute monarchy a legitimate form of government?

What makes these all **questions of value** is that people's beliefs about them will vary depending on what they think is important (on what they **value**). Remember: Questions of value are not just matters of opinion; they're matters of good reasons, evidence, and argument. We not only *can* reason about values, we *must* reason about values if we're going to get agreement without manipulation or coercion. It might not seem important to reason about what people value in a car, but marriages have broken up over less!

Whether Chevrolets are good cars is a question of **pragmatic** value—how well something works, fulfills its function, or lives up to relevant criteria—and the answer depends on what you value in a car. (Obviously, you have to know some facts about cars to answer this question. But even when people agree on the facts, they still may value different things.) The second question is also an issue of pragmatic value, which depends on what you value in an economy. Whether Beethoven is the greatest classical composer is a question of **aesthetic** value, which concerns the degree of satisfaction provided by objects and experiences according to one's tastes.

Questions of **moral** value, sometimes called **ethics,** have to do with what is right or wrong, good or evil. Whether nonhuman beings should have rights is such a moral question because it involves judging what would be right to do. Whether monarchy is an effective form of government is a pragmatic question, but whether it is a legitimate or wise one is a moral question. Again, moral questions are not just matters of opinion. Moral beliefs, like other beliefs, can be argued for and can be well justified or not. The more rational we are about morality, the more our moral values should be supported by good reasons.

Questions of Concept

Questions of concept are issues that depend on how one or more key terms is used. Here are some examples:

Should mini-vans be considered automobiles or buses?

What exactly is classical music?

Do people have a right to clean air?

Should euthanasia be considered murder?

To answer the first of these questions, we would need to know what defines whether something is an automobile or a bus. (Again, this involves knowing some facts about mini-vans, for example. But we also need to understand what we mean by these expressions to answer the question.) To answer the second, we would need to know what is meant by "classical music." To answer the third, we'd need to know what is meant by having a right to something and then decide whether clean air is something we have a right to. To answer the fourth question, we'd need to know not only what is meant by "murder" but also "euthanasia." (Note that we might then have to go on to make a moral judgment about whether or not it is right to act on our current understanding.)

Be careful not to confuse questions of concept with questions of fact. For example, "What is a civil right?" is a question of concept, whereas "What is the dictionary definition of 'civil right'?" is a question of fact. Similarly, "Should euthanasia be considered murder?" is a question of concept, whereas "Does the law now consider euthanasia to be murder?" is a question of fact. Why it is not always possible to settle questions of concept by turning to dictionaries, and what we should do instead, are the topics of Chapter 5. For the moment, remember that dictionaries only report the ways in which people use terms, and people use terms in confusing ways!

Questions of Interpretation

Questions of interpretation involve making judgments about how best to organize, understand, or explain data. In this case we may know many facts; the question is how to understand them. Here are several questions of interpretation:

Why is GM's Chevrolet Division losing market share?

Would more financial support for public schools solve the problem of uneducated high school graduates?

Why did the North win the Civil War?

Can a political party win the White House without running a negative campaign?

Chevrolet's market share is a function of many variables, including foreign competition, price, engineering, advertising, and many more. The interpretive question is which of all the variables plays the most important role in causing Chevrolet to lose market share. Similarly, what is primarily responsible for poor educational performance among high school graduates requires judging among many possible explanations, not enough funding being only one of them. Historians constantly face the task of weighing the variables that determined past events. Whether or not to run another negative campaign is an interpretive question both political parties will have to answer soon.

Again, the important thing about questions of value, concept, and interpretation is that to decide what is reasonable to believe will have to involve argument—giving reasons. The only requirement for resolving questions of fact is that the information you find must be true or reliable. What makes beliefs about values, concepts, and interpretations worth believing is the reasons you can give to support them. The stronger the reasons, the more likely other people will agree with you and the more rational you are to hold the belief you do. But what makes reasons or arguments logically strong?

There are five important criteria for good arguments in logic. They can be summarized in the following rules:

▲ Use reliable forms of argument.

▲ Define your terms clearly, accurately, and without bias.

▲ Make sure your reasons are relevant to your conclusion.

▲ Offer enough reliable information to persuade a reasonable person.

▲ Make sure it's clear how your reasons prove your conclusion.

We will discuss each of these criteria in the next five chapters.

SUMMARY

There are five important uses of language: the informative, the interrogative, the directive, the expressive, and the persuasive. Of these, the informative and the persuasive uses are of particular interest in logic. They differ from each other in that an informative language use offers no reasons or other mechanisms to inspire belief, whereas persuasive language uses involve trying to influence people's beliefs. Arguments are one form of the persuasive use of language, but there are others, such as the psychological mechanisms association and projection. Because logic is both a tool for influencing other people's beliefs and a method of deciding what to believe, it is relevant to situations in which there are differing beliefs that cannot be resolved merely by finding out the right information. Logic has its main applications to questions of value, concept, and interpretation.

EXERCISE I

Decide what the main language use is in each of the following expressions. If an expression can be interpreted in more than one way, explain what they are. Be complete.

1. Ouch!

2. There are thirty desks in room 305.

3. How long does it take a Datsun 280Z to go from 0 to 60?

4. Take out your books and turn to page 68.

5. You should not try to work so many hours and take a full load at the same time because there's just not enough time for both.

6. You're not getting into a dangerous sport like skydiving, are you?

7. Can't you turn down that stupid boom box?

8. If you want some good Italian food, the O Solo Mio serves authentic north Italian at reasonable prices.

9. Didn't I see you with that genius from the chem class last Saturday night?

10. Go ahead. Take a test drive. You'll feel the difference from the moment you turn the key.

EXERCISE II

For each of the following expressions, decide what its main use is. Again, if an expression has more than one purpose, explain. (Jan and Amy are both students having lunch at the college snack bar.)

1. Jan: I hear you're thinking about majoring in philosophy.

2. Amy: Yeah, I sort of like it, and it's really interesting.

3. Jan: Are you crazy? What kind of job are you going to get with that kind of a degree?

4. Amy: Any kind I want. Philosophy qualifies you for almost anything. Anyway, you should think about something besides getting a job.

5. Jan: Hey, I like to eat. Which reminds me — can't they make anything decent in this place?

6. Amy: Watch it! You just knocked over my Coke!

7. Jan: Oh no! Quick, gimme some napkins!

8. Amy: Besides, philosophy teaches you to concentrate.

9. Jan: Don't start that again.

EXERCISE III

Write at least one example of each of the language uses discussed in this chapter: informative, interrogative, directive, expressive, persuasive.

EXERCISE IV

In each of the following cases, decide what kind of question is the main problem to be resolved. Be very specific. If it's a question of fact, explain exactly what fact(s) would be needed and how you would go about getting them. If it's a question of value, explain what value(s) are involved. If a question of concept, identify it and explain what ambiguities cause trouble. Or if interpretation, discuss what the possibilities are. Remember that some examples involve more than one kind of question.

1. Judith wants to go to law school, and she wants to know which undergraduate major has best prepared students to score high on the LSAT (Law School Admissions Test).

2. Amy and Jan disagree about what's most important in selecting an undergraduate major. Jan thinks it's being vocationally

trained for employment, whereas Amy thinks it's studying something interesting that provides broad preparation.

3. Mai-Ling has received a memo from her principal advising her of a new dress code she must enforce in her class. Among other things, the code says, "All students will be well groomed, and will dress in an appropriately academic way."

4. Barbara thinks it is sometimes ethical to disconnect life support systems in hospitals when the patients are "just human vegetables," but David thinks a doctor's obligation is always to sustain life no matter what the condition of the patient is.

5. Andrew is writing an investigative article on why tuition increases have consistently outpaced inflation. He thinks expensive new programs and large administrative salaries may be the main factors. But he wonders if large enrollment increases or state-funding cutbacks may be part of the problem.

6. Rico thinks that both rock-and-roll and country/western music are valid musical art forms and wants the curriculum committee to OK them for general education credit under the "arts" category.

7. Diane wants to explain the movements toward more capitalistic economies in Communist countries for her international economics class. She thinks consumer dissatisfaction is important but also that low productivity and poor morale may be involved.

8. Because of several accidents, Jim's insurance company will cover only "strictly necessary travel, such as that minimally required for transportation to place of employment."

9. Teresa is writing a paper on election campaigns in South American democracies for her political science class. Should she include Nicaragua, Panama, and Cuba in her study?

10. Jack is a strong pro-life advocate who argues this way: "It's always wrong to kill an innocent person, and a fetus is an innocent person. Since abortion involves killing fetuses, abortion is always wrong."

4 Use Reliable Argument Forms

O nce we have a sense of what arguments are and what they are used for, we need to begin to distinguish good arguments from bad and learn to use the good ones. In addition to the five rules for good arguments mentioned at the end of the last chapter, there are some basic kinds of arguments that are reliable as long as the reasons they depend on are true. The main purpose of this chapter is to introduce five of these. Four of them fall under the general category called *deductive* arguments, and one falls under the category called *inductive* argument. We'll also look at the differences between deductive and inductive arguments and talk about strengths and weaknesses of each. Finally, we'll see what happens when these reliable kinds of argument are used improperly.

ARGUMENT FORM
VERSUS ARGUMENT CONTENT

There are probably an infinite number of arguments that people can use to try to influence other people's opinions. Not all of them are logically convincing, however. And unfortunately, the ones that are not logically convincing outnumber the logically reliable ones by a huge margin. People who have studied logic have found that most of the reliable arguments fall into just a few different groups, depending on how they are put together. So in this chapter, we'll start with some of these reliable patterns of arguments.

Probably the best way to understand what we'll be trying to do in this chapter is to compare giving an argument with writing a sentence. In order for an English language sentence to make sense, you not only have to use words people understand but also have to put those words in an order that shows how they're related to each other. For example, the sentence "Shawn's dog barks too much" makes sense, and if you know about Shawn and his dog, you can decide whether or not what the sentence says is true. But this sentence does not make sense: "Much too barks dog Shawn's." It doesn't make sense because although the same words appear in both sentences (both sentences have the same content), the content is mixed up in the second sentence. By reversing the order of the words in the second sentence, the way we usually indicate who owns what and who's doing what — the grammar of the sentence — gets lost.

Arguments are like sentences in that they have both content and grammar. Some arguments are like well-written sentences in that their content is true and their grammar is accurate, so that the true reasons given in the argument are clearly, relevantly, and completely connected up with their conclusions. These are the most reliable arguments in logic. Now, just as there are many ways to combine the words in the previous sentences that don't make sense, there are many ways to put together reasons and conclusions that won't make logical sense either. So what we're doing in this chapter is looking at some of the ways to construct arguments that will make sense. We're looking at the grammar of logical arguments, which is called the argument's **form**.

There are differences as well as similarities between the grammar of sentences and the grammar of arguments. One important difference is that the order in which words are presented makes a tremendous difference in sentences, but the order in which reasons are presented makes no difference in logic. That is, the following two arguments have the same form and are equally good arguments:

> If Jennifer is at the library, she's studying with Karen. But if she's with Karen, she won't get much work done. So if Jennifer is at the library, she won't get much work done.

> Jennifer won't get much work done even if she is at the library. That's because she won't get much done if she's with Karen. And if she's at the library, she's studying with Karen.

RELIABLE ARGUMENTS AND WHAT TO WATCH OUT FOR

So we'll need to look carefully at what does make a difference in the grammar of arguments. To begin, we'll look at some examples. Suppose Ryan answers the telephone and it's a call for his sister Jennifer from her boyfriend. When Ryan tells him Jennifer is not home, her boyfriend wants to know if Ryan can tell him where Jennifer is. So Ryan reasons this way:

> Jennifer said either she was coming straight home after school or she was going to the library with Karen to work on a research paper. She's not home. So she must be at the library.

Leah's grade-point average is slipping because she is working so many hours at the 7-11 convenience store she doesn't have time to study. She reasons:

> Either I can work a lot of hours at the 7-11 and barely get by in my courses or I can work fewer hours and study more so I can get better grades. I can't afford to just get by. So I guess I'd better cut back on my hours and study more.

Marco has a different problem:

> If I take band I won't get a scholarship, but if I go out for football I might get one. I need the scholarship. And you're only allowed either to take band or to go out for football. So I suppose I'd better go out for the team.

Now, each of these examples of reasoning has different content. The first example is about locating Jennifer, the second about cutting

back on work hours, and the third about deciding whether to go out
for sports. But the pattern involved in each piece of reasoning is the
same. In each case, Ryan, Leah, and Marco see some alternatives that
can't both be true. Then they think of a reason why one of the
choices is the wrong one or less desirable than the other. They conclude that the other choice is the right one. In Ryan's case, the form
of the argument is:

> Jennifer's at home (H) *or* Jennifer's at the library (L).
>
> She's not home (not H).
>
> So Jennifer's at the library (L).

In Leah's case, it's:

> Work a lot of hours (W) and get by (G) *or* work less (L) and
> study more (S) (that is, [W and G] or [L and S]).
>
> She can *not* keep working a lot and getting by (not [W and G]).
>
> So she needs to work less and study more (L and S).

And for Marco, the argument is:

> He can either take band (B) *or* go out for football (F).
>
> He can *not* take band (and still get a scholarship) (not B).
>
> So he should go out for football (F).

Or, more simply, the form of each of these arguments is:

> (A) or (B)
>
> not (A)
>
> Therefore, B

Dilemma Versus False Dilemma

The argument form shown above is called **dilemma** because people
using it are choosing between two (or more) alternatives.[1] Dilemma

---

1. Among philosophers, many reliable argument forms have traditional names.
For example, this argument form is often called "disjunctive syllogism" because
it involves an "either . . . or" statement, which logicians call a "disjunction,"
another premise, and a conclusion drawn from it, the collective name for which
is a "syllogism." The traditional names of argument forms we'll look at in this

works like this: First you list all of the available options; next you rule out those that won't work; and then you conclude that the one that remains is the best or true choice. Dilemma is a **deductive** argument form, which means that it's a kind of argument set up so that, if the reasons are true, the conclusion has to be true as well. The reason to point it out to you is that *as long as the content of the reasons is true, the conclusion of any argument with this form must be true as well.* That is, since the form of this argument is *deductively valid* (is set up so that if the reasons are true, the conclusion has to be true as well), any argument with the form

(A) or (B)

Not (A)

Therefore, B

will have a true conclusion if the reasons are true as well. (Arguments that are *both* valid and have true reasons are **sound.**)

Another way to put the same point is that if there's a problem with an argument set up as a dilemma, the problem must be with the content. And usually, when dilemmas are not reliable, it's because some possible alternative has been overlooked. Look back at the earlier examples. If Jennifer could have gone somewhere besides home or the library, then Ryan's reasoning wouldn't hold up. If Leah could find something else to cut back on so she could both work and study more, then her argument wouldn't necessarily be correct. And if Marco could get the school system to make an exception in his case, he might not have to choose between music and athletics, so his reasoning wouldn't work.

When other choices are overlooked, deliberately or not, the valid argument form called dilemma becomes a **fallacy,** or bad argument, called **false dilemma.** That fallacy will be discussed more fully in Chapter 7. The argument Calvin gives in the cartoon in Figure 4.1 is a false dilemma because some other alternatives are overlooked, namely living sensibly, taking only reasonable risks. Meanwhile, all

---

chapter will be given in footnotes like this one. It is not necessary to remember these traditional names unless your teacher asks you to do so. Also, not all logic books use these names in quite the same ways. I'll stick fairly close to the way Howard Kahane uses them in *Logic and Philosophy,* 6th ed. (Belmont, Calif.: Wadsworth Publishing Company, 1990).

Figure 4.1

you need to remember is that a dilemma where no other possibilities are overlooked is a reliable argument.

Now we can make a more general point about soundness and validity. When you're judging how rationally convincing an argument is, you'll need to look at two things. One is whether the argument will prove its conclusion if its reasons are acceptable. The other is whether the reasons are good enough and strong enough to prove the conclusion. If you know that an argument's form is valid, you can direct your attention to the quality of the reasons. So, recognizing valid argument forms can help you reason better and focus your attention when you evaluate arguments.

Implication Versus Affirming the Consequent

Another reliable argument pattern that is deductively valid is called **implication.**[2] Here are several examples:

Ryan reasons, "If Jennifer has gone to the library, she's studying with Karen. Since she's at the library, Karen must be with her."

Leah reasons, "If I want to keep a high grade-point average, I can't work as many hours as my boss wants me to. I really need a high GPA. So I guess I'll have to tell my boss I need a shorter work schedule."

And Marco reasons, "If I want a scholarship, I'll be better off going out for football than playing in the band. I've got to get a scholarship if I'm going to afford college. So I'd better go out for football."

---

2. The traditional name for implication is "modus ponens."

Each of these arguments has the same form. It involves two reasons and a conclusion, and the reasons must include a statement that whether one thing is true depends on something else being true. Then, when the first part of the implication, called the *antecedent*, is seen to be true, the second part, called the *consequent,* is recognized as true also. This second part is the argument's conclusion. So the argument pattern called implication has the following form:

If (A [the antecedent] is true), then (B [the consequent] is true).

(A [the antecedent] is true.)

So (B [the consequent] is true also).

In Ryan's case, A stands for "Jennifer is at the library" and B stands for "Jennifer is with Karen." In Leah's case, A stands for "Leah wants to keep a high GPA" and B stands for "Leah can't work as many hours as her boss wants her to." And in Marco's case, A stands for "Marco needs a scholarship" and B stands for "Marco should go out for football instead of band."

Now, because implication is deductively valid, any argument that fits this pattern will have a true conclusion if the reasons it depends on are true. But the argument won't be reliable if the form is reversed—if the consequent is affirmed.[3] That is, not only is the next example an unreliable argument, but any argument that fits this pattern will be unreliable, too:

If Leah wants a high GPA, she'll have to work fewer hours. She's going to cut back twenty hours next week. So she'll definitely get a higher GPA.

Of course, just cutting back on work hours won't guarantee a higher grade-point average. Leah will have to study, do well on exams, and so on. But also, any argument with this form will tend to give conclusions that can't be trusted. This argument has the form:

If (A is true), then (B is true).

(B is true).

So (A is true also).

---

3. There are exceptional cases where affirming the consequent is not invalid, but they are rare enough that we will not discuss them here.

So does this one:

> **If Jennifer is at the library, she's with Karen. I just saw Jennifer with Karen at McDonalds a few minutes ago. So Jennifer must be at the library by now.**

But, of course, Jennifer might still be at McDonalds. So this argument, and any argument with an invalid form, can't be trusted. Be careful to stick with reliable argument forms and not mix them up with others that look similar, but aren't the same.

Chain Argument Versus Inconsistent Terms

The third deductively valid pattern is called **chain argument.**[4] Chain arguments involve reasons that overlap in the following way:

> **If (A is true), then (B is true also).**
>
> **If (B is true), then (C is true also).**
>
> **So, if (A is true), then (C is true).**

Here are several examples of chain arguments:

> If Jennifer is at the library, she's studying with Karen. But if she's with Karen, Jennifer will probably spend more time talking about her boyfriend than studying. So if they went to the library, Jennifer's probably talking about her boyfriend.

> If Leah wants to keep a high GPA, she'll need to cut back on her work hours. But if Leah cuts back on her work hours, she won't make enough money to pay for a new car. So if Leah wants to keep her grades up, she can't afford a new car.

> If Marco wants an athletic scholarship, he'll need to attract the college scouts. If he's going to attract the scouts, he'll need to avoid injuries and get a lot of playing time. So if he wants a scholarship, he'll need to get a lot of playing time and not get hurt.

Chain arguments work when you recognize the right kinds of connections between the reasons. Problems with chain arguments mostly occur when the terms are *inconsistent*—when the overlapping

---

4. The traditional name for chain argument is "hypothetical syllogism."

term is not used in the same way in different sentences (see "equivocation" in Chapter 8).

Denying the Consequent Versus Denying the Antecedent

The last deductive argument pattern we'll present here is called **denying the consequent**.[5] Here is a series of examples of this valid form of argument.

> If Jennifer is going to get to the library, Karen has to drive her there. But Karen can't drive her; her car is in the shop. So Jennifer must not be at the library.

> If Leah is going to keep a high GPA, she'll need to cut back on her work hours. But her boss won't let her cut back at all. So Leah's GPA is going to suffer.

> If Marco is going to get an athletic scholarship, he'll have to avoid injuries and get a lot of playing time. But he sprained his ankle last game and won't play again this season. So it looks as if he won't get an athletic scholarship after all.

All of these arguments have the following form:

If (A is true), then (B is true also).

(B is not true) or Not (B is true).

So (A must not be true either) or Not (A is true).

And, as before, any argument that has this form will have a true conclusion if both of the reasons are true. But in using this kind of argument, we need to remember that the only way the consequent can be true is for the antecedent to be true. If the consequent doesn't depend on the antecedent, denying the consequent won't be reliable. So, for example, if somebody else could have given Jennifer a ride, or if Leah could keep up her GPA without cutting back on her work hours, or if Marco could get an athletic scholarship without getting a lot of playing time, the arguments won't work.

Another source of confusion is illustrated by an argument like the one following:

---

5. The traditional name for denying the consequent is "modus tollens."

> If Jennifer is at the library, she's with Karen. Nobody's seen her at the library. So she must not be with Karen.

Here what's being denied is the *antecedent,* not the consequent, and not only this argument, but any one with this form is unreliable as well:

> If (A is true), then (B is true also).
>
> (A is not true.)
>
> So (B must not be true either).

Again, what's crucial is to not confuse two argument forms that seem similar. Only denying the consequent is deductively valid.

DISTINGUISHING DEDUCTIVE AND INDUCTIVE ARGUMENTS

So far, all of the reliable patterns of argument we've looked at are deductively valid, which, you'll remember, means that if we assume their reasons are true, their conclusions cannot be false. Probably these argument patterns have seemed pretty simple or even obvious to you, and sometimes they are. But not always. And especially not when they're combined to create longer, more complex arguments.

But not all reliable patterns of argument are deductive. Some are inductive. The best way to understand the difference between inductive and deductive arguments is to say that while valid deductive arguments with true reasons guarantee that their conclusions are true, valid **inductive** arguments with true reasons make their conclusions more likely or probable, but it's still possible that the conclusion is false. This is because inductively valid arguments present evidence to support a conclusion. Giving examples, specific cases or instances, or experiences to lead to a conclusion will tend to support that conclusion, but since it is always possible that some other examples, cases, instances, or experiences might be found that point in a different direction, inductive conclusions are always only probable, not certain.

Here are some examples of inductive arguments.

> Last Monday, when Jennifer went to the library, she went with Karen. She did the same thing last week and the week before.

In fact, every time Jennifer has gone to the library this semester, she's gone with Karen. So probably if Jennifer goes to the library this Monday, she'll take Karen with her.

Four people I know have been doing poorly on their exams lately. Leah is working a lot of hours at the 7-11. John just got assigned extra hours at the department store. Joanne has been called in for extra weekends at the A&P. And when I had to work extra hours at Stop and Go, my grades dropped through the floor. I guess people who have to work a lot of hours can't really expect to keep up their grade points.

If Marco goes out for football, he'll probably get a college scholarship. After all, David was on the football team, and he got a fat scholarship to Central. Rod was on the football team, and he got a scholarship to Eastern. Walt was on the football team, and he got a scholarship to Northern State.

What makes these arguments inductive is that the reasons given to support their conclusions can give us only a probability that the conclusions are true. The weaker the support offered by the reasons the weaker the inductive argument. In the first example, what Jennifer has done on her trips to the library this semester—gone there with Karen—is used as evidence that she'll probably do it again. In the second case, the fact that four people did poorly on exams when they had to work more hours than before is used as evidence that most people will have trouble keeping up their grades if they have to increase their work hours. And the third argument relies on three football team members' getting scholarships as evidence that if Marco goes out for football, he'll probably get a scholarship too.

It's easy to see that these arguments are not conclusive in the way that sound deductive arguments are. (Sound deductive arguments are valid and have true reasons.) Jennifer might decide to go to the library alone, so the evidence about what she's done this semester doesn't guarantee anything about what she'll do this Monday. It's always possible—though not very likely—that something besides working extra hours caused the grade problems for the four students. (Maybe none of them took very good notes in class and it's just now catching up with them.) And in the third case, just being on the football team is probably not enough to get you a scholarship; you have to be good at football too. So none of these arguments is necessarily convincing.

What Makes an Inductive Argument Strong

On the other hand, some inductive arguments are more reliable than others. Of these three examples, the first and the middle ones are the most reliable and the last one is the least. What makes the first one reasonably good are the large number of cases in which Jennifer has gone with Karen and the fact that there are no cases when she hasn't. (Of course, the argument would be even stronger if we knew that Jennifer and Karen had not got angry with each other, or if Jennifer needed Karen to give her a ride. But this illustrates another important fact about inductive arguments: They're used when we don't have all the information that would be useful to decide what's really true.) The second argument is reliable because there's a strong connection between working too many hours, not having enough time to do your homework, and doing poorly in your classes. (Again, the argument would be stronger still if more examples were mentioned.) But the third argument is not very convincing, because we know that just being on the football team doesn't guarantee a scholarship, and there are probably a number of other guys who were on the team and didn't get one. Since there's (probably) evidence against the conclusion of the third argument, it's not as convincing as the other two.

How much support the evidence provides in an inductive argument does depend on whether it's all true, just as in the case of deduction. Obviously, if it isn't true that Jennifer has gone to the library with Karen in the past, then that can't be evidence that she will in the future. But it also depends on these three other factors:

- whether or not the examples cited are true, accurate, and representative (not unusual in some way)
- whether enough evidence is provided
- whether there is other evidence pointing to a different conclusion

In the first two arguments given earlier, all of these criteria are fulfilled. (At least, they are if we assume the information is true.) But in the third, none of them is.

Since every case of Jennifer's trips to the library is considered in the first argument, we don't have to worry about whether the examples are representative of her trips to the library; we've got the complete list. In the second case, although four cases might be too few if the conclusion is controversial, there's every reason to think that

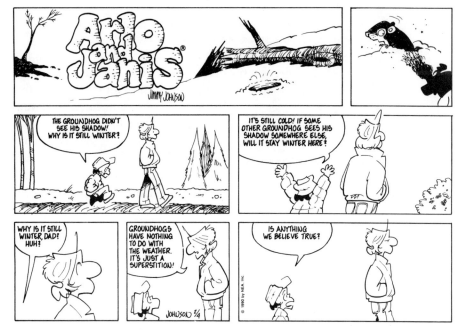

Reprinted by permission of NEA, Inc.

working a lot of hours makes it hard to keep up a high grade-point average. But the third argument has many problems. David, Rod, and Walt are *not* representative members of the football team precisely because they got scholarships and others probably didn't. They are not enough examples to consider because football teams often have at least twenty or thirty other players, most of whom aren't "stars." And there is good reason to suspect that most of these other players didn't get scholarships, so they would probably count as evidence against the conclusion. This is a hasty generalization. Later on, in Chapter 9, we'll come back to what happens when inductive arguments go wrong in this way.

Although no inductive arguments are as strong as a sound deductive argument, and inductive arguments can go wrong when they violate the criteria we've just listed, it's important to remember that strong inductive arguments are very valuable and quite reliable. This is because inductive arguments play so important a role in situations of uncertainty, and there are many of those situations. So it's logical to add strong inductive arguments to your set of reliable argument forms.

SUMMARY

In this chapter we discussed several types of reliable arguments. We also distinguished between deductive and inductive arguments. Deductive arguments guarantee that their conclusions are true if their reasons are true and if their form is valid. And we examined four valid deductive argument forms: dilemma, implication, chain argument, and denying the consequent. Each of these argument forms can easily be misused, though, so we need to avoid false dilemmas, affirming the consequent, denying the antecedent, and inconsistency in chain arguments. Inductive arguments offer evidence for their conclusions and are reliable when that evidence is true or representative enough to support the conclusion, and when there is no counterevidence pointing to a different conclusion. If you rely on these argument forms, your reasoning will improve dramatically.

EXERCISE I

For each of the following examples, decide whether it is deductive or inductive. Then decide whether it is an example of one of the argument forms we've discussed in this chapter. If it is, decide which one. Don't worry too much about how convincing these arguments are.

1. If the Detroit Lions really want to be Super Bowl contenders, they're going to have to get some good split receivers. Their coach, players, and owner all say they want to be contenders. So they'll go after some good split receivers.

2. When the Miami Dolphins were a Super Bowl team, they had a big running back. It was the same with the Washington Redskins. And when Pittsburgh was a contender, they had a big running back. So a team that wants to be a contender probably needs a big running back.

3. Jan knows that anyone who wants to look good and feel good has to exercise and not eat too much. But Jan never exercises, and she has no self-control where food is concerned. So Jan must not care how she looks or feels.

4. Alisa, Amy, and Arlene have each lost ten pounds since the holidays, and they all work out for an hour every morning in the gym. So if Jan wants to lose weight, she probably should be working out every day.

5. Mario studies for three hours every night, and he's got an A–grade-point average. Michelle studies for two hours every morning, and she's close to an A too. Michael studies for an hour or two every evening after work, and he's doing well too. So it looks as if studying regularly is important if you want to get a high grade-point average.

6. If Maxine wants to get into medical school, she'll need to keep a high grade-point average. But if she's going to keep a high grade-point average, she can't work so many hours that she doesn't have time to study. So if Maxine wants to get into med school, she can't work too many hours.

7. Either a Republican or a Democrat will win the next presidential election. But the Democrats don't have any candidates who can get a majority of voters to elect them. So the next president will be a Republican.

8. Republican candidates won in all but one of the last six presidential elections. Therefore, a Republican will probably win the next one too.

9. When Kay put a big fern near a window facing south, it grew like crazy. When she moved it back to a north window, it didn't grow very well. The same thing happened with two other plants she put near the windows. So probably, if she wants her plants to grow, she needs to put them in a window facing south.

10. If plant fertilizer is the main thing Kay's fern needs, fertilizing it and leaving it in the north window should make it grow well. But no matter how much fertilizer it got, the plant in Kay's north window didn't grow. So fertilizer must not be the main thing it needed.

(These examples involve more than one argument form.)

11. If Terrell wants to make the basketball team, he either has to improve his outside shooting or has to be a lot more aggressive rebounding underneath the basket. He really wants to be on the team. But he's just not big enough to be aggressive under the basket. So he'll have to improve his outside shooting.

12. Sweden spends a lot of money on child-care services and has fewer social problems than the United States has. The same is

true of Germany, France, and most other European countries. So if the U.S. wants to avoid serious problems down the road, it should be spending money on child care. Unfortunately, no new money is being spent on it. So we better get ready for serious social problems in a few years.

13. If Maya buys a new Toyota, she'll have expensive car payments to make. But she can afford a used Chevy. She'd like the Toyota, but if she's making expensive car payments, she's not going to be able to afford tuition for college. She has to go to college. So she should buy the Chevy.

14. People who want good jobs in the 90s should get some training in how to use computers. But if people are going to get training in computers, the high schools will have to buy a lot more computers, people will have to buy their own, or more people will have to join the military. But the military is taking fewer new people all the time. And most school districts won't pass taxes to pay for more computers. So people who want good jobs in the 90s will have to buy their own computers.

15. Hamid has saved enough money to buy either a pair of expensive basketball shoes or a personal stereo, but not enough for both. Most of the guys he hangs around with have gone for the shoes. So Hamid will probably not get a personal stereo.

EXERCISE II

For each of the five types of arguments discussed in this chapter, write *one* good, original argument of your own that has the same form. That is, come up with arguments that have content you haven't found in this book.

EXERCISE III

As in Exercise I, identify what kind of argument appears in each example below, whether inductive or deductive. But since these arguments are fallacies (mistaken versions of the good arguments we've discussed), explain what's wrong in each case. If the problem has to do with the argument's form, explain precisely what's wrong.

1. Aaron's father is an investment banker, and he's making a lot of money. So if I want to be rich, I should consider a career in investment banking.

2. If a person is interested in the liberal arts, it makes sense for her to major in English or philosophy. But I have no interest in the liberal arts. So it's pointless for me to major in English or philosophy.

3. Professor, you've always said that if you want to do well academically, you'll have to study hard. I studied hard for this exam, so I don't see how you can give me a D on it.

4. The last two student government presidents have been members of the Sigma Sigma sorority. I guess if you're not in Sigma Sigma, you don't have a chance to get elected.

5. If a person is going to get into Sigma Sigma, she has to be either rich or super attractive. Well, I'm pretty well off. And my boyfriend thinks I'm gorgeous. So I should have no trouble getting in.

6. "Jumbo" Elliott is a 285-pound tackle who got a big scholarship to the University of Michigan right out of high school. "Fat Eddie" Jackson got an academic scholarship to Albion College, and he weighs 290. Since I weigh 180, all I need to do is gain 100 pounds to get a scholarship.

7. Professor Torres said if I want to do well in his Spanish class, I'll have to study. I've been studying hard for my math exam. So I guess I'll do OK in Spanish, too.

8. Look, you either buy the fine Beretta or settle for some broken down clunker. You don't want an ugly, unreliable car, do you? So buy the Beretta!

9. If you're going to get a job in a very competitive field, you have to be good. And if someone is a good person, she's honest, caring, and loyal. Since I'm one of the most honest, caring, loyal people I know, I should have little trouble getting a job, no matter how competitive the field.

10. People who love wild animals would never buy a fur coat. But if no one buys fur coats, then lots of fur-bearing animals will not be raised. And if lots of fur-bearing animals are not raised, there will be fewer mink, fox, and raccoon. So people who love animals are actually helping to reduce the numbers of mink, fox, and raccoon found in nature.

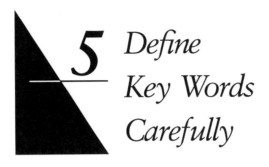

5 Define Key Words Carefully

You can't think clearly in terms you don't understand. Nor can you persuade anyone else without using language they understand in the same way you do. These are two reasons why defining your terms clearly is crucial for logic. Another important reason is that many controversial issues are made difficult when people use terms without fully understanding them. So even a start on resolving disputes requires being able to define your terms. Finally, many issues involve questions of concept, and these can be resolved by providing persuasive, "intensive" definitions. In this chapter we will discuss what makes a definition good, how to develop a good definition, how to resolve questions of concept, and what can go wrong with definitions.

Figure 5.1
Calvin and Hobbes © 1987 Universal Press Syndicate. Reprinted with permission. All rights reserved.

WHY PRECISE DEFINITIONS ARE IMPORTANT

In the cartoon in Figure 5.1, Calvin and his mother aren't "speaking the same language" because they have different things in mind by the word *snack*. This is not an unusual problem. Clear reasoning, effective communication, and all logical thinking require words and expressions to be clearly understood by all parties. Without an accurate and precise understanding of the meaning of a term, you cannot use that term accurately or precisely. And unless all parties to a discussion share the same idea of a term's meaning, communication, in the sense of sharing an idea, cannot take place.

You may think this is too small a problem to take up a whole chapter in a logic book. After all, you might think people generally know what they mean, and if not, a good dictionary ought to settle the question. If people could just take the time to look up every unclear word or phrase in a good dictionary whenever they felt unsure about it, disagreements about meaning would disappear, and much personal thinking, speaking, and writing would be clearer (and better spelled).

There is much to be said for using a good dictionary. Using one to identify the meaning of unfamiliar words and phrases helps increase your vocabulary and refine your use of language. It also can help coordinate your spellings with standard grammar. Of course it is easy to skip over unfamiliar expressions and hope to guess their meanings from the context, such as long words in Russian novels. But you really should look them up. Not only does the meaning of key words or phrases change the context, but also the guess you make may be wrong and may lead you to embarrass yourself next time you try to use the word.

Problems with Dictionary Definitions

Although dictionaries can go a long way in helping people to understand clearly and communicate effectively, dictionaries alone won't solve all the problems of definition that you will encounter in logic. To see why not, we need to make some distinctions.

- A **lexical**, or **reportive, definition** lists the ways in which most people who speak the same language use the term being defined.

- A **stipulative definition** specifies a particular meaning for a term within a given context or situation.

Dictionary definitions are lexical definitions that report the ways in which people use words, with the most frequent use listed first. Here is a lexical definition:

> **love** (luv) *n.* warm liking or affection for a person, affectionate devotion; *there's no love lost between them,* they dislike each other. 2. sexual affection or passion, the relation between sweethearts. 3. God's benevolence toward mankind. 4. strong liking for a thing, *love of music.* 5. affectionate greetings, *send one's love.* 6. a loved person, a sweetheart, *(informal)* a familiar form of address. 7. (in games) no score, zero; *love all,* neither side has yet scored; *a love game,* in which the loser has not scored at all. **love** *v.* (**loved, lov • ing**) 1. to feel love for. 2. to like greatly, to take pleasure in having or doing something. □ **for love,** because of affection; without receiving payment; *cannot get it for love or money,* by any means. **In love,** feeling love (especially romantic or sexual love) for another person. **love affair,** a romantic or sexual relationship between two people who are in love. **love apple,** *(old use)* the tomato. **love beads,** a long string of beads worn by members of both sexes to indicate freedom from traditional attitudes and customs.

This lexical definition comes from the *Oxford American Dictionary,* and it means that *love* (which is pronounced "luv") is a noun most commonly used to mean "warm liking" and less commonly used to mean "sexual affection," "God's relation to mankind," and so on. Why wouldn't this be enough to settle disputes about meaning?

Imagine a situation in which it is very important that someone understand what someone else means by a term. Here is an example.

Diane is jealous that Steve continues to spend time with his former high school girlfriend, Shelly. Tortured by doubts, Diane

confronts Steve and demands that he explain exactly what his feelings are for her and for his former girlfriend.

"Steve, I've got to know. It's just tearing me up. You're always spending time with Shelly. What's going on between you?"

"Well," Steve replies, embarrassed, "Ah, she's a friend, you know; I, ah, like her."

"You *like* her, Steve? What exactly does that mean?"

"Oh, c'mon Diane; I don't know. She's . . you know, a friend. I just like hanging around with her sometimes."

Angry, now, Diane continues, "'You *like* hanging around with her?' How much? Why can't you give me a straight answer? What do you mean, you '*like*' her?"

This conversation could go on forever. The problem is that Steve is replying to Diane's demands for a definition of *like* with evasive answers. That is, his answers give her as little information as he can get away with. Many ordinary language situations are similar to this one because, like Steve, people often use language vaguely or ambiguously. An expression is **vague** if its meaning in the context cannot be clearly determined because it is not sufficiently specific. And an expression is **ambiguous** if its meaning in the context cannot be clearly determined because there is more than one possibility and you can't tell which is meant. So one problem with dictionary definitions is this: They will preserve all of the vagueness and ambiguity that occur in ordinary language.

Of course, vagueness and ambiguity have their uses. There are situations in which people may not know specifically what they feel, so their truthful answers will be vague in this respect. Or they may not wish to overstate their evidence. Or they may wish to leave tactless details unmentioned. Or they may speak ambiguously because their beliefs are many sided and flexible. In general, however, it's best to be very precise about what we think, replacing vagueness and ambiguity with a precise idea of what needs to be discovered, better understood, or communicated.

There are problems besides vagueness and ambiguity in dictionary definitions. Let's continue this example. Trying not to be put off by Steve's vagueness, Diane says:

Don't play with my feelings, Steve. You *like* to spend time with Shelly. Do you *love* her?

Of course, Steve may not know what he feels for either of them. Suppose he tries to find out by looking up the meaning of *love* in the dictionary. Dramatically turning his back and slipping the *O.A.D.* out of his trenchcoat pocket, Steve finds the above definition, realizes the #1 definition is only "warm liking," and says:

> **Diane, I've known Shelly for years, and we've shared lots of time together. Of course I *love* her.**

But it's unlikely that Diane will be reassured, even if she's using the same dictionary. Why not?

In addition to being vague, the word *love* is ambiguous, and the ambiguity isn't resolved by the dictionary. This is because even if the individual definitions are clear, Diane can't tell from the context which one Steve is using. If she's not thinking, only being jealous, she may not realize the problem and may assume Steve means #2, "sexual affection or passion," which is what she's afraid of. The general problem is that even though the dictionary lists usages in order of frequency, there is no ensurance that the order will be followed in any given situation.

But suppose that instead of slapping Steve across the face, Diane turns to her own dictionary, the *American Heritage Dictionary,* and finds this entry:

> **love** (luv) *n.* 1. a. An intense affection for another person based on familial or personal ties. b. A strong affection for or attachment to another person based on regard or shared experiences or interests. 2. An expression of one's affection: *send him my love.* 3. a. An intense attraction to another person based largely on sexual desire. b. The deep affection, tenderness, and concern felt for a person with whom one has or wishes to have a relationship based on sexual attraction. c. The person who is the object of such an attraction: beloved. 4. a. Intense sexual passion. b. Sexual intercourse.

After reading it, Diane might say to herself, "Hmm. Does he mean 1.a or 1.b? That wouldn't be so bad. But what if it's 3.a or 3.b?" Diane, trying to let just enough pain into her voice, says:

> **OK, you *love* her. Now what do you mean by that?**

Steve might be puzzled at this. Since nonromantic affection is the first listing in the *O.A.D.,* he used it. But it isn't quite accurate. Steve and Shelly more than like each other "warmly." In their hearts, there are still the burning embers of those romantic nights at the beach, the night after the prom . . . The problem is, there is no dictionary definition for "stronger than 'warm liking' but less than 'sexual passion' although it's still a possibility we want to keep open." Suppose Steve were to say:

Diane, there are simply no words to describe how I feel about Shelly.

That, too, would be a bad move because "there are no words" has a nondictionary meaning too—that his actual feelings for Shelly are too intense or romantic for words. The problem now is that dictionaries usually don't include idioms, or slang. Besides, these change so rapidly that dictionary definitions of them can be silly.

CRITERIA FOR GOOD DEFINITIONS

To clear all of this up, Steve and Diane will have to toss their dictionaries and *stipulate* a precise meaning of *like* and *love* as they intend them. Perhaps their abilities to do this will be affected by their emotional states—it's hard to reason well when you're jealous or defensive. So suppose that Shelly, walking her St. Bernard in the park, overhears this conversation and talks to the two of them.

> **"Look, Angel," she might say to Diane, "Not so fast. It's easy to see the definitional problems of three little people may not amount to a hill of beans in this crazy world, but inside us, we both know you belong with Steve. He said he loves me. But tonight you've said a great many things. You thought he meant it was still hot stuff between us. But that was all over long ago. Oh he might have pretended, once in a while, and I might let him pretend. But the kind of love Steve has for me isn't the hot stuff; it's friendship; you know, mutual respect and enjoyment based on shared interests. You—you're all romance and excitement. Look at him; he's crazy about you. Now go on. Get out of here, both of you."**

Shelly's stipulative definitions are *friendship* as "mutual respect and enjoyment based on shared interests" and *love* as "romantic attraction and (sexual) excitement." Her stipulative definitions have several advantages:

◂ They're clear, in that they specify meanings understood by all parties and they eliminate the confusion.

Figure 5.2

▌ They're accurate, in that the meanings she specifies are close to the way people normally intend these terms to be understood in situations like this.

▌ They're unbiased, in that they don't involve any strong emotional connotations and are acceptable to all parties to the discussion. (More about this later.)

And these are the most important criteria for good definitions generally: They need to be clear, accurate, and unbiased. Of course, some terms are impossible to define without emotional bias, even if the definitions are clear. Note that Calvin's definition of a *doofus* (Figure 5.2) is the same as his definition of *nimrod* and that Suzie doesn't care for either of them.

Ostensive, Extensive, and Intensive Definitions

So, how do you go about giving good stipulative definitions? There are three strategies, each of which has advantages and disadvantages.

▌ An **ostensive definition** gives a word's ostension, which is one or more examples of things referred to by a term or an expression.

▌ An **extensive definition** gives a word's extension, which is a *complete* list of things referred to by a term or an expression.

▌ An **intensive definition** gives a word's intension, which is the common features shared by everything correctly referred to by a term or an expression.

Most words and expressions are learned by ostension. For example, if you took your two-year-old nephew to the fruit stand and taught him what *apple* means by pointing to a Jonathan or a Delicious, you would be giving a definition by ostension. Similarly, if someone asked you to define *automobile* and you said, "Well, that Mercedes-Benz over there is an automobile, and so is that Chevette," you'd have given an ostensive definition. And if you are able to give an ostensive definition by citing just one perfect example ("What I mean by a 'real baseball player' is someone like Ricky Henderson"), that perfect example is called a **paradigm case.**

Ostensive definitions are usually easy to give. Unfortunately, they are also easy to misunderstand, because they don't explain why a term applies to an object. When you point at a Jonathan, your nephew might think you're defining *red* rather than *apple,* or *Jonathan apple* rather than *apple,* or even *pile of fruit.* In short, there's no logical guarantee that any ostensive definition will be understood. But there's another problem with ostensive definitions. Often there's nothing to point to as an example, as in the case of *unicorn* or *triangularity* or *justice.* And in formal writing, people aren't interested in examples. Instead, they want precision.

Extensive definitions are clear, because they list everything to which a term properly refers. If you define the expression *solar planet* as "Mercury, Venus, Earth, Mars, Jupiter, Saturn, Uranus, Neptune, and Pluto," you've given the extension of *solar planet,* and identified exactly how the term is used. The problems for extensive definitions are that there aren't many things that can be listed completely (e.g., *real number* cannot), that some complete lists are inconveniently long (e.g., *American states*), and that an extensive definition does not specify what makes a term apply to what it does.

Necessary and Sufficient Conditions

The most useful definitions for most purposes in logic are intensive definitions because they settle questions of concept by identifying exactly when a word applies. If you defined *automobile* as "an enclosable land vehicle with a trunk or rear passenger area, designed to transport up to six to nine passengers, usually powered by an internal combustion engine," you'd have given an intensive definition by spelling out what characteristics all and only automobiles have. More specifically, you would have given *necessary and sufficient conditions* for being an automobile. **Necessary conditions** are features that must

Figure 5.3
Calvin and Hobbes © 1987 Universal Press Syndicate. Reprinted with permission. All rights reserved.

be present for an object to count as an example of the term in question. (It's a necessary condition of being an automobile that an object be a land vehicle, for example, but it's not sufficient because although trains are land vehicles they're not automobiles.) **Sufficient conditions** are enough to make the object count as an example of the term in question. (Being a Mercedes-Benz is a sufficient condition for being an automobile, but not a necessary one.) The best intensive definitions give both necessary and sufficient conditions and nothing more.

One danger of an intensive definition is that it must not just reflect your personal opinion about something. Like all definitions, it needs to be accurate. It needs to represent how the concept is used in society generally. In the cartoon in Figure 5.3, Calvin's definition of *happiness* as "being famous for your financial ability to indulge in every kind of excess" does not reflect either necessary or sufficient conditions, because people can be happy without being rich and rich without being happy. Instead, it only represents his opinion.

So, how can you be sure you're not just expressing an opinion, rather than giving a good intensive definition? A good way to develop an intensive definition is to start with the general category something belongs in (called its **genus**) and then identify the features that make it different from other, similar objects (called **differentia**). In the automobile case, the genus is "vehicle." "Land" differentiates automobiles from airplanes and boats. "Typically powered by an internal combustion engine" differentiates them from bicycles and golf carts. "Enclosable" differentiates them from motorcycles. "Designed to transport up to six to nine passengers" distinguishes them from buses and trains. "With a trunk or rear passenger area" distinguishes automobiles from trucks. So the result should uniquely pick out automobiles and explain the reasons why.

Counterexamples

You can test the accuracy of the intensive definition of *automobile* by trying to think of something that is obviously an automobile but doesn't fit the definition or something that obviously fits the definition but isn't an automobile. Something of either kind is called a **counterexample**, and if there are counterexamples to a definition, the definition is inaccurate and needs to be corrected. It's important to remember, however, that counterexamples need to be obvious rather than questionable. For example, a mini-van should probably not be considered a counterexample to the definition of *automobile* because it's not obvious whether we should consider a mini-van an automobile or not.

DENOTATION AND CONNOTATION

Last, in addition to being clear and accurate, definitions need to be emotively neutral. Words have both **denotation,** which is what a term literally refers to, and **connotation,** which is what emotional responses are associated with a term. All terms have positive, neutral, or negative connotation; what logic requires is to give definitions in the most neutral terms as possible.

It is easy to think of words with the same denotation and different connotations. Some examples follow.

Positive	Neutral	Negative
slender, slim	thin	skinny
assertive, strong	aggressive, intense	pushy
freedom fighters	rebels	terrorists
economical	inexpensive	cheap

Remember, all of these examples are relative in the sense that *thin* is less positive than *slim* and less negative than *skinny.* Even a relatively neutral term such as *aggressive* may have a somewhat negative connotation; the point is, it's *relatively* neutral.

Problems arise because people's attitudes are influenced by connotations, so that when a definition is not neutral, people are not always able to think clearly. Of course this is what is intended by people who use biased language to influence other people's ideas instead of giving them reasons. As effective reasoners, however, we need to recognize biased language and resist it.

Here is an example of biased language at work. It is taken from a pamphlet urging people to sign an anti-abortion petition.

> **Thousands of beautiful, healthy, unborn babies are being slaughtered every day at your expense! In spite of the best efforts of your neighbors of the Right to Life, legislative liberals and a misguided governor have conspired to continue the killing. But now, you can help. Sign the petitions being circulated by the caring people in your neighborhood. Cut off publically funded abortions. Call 1-800- --- ----.**

Without debating the moral issues involved here, notice how the writer has used connotation to influence people's beliefs. By defining *fetus* as "beautiful, healthy, unborn babies," the writer arouses positive feelings toward his cause, while using *slaughtered* to mean "aborted" directs negative attitudes toward those who disagree with the writer.

The best way to ensure that your definitions do not involve biased language is to use expressions all sides will accept. If all parties agree that their views are described fairly, it is likely that the descriptions of their positions are emotively neutral. (In a "pro-choice" pamphlet, "pro-lifers" are described as "fundamentalist bigots." Would they feel comfortable with that description? If not, it's biased!)

Unfortunately, some topics have become so emotionally charged that there are no neutral ways to talk about them. The word *gay*, for example, was once used to define *homosexual* positively, but it has mostly lost that positive connotation. And perhaps there is no positive way to define *fat* or *ugly* or *murder*. What is required for unbiased definitions is only that you use the most neutral expressions you can.

Summary

Effective reasoning requires you to define your terms carefully. The best definitions are clear, accurate, and emotively neutral. Since dictionaries offer only lexical definitions, and these are often inadequate in many respects, it is often necessary to stipulate a definition. Although some definitions can be given by ostension and extension, the most useful definitions in logic are intensive, because they offer necessary and sufficient conditions for applying a term correctly. The best strategy for working up a good intensive definition is to start with a genus and add differentia. You can test the accuracy of your definition by the method of counterexamples. You can test your definition for bias by deciding whether all parties to a dispute would accept your definition. And you can test for clarity by making sure your definition is free of any ambiguity or vagueness and can be easily understood.

EXERCISE I

Give good definitions of each of the following, explaining how your definitions meet the criteria of clarity, accuracy, and neutrality. Identify any ambiguities you'll have to resolve before you can give a definition. If there is a problem giving a definition of the required kind, explain what the problem is. (Note: Explaining how you would go about giving a definition is not the same as giving the definition.)

1. Give good ostensive definitions of: (a) pen, (b) desk, (c) integer, (d) war, (e) triangle, (f) illusion.

2. Give good extensive definitions of: (a) positive integers smaller than 3, (b) American states bordering the Great Lakes, (c) major American automobile makers, (d) twentieth-century wars in which Americans were combatants.

3. Give good intensive definitions of: (a) pen, (b) desk, (c) war, (d) religion. In each case identify genus and differentia.

EXERCISE II

Use the method of counterexamples to disprove the accuracy of the following definitions.

1. *Love* means sincerely caring about someone.

2. An *airplane* is a heavier-than-air device that flies.

3. *Tea* is a warm beverage people drink instead of coffee.

4. *Rights* are freedoms you're guaranteed by the Constitution.

5. *Intelligence* is the ability to solve problems.

EXERCISE III

Identify any ambiguity, vagueness, unclarity, inaccuracy, or bias in the following definitions and sentences. Then write a definition that solves the problem(s) you've identified.

1. *Harmful* means "capable of causing harm."

2. A *dog* is man's best friend.

3. A *hunter* may be defined as one who enjoys inflicting pain and suffering on animals.

4. A *politician* is a person who nobly sacrifices his personal fortune for the good of his fellow citizens.

5. Your *mother* is the one who always loves you, no matter what.

6. *Deterrence* means stopping crime before it happens.

7. *Communism* is an antireligious political system that disregards human rights and confiscates private property.

8. A *conservative* is a person who recognizes the folly of throwing money at social problems.

9. *Meat* is food made from the corpses of dead animals.

10. *Taxes* are simply legalized theft.

11. *Money* is a medium of financial exchange.

12. "Poetry is the kind of thing that poets write." (Robert Frost)

13. A *drug* is any substance that has an effect on the body or mind. (National Clearing House for Drug Abuse)

14. An *expense* is any expenditure or cost incurred by a business. (Financial Accounting)

15. *Leadership* is the act or process of leading.

6 Make Reasons Relevant

One of the important criteria for good arguments is relevance. This is because people who cannot see that your reason is relevant to your conclusion usually will not be persuaded by it. So it's important to make clear how your reasons and conclusion connect up with each other. Reasons are logically relevant to their conclusions when the truth of the reason affects the truth of the conclusion. But people sometimes see things as personally relevant when there's no logical connection. Since logical truth relations are often difficult to determine, we need a clear understanding of how relevance works in actual arguments. So in this chapter we'll examine some arguments in which reasons that are relevant help to prove their conclusions and also look at some arguments in which reasons that appear relevant but aren't are used to manipulate people into accepting unwarranted conclusions. These arguments, which are called fallacies of relevance, fail due to problems in the relation between the reasons and conclusion.

EXAMPLES OF RELEVANT AND IRRELEVANT REASONS

Suppose that Alan and Maribeth are on their way to play tennis together for the first time. If Alan wanted to gain a slight psychological edge, he might give Maribeth the following argument:

> You know, I hope you don't mind losing. You see, I'm sure to win because I'm wearing an extremely expensive new tennis outfit.

Now this argument probably would not convince Maribeth that Alan is sure to win, because there's no evidence of a close connection between expensive clothes and winning at tennis. That is, since people who wear expensive outfits often lose, and people who wear old gym shorts often win, there doesn't seem to be a relevant connection between the cost of your clothes and your chances of winning. To make this argument more effective with reasonable people, Alan would have to show that there is a connection between expensive clothes and winning, and explain what that connection is in a convincing way. Maybe he could try to show that wearing expensive clothes improves people's confidence so much that their skills improve enough to ensure their winning. But since this probably isn't true, it shouldn't persuade a reasonable person either.

So Allen might give Maribeth another argument, such as this:

> Well, I've also got another advantage that guarantees my winning. You see, I use the same kind of tennis balls they have at the US Open.

But again it's unlikely that Maribeth would be very intimidated, because the reason still doesn't seem very persuasive. The reason is not persuasive because *both players* will be using the same tennis balls, so they can't give one player an obvious advantage over the other. Besides, any regulation tennis ball, including the kind of tennis ball that is used at the US Open, will be nearly identical with any other new tennis ball. So this reason isn't relevant either, and these facts explain why. It's hard to imagine anything that would make this argument work; maybe if Maribeth were used to playing with old, mushy tennis balls that hardly bounce, Alan would have a relevant advantage if they used balls he was much more comfortable with. But that's assuming a lot of unusual circumstances as background information.

Now suppose Maribeth gets tired of Alan's attempts to manipulate her and she replies with the following argument:

It's good to hear an intermediate player trying to build up his confidence. Usually when people realize that I'm the #3 ranked women's singles player in the world, they get a little intimidated. I'll probably win, but at least maybe we can have a good match.

Here, the conclusion is that Maribeth will probably win, and the reason is that she's the #3 ranked women's singles player in the world, whereas Alan is only a mediocre intermediate. If Alan is reasonable and she's telling the truth, he should be pretty worried, because being ranked #3 is very good evidence that she'll probably win. This is because WTA rankings depend on such relevant things as how many matches you've played and won, who your opponents were, and so on. And to be ranked #3 means you've defeated many players who are far better than Alan is. So if he understands the relevance of these points, he is very likely to be convinced.

RELEVANCE AND
BACKGROUND INFORMATION

The moral of these examples is that arguments are most effective with reasonable people when they offer true information that is relevantly connected to their conclusions. If the connection between your reasons and conclusion is not obvious background information, you will need to make it clear by providing supplementary explanations. While all arguments presuppose some background information (see Chapter 7), relying on your audience to find the connection between your reasons and conclusion all by themselves can be risky. It is a much better strategy to supply any connecting information your audience might need to understand the relevance of your reasons.

Here are several examples of arguments in which the relevant connecting explanation appears in parentheses:

You should rent with Thrifty Rent-a-Car. We guarantee the lowest rates in the business. (One important consideration in choosing a car rental company is low rates.)

The average person will change jobs seven times during his working life and change careers at least twice. So more people should major in liberal arts areas. (Majoring in liberal arts areas helps prepare people broadly enough that they can make successful job and career changes.)

Animals have nervous systems that are very similar to those of people. So it's immoral to use animals for painful experiments that do not benefit them directly. (Animals probably experience pain, and it's immoral to subject anything to painful experiments unless it benefits them directly.)

You will notice that the closer the connection between the reason and the conclusion, the less controversial the connecting information needs to be. And the less controversial the connecting information is, the more convincing the argument becomes. Most reasonable people have little difficulty seeing the relevance of cost in deciding what car rental company to pick. Many college students, however, do not understand the relevance of liberal arts courses to being prepared for career changes. And probably even fewer people see the connection between the type of nervous system something has and the morality of doing experiments on it. This is why the connecting information in these examples has to be more detailed and may involve some controversial statements. (Is it necessarily immoral to do painful experiments on something that doesn't benefit directly? This is a question of value that reasonable people may disagree over. So probably even more argument will be needed to make the nervous system–morality argument successful.)

PERSONAL RELEVANCE VERSUS LOGICAL RELEVANCE

Arguments in which the relevance of the reasons to the conclusion depends on true information, or information that is well justified and generally accepted without further elaboration, can be considered good arguments, at least as far as the criterion of relevance is concerned. But some arguments make use of reasons in which the relevance to the conclusion depends on false information, or information so unusual or controversial that the strength of the argument is undermined. Yet some of these arguments still convince people. Often, this is because if people believe false things, they may come to accept a conclusion, even though they would be unreasonable to do this. We need to examine this issue further.

Let's go back to the tennis ball example, the argument that I'm sure to win because I'm using the same kind of tennis balls as the US Open uses. Suppose you have a lucky tennis ball—one that you've won with in the past. And suppose that you have the strange (false) belief that you can't win unless you play with your lucky tennis ball. Would that make my argument about tennis balls logically successful? The answer is no. This is because even though you personally might be influenced by my argument, there is no interpersonally reliable connection between the truth of my reason and the truth of my conclusion. Instead, the supposed connection depends on a personal belief you have that is false, and which people in general will not share.

This case illustrates an important distinction, between *personal relevance* and *logical relevance*. A sentence is **personally relevant** for someone if it would tend to influence that person's beliefs, feelings, or attitudes. But a sentence is **logically relevant** to a given conclusion (for anyone) if the truth of that sentence affects the probability that the conclusion is also true. Note that whereas personal relevance is always **subjective** and relative to some particular person (because it depends on that person's own beliefs, feelings, and attitudes), logical relevance is **objective** (doesn't depend on personal opinions, feelings, or attitudes). If something is logically relevant for someone, it's logically relevant for everyone because truth relations are interpersonal, not individual. Of course, people may disagree about what's true. And people may have various contributions to make as they work toward finding out what's true. But that doesn't change the fact that the yardstick for truth is not for individual adjustment according to our individual wishes.

Here are some additional examples that show the differences between personal relevance and logical relevance.

Jane thinks aliens have kidnapped all American politicians and replaced them with mindless robots. This is why she accepts the following argument: Aliens have visited the earth, so everyone should always ignore American politicians. "Aliens have visited the earth" has no logically relevant connection to "Everyone should always ignore American politicians." It's only Jane's strange (and groundless) belief that makes it seem personally relevant to her.

At an expensive restaurant, Alan reasons: "That man is wearing a polyester suit, so he'll be surprised they don't serve hot dogs here." This is because Alan thinks anyone who has ever worn a polyester suit has bad taste and that everyone who has bad taste prefers hot dogs to any other menu item. Of course Alan's beliefs are false, since the man need not prefer (let alone order) hot dogs. But Alan's reasons have personal relevance for him, however ridiculous they are in reality.

Andres is furious at the officials of the Detroit Pistons/Chicago Bulls basketball game he's watching because they keep calling Michael Jordan for traveling. But Andres believes that Michael Jordan can do no wrong. So he concludes that the officials are throwing the game to Detroit.

Because of the distinction between personal relevance and logical relevance, we are now in a position to see how some arguments can go wrong. When arguments offer personally relevant but not logically relevant reasons to support their conclusions, reasonable people should not believe those conclusions. Arguments that do not offer relevant information, or fail to make the relevance of their reasons clear by relying on true connecting information, are bad arguments.

Traditional logic books call arguments in which there is no relevant connection between reasons and conclusions *non sequiturs*. In real life, however, no one gives such arguments as "Invest $4,000 in the Big Bucks Mutual Fund; our brochure was typeset in Oregon" because reasonable people generally don't see "having been typeset in Oregon" as a relevant consideration when they're deciding where to invest their money. Instead, people usually offer reasons that have an *emotive* or *associative* connection, rather than a logically relevant connection, to their conclusions, relying on people's emotions to substitute for effective reasoning. Arguments that work this way are called *fallacies of relevance.*

AVOID FALLACIES OF RELEVANCE

What all **fallacies of relevance** have in common is that they offer reasons which have no connection of evidential support to the conclusions they're used to persuade people of. The fallacies rely on various feelings or attitudes to inspire belief. There are three common kinds of fallacies of relevance: appeals to emotion, appeals to irrelevant association, and appeals to irrelevant authority. In this chapter, we will examine only appeals to emotion and association. Appeals to irrelevant authority will be covered in Chapter 11.

Appeals to Emotion

All logically improper appeals to emotion make wrongful use of strong feelings, substituting them for clear reasoning and reasonable evaluation of evidence. It is very important to see that *not all emotional appeals are fallacies*, only the ones that substitute emotion for evidence are fallacies. It is perfectly proper to put your arguments in terms that appeal to people's hearts as well as their minds. The problem we're concerned with here arises only when the appeal to people's hearts replaces an appeal to their minds. There are fallacies of relevance (emotion) that correspond to each of the strong human feelings, but some are more common than others. Here are some common examples.

Appeal to Pity When a student asks for a better grade because his car broke down, or because if he gets a "D" he'll lose his scholarship, he's committing **appeal to pity,** a fallacy of relevance that substitutes feeling sorry for someone for good reasons. (Car breakdowns and losing scholarships are not relevant to assessing the academic quality of a student's work.)

There are many examples of appeals to pity. We are all familiar with the sad faces of children like those in the Rescue the Children ad in Figure 6.1, appealing to us to donate money to the organization sponsoring them. As a means of arousing our lazy consciences, such pictures can perform a perfectly valid function. They become fallacies when the sorrowful pictures are *all* that is offered to justify the appeal for funds. Here are some considerations that reasonably should be relevant to determining whether or not to contribute to Rescue the Children.

- Will these children benefit from your gifts?

- How, exactly, will your contribution be used to benefit them? (e.g., clothes? . . . food? . . . education? . . . employment? . . . employment for their parents?)

- What percentage of the funds contributed is spent on administrative costs, advertising, and the like, as compared with other, similar agencies?

If he were your child — would you let him starve?
Rashmi is only one of a thousand homeless waifs begging
for a little food in the filthy streets of India. At night, when
he tries to sleep in his cardboard hovel, cold and hunger
will torment his frail body. But you can help children like
Rashmi. For only $20 a month you can shine a ray of
hope into his dark life. So please hurry. Every day
thousands of children die of neglect and malnutrition.
$20 to Rescue the Children. It's not much, but it can make
a world of difference.

Figure 6.1

Next, think about the example in Figure 6.2. Here, as in Figure
6.1, the appeal to pity is probably based on a feeling of parental affection (why *is* it that impoverished suffering adults appear less often in
such ads than attractive but suffering children?), and it urges contributions to the United Way. The same rational considerations just
mentioned seem relevant here as well, but here the appeal to emotion
is also used to ignore a particularly difficult moral question, namely,
"Should we, morally, say 'yes' to funding extremely expensive neona-
tal life support, as opposed to making the same investment in school

IT COSTS A LOT TO SAY YES TO A MIRACLE.

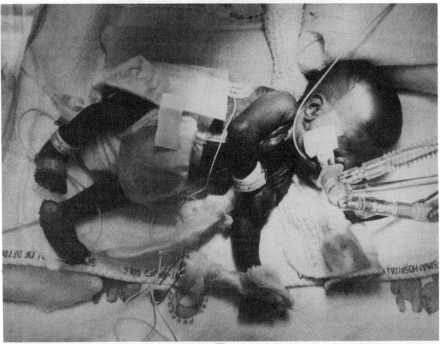

BUT WE CAN'T AFFORD TO SAY NO.

Ten years ago, this newborn would never have come home from the hospital. Today, thanks to medical research, new methods of treatment exist that increase the chances of a happy homecoming.

To encourage more miracles, the United Foundation Torch Drive supports 13 agencies that conduct research into heart disease, cancer, kidney disease, cystic fibrosis, arthritis, hemophilia and sickle cell anemia. Last year, you helped fund this research with $1.7 million. This year, we need to do more. Your contributions must help more people in need of new treatments.

So please give more to the Torch Drive and help fund 153 health and human service agencies in the tri-county area. Agencies that not only provide medical research, but also provide services to the elderly, the handicapped, the unemployed, the homeless and many others. It costs a lot to say yes. But, to save just one life, we can't afford to say no. **GIVE...FOR ALL THE GOOD YOU CAN DO.**

United Way
Michigan State Solicitation MISC 2123

Figure 6.2

lunch programs, public health, or care for the elderly?" The answer
to this question of value, which we as a society cannot avoid facing,
will be very difficult. But merely assuming that babies have a better
moral claim because they're pitiable prevents us from thinking about
this problem in a rational way.

Appeal to Sex In another widespread but irrational means of persuasion, the **appeal to sex**, an association or suggested linkage is
established between a sexually attractive image and a belief otherwise unrelated to it. Some of the more blatant cases of appeal to sex
occur when models in swimming suits or low-cut coveralls appear in
auto parts ads, but stylish-looking men in Armani suits selling panty-
hose or perfume are also appealing to sex. In Figure 6.3, *Ms. Magazine* has assembled a collection of ads that attempt to sell boats and
watches (among other things) through sexual appeals.

Some television ads appeal to sex to sell beer, as do Coors "Silver
Bullet," Budweiser, and Michelob Dry ads, which imply that there is
some close connection between being surrounded by extremely
attractive people and drinking their products. And in spite of taking
their ads off the air, cigarette companies often find ways to appeal to
sex in movies, for example. After all, one picture of Michael Douglas
(in *Black Rain*) or Kathleen Turner (in *Body Heat*) smoking Marl-
boros sends a far more powerful message than does a shelf full of the
Surgeon General's reports (at least, the tobacco companies hope so).

The point, and what makes these ads and images irrelevant
appeals to sex, is that whatever reasons might have been given for
buying shirts, boats, beer, and watches are replaced by various
images of sexual satisfaction that are psychologically but not rationally connected with buying these products. Since that is no reason to
suppose that buying any of them is directly connected with sexual
experience, being influenced in this way represents fallacious reasoning if there is any reasoning going on at all.

However, it is worth pointing out that not all ads which feature
attractive people, even if they are flirting with each other or cele-
brating their own attractiveness, are necessarily appeals to sex. Many
cosmetic ads, for example, feature beautiful women and attractive
men, sometimes in poses some people would consider suggestive.
But such ads may not appeal to sex if the products they advertise
are relevantly connected to a person's attractiveness. Also, remember that appeals to sex directed toward men will typically feature
women in seductive poses, whereas those directed toward women

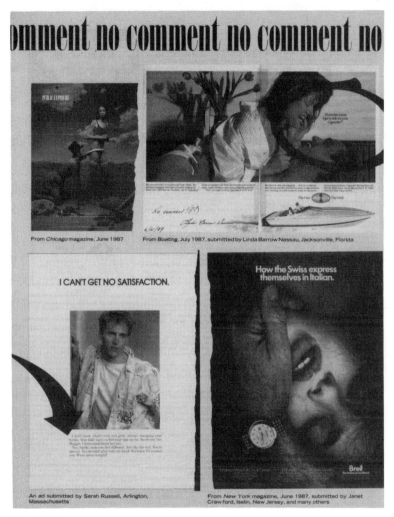

Figure 6.3

will usually feature men. Thus, an attractive woman modeling make-up to women consumers is not as likely to appeal to sex as if she were selling dirt bikes to men.

Appeal to Fear A motivator as strong as sex is fear, and those who threaten, explicitly or implicitly, in place of reasoning relevantly, commit the fallacy of **appeal to fear**. In the cartoon in Figure 6.4, Motley's persuasiveness regarding the mouse's diet is surely not

Figure 6.4
Reprinted by permission of UFS, Inc.

primarily rational, nor is the parent's or boss's who deals with disagreement by pointing out, "If you don't like it, get out!" Also, many American politicians have relied on fear to justify their unwillingness to agree to arms control treaties with the Soviet Union.

Appeal to Anger The **appeal to anger** relies on the fact that people who are angry will often not require a rational demonstration that their anger is properly directed. Hitler, for example, effectively used the appeal to hate to pass from "That man is Jewish" to "That man should be killed," just as many racists have used it to argue from "That woman is black" to "That woman has no rights." Recently, a number of Islamic leaders have used the anti-Western anger and feelings of persecution felt by many Moslems to justify policies for which no rational defense exists, such as terrorism and kidnapping hostages.

Appeal to Hope Another fallacious emotional argument is the **appeal to hope**, in which the gap between the reason and the conclusion is bridged by playing on people's strong optimistic desires. Quacks who sell fake "cures" to people suffering from chronic diseases often try to manipulate their clients' desperation to cover the lack of evidence that their bracelets, ionizers, electromagnetic field generators, and other rubbish will actually cure anyone. Similarly, those who advertise dramatic weight losses by diet pills or other effortless means are playing on the hopes of their customers rather than offering evidence about the effectiveness of the pills or whatever. And state lottery ads appeal to hope when they argue that you should buy lottery tickets on the grounds that you might win, covering up the fact that your actual odds of winning are very small.

Appeal to Excitement A final emotional appeal is the **appeal to excitement.** This fallacy of relevance occurs when the arguer uses that fact or possibility of people being excited or enthusiastic about something as a reason to believe it. Car and appliance dealers often advertise appeals to excitement ("Sunday—for 12 hours only—make a deal during the greatest sale in history!") as a substitute for relevant evidence that their prices are lowest or their service is superior. Politicians and religious revivalists often rely on the effect of mob emotion to convince people to believe them. And sensational magazines, such as the *National Enquirer,* similarly offer no proof of their dramatic stories beyond their entertainment value, relying on people's taste for excitement to substitute for intelligent appraisal of truth.

Appeals to Irrelevant Association

Not all fallacies of relevance involve emotional appeals. Some rely on **irrelevant association,** the willingness of people to see things as connected when they aren't. Two kinds of irrelevant association are particularly common. They are arguments of simple irrelevance and appeals to ignorance.

Arguments of Simple Irrelevance When people give reasons that may have some topical association with the conclusion but have no evidential relation to it, they are using **arguments of simple irrelevance.** A city commissioner who argues that the community can afford to build a new swimming pool because the old pool is too small and the neighborhood children need "wholesome summer recreation" is committing this fallacy because pool size and children's needs are not relevant to the city's finances. So is the parent who argues that his children's tastes in gym shoes are too expensive on the grounds that the shoes are more expensive than those the parent bought for himself.

Argument from Ignorance The other common fallacy of association is **argument from ignorance.** Arguments from ignorance can take two forms. One is an argument that since something has not been proved to be false, it must be true. The other is an argument that since something has not been proved to be true, it must be false. A believer in astrology who argues that the stars strongly influence people's lives since no one has ever shown they don't commits the first form of this fallacy. The smoker who tries to convince herself that smoking isn't

really that harmful because no one has ever conclusively demonstrated a true cause-and-effect relation between smoking just by itself
and lung cancer is committing the second form of argument from
ignorance.

The catalog of fallacies of relevance can be extended indefinitely.
You can probably think of other examples, now that you have the
basic idea. Bear in mind though, that the foregoing fallacies are only
a small sample of the infinite ways in which reasoning can go wrong.
To avoid these fallacies, then, does not guarantee that your reasoning
is rationally defensible or that you have not been deceived. What is
far more important is to remember and observe the criteria for good
argument, one of which is that a rational person will be persuaded by
relevant information. Always keep in mind that you need to make
sure the connection between your reasons and your conclusion is
very clear.

SUMMARY

One of the requirements for a good argument is that the reasons must
be relevant to the conclusion. Something is relevant to something else
in the logical sense when the truth of one has a bearing on the truth
of the other. Put another way, reasons need to have a clear, evidential
connection with what they are reasons for. When people offer reasons that have no connection of evidential support to the conclusions
they're used to persuade other people of, they are using fallacies of
relevance. In this chapter, we looked at two kinds of fallacies of relevance. The first type, improper appeals to emotion, makes wrongful
use of strong feelings (e.g., pity, anger, sex), substituting them for
clear reasoning and reasonable evaluation of evidence. The second
type relies on irrelevant association, the willingness of people to see
things as connected when they aren't.

EXERCISE I

You are a member of the admissions committee, evaluating applications for two positions in next year's law school class. There are three
applicants. You are required to consider the probability of each
prospective student's success in law school and the law school's need

for a representative and diverse student body. For each of the following statements, decide whether it is or should be considered relevant to determining who to admit. Be prepared to explain why, in each case. Then write a short letter to the dean, explaining who you want to admit and why.

1. Amy graduated with a 4.0 GPA in philosophy, with minors in political science and English.

2. Khalid is a vegetarian.

3. Carolyn decided to apply to law school when she couldn't get a graduate fellowship in history.

4. Amy has always wanted to be a lawyer, arguing "cases" with her father when she was a child.

5. Khalid's GPA is 3.87, he majored in economics, and his LSAT (Law School Admission Test) scores were in the top 10 percent.

6. Carolyn was editor of her college newspaper.

7. Amy's parents both received advanced degrees. Her father has an M.B.A. and her mother has an M.D.

8. Khalid has listed your school as his third choice.

9. Carolyn is a minority student who comes from an extremely disadvantaged home.

10. Amy has two children for whom she is the sole means of support. (Her parents refuse to have anything to do with her.)

EXERCISE II

Determine whether any fallacies of relevance occur in the following arguments. If so, use the available information, add what you need, and give a better argument for the same conclusion. Note: it may be difficult to give a good argument for some of these conclusions. In that case, explain why.

1. The Soviet Union has consistently supported terrorist revolutions throughout the world. Its official ideology still endorses violence against democracies, including the United States.

Whatever the current Soviet leadership says, we risk annihilation if we agree to reduce our military forces.

2. The power of the Energy Crystal can focus your own healing energies to relieve suffering that medical science cannot reach. Harness the power of your inner light today for only $39.95.

3. Professor, during the first part of this class I was living with a bunch of rowdy guys who never studied and I had to miss a lot of classes because they were always using my car. I know I haven't done so well so far, but I really need to pass this class to stay eligible.

4. Father's Day comes only once each year. And you were thinking of buying him an inexpensive scotch? Isn't he worth the best? Glendornoch.

5. Senator, I want you to know that we environmentalists have carefully monitored your voting record, and it hasn't been too favorable to the environment. I think our organization might be willing to forget that if you come out strongly against the proposed nuclear plant.

6. Can we afford to fund the All-City Summer Basketball Tourney? We can't afford not to. Our children need good, clean summer recreation.

7. No one has convincingly proved that being able to write well necessarily affects a person's career. So there's no good reason to expect graduates of this college to pass English competency tests for graduation.

8. Who is sapping America's economic strength? Crummy welfare cheats! Who is taking your hard-earned tax dollars to buy drugs and Cadillacs? Crummy welfare cheats! Who is taking a free ride on the backs of us working people? Crummy welfare cheats! So who should we cut off without a penny? Crummy welfare cheats!

9. I will not deny that I have made some mistakes during my long career of public service. Videotape doesn't lie. I did take the money. But I want you to remember one thing. I have been the victim of a cruel government vendetta. The FBI has been out to get me for years. So I am confident that the jury will find me not guilty.

10. President Baker, your contract is coming up for renewal next year, and the board will be looking over your decisions very carefully. Now I notice you're thinking of caving in to those faculty radicals who want you to slash the sports budget. I'd think again if I were you.

11. Although some twenty space probes have been launched by scientists from the United States and other countries, none has so far found evidence of extra-terrestrial life forms. We should therefore conclude that the search for alien life is futile.

12. Discuss the appeal made by Columbia House (a record/CD club) to get people to sign up.

> **Due to the exclusive nature of this special membership offer, please respond immediately.**

13. Find and bring to class an ad that you think appeals to sex. Be sure you can explain why the image in the ad is not relevantly connected to the product it advertises.

14. Discuss the U.S. Council for Energy Awareness ad in Figure 6.5, on the following page.

AMERICA'S NEXT HOSTAGE CRISIS?

According to the latest figures, America is now importing almost 50 percent of all the oil we use. If our oil imports continue to rise, another energy crisis could be triggered, one that could hold America's economy hostage again.

But the more we use nuclear energy, instead of imported oil, to generate electricity, the less we have to depend on foreign nations.

Our 112 nuclear electric plants already have cut foreign oil dependence by 4 billion barrels since the oil embargo of 1973, saving us more than $115 billion in foreign oil payments.

But 112 nuclear plants will not be enough to meet our growing electricity demand. More plants are needed.

We can help keep America from being held hostage and maintain our energy indepen-dence by relying more on our own resources, like nuclear energy.

For a free booklet on nuclear energy, write to the U.S. Council for Energy Awareness, P.O. Box 66103, Dept. RF01, Washington, D.C. 20035.

Nuclear electricity and energy independence

U.S. COUNCIL FOR ENERGY AWARENESS

Nuclear energy means more energy independence.

Figure 6.5

7 *Make Reliable Assumptions*

E very argument presupposes a large amount of shared background information between speaker and audience. This shared
background information is the set of assumptions the argument
depends on. It's important to rely on assumptions that are true or
reasonable and which are already accepted by the people you're trying to convince. Otherwise, your argument will not be accepted
because your audience won't agree with you at the start. In this section, we'll discuss the role of assumptions and what it is reasonable
to assume your audience knows.

ALL ARGUMENTS INVOLVE ASSUMPTIONS

Diane and Alan are planning to go out to dinner to celebrate the end of a long week. Both enjoy Italian food, and there are two good Italian restaurants in the area. Giovanni's, however, specializes in veal entrees, and Alan won't eat veal because he believes that veal farming causes immoral cruelty to animals. So Diane offers Alan this argument:

> **Since we'd like to eat Italian, we can go either to Giovanni's or to the O Solo Mio. Although both got good restaurant reviews, you'd probably not enjoy Giovanni's because it specializes in veal dishes. So let's go to O Solo Mio.**

It's likely that Alan will be persuaded by this argument because Diane is using the reliable deductive argument form "dilemma," and she is assuming what she already knows about Alan's attitudes and beliefs. Specifically, the hidden assumptions behind Diane's argument include all of the following (and more!):

1. Alan and Diane speak the same language and understand basically the same things by the terms of the argument.

2. They're going out to dinner, and they'll choose an Italian restaurant.

3. There are only two options, Giovanni's and O Solo Mio.

4. Restaurants that get good reviews have about the same level of features that make restaurants good (large menu, outstanding food, reasonable prices, excellent service, enjoyable atmosphere, etc.).

5. Alan thinks eating veal is immoral.

6. Alan would be less comfortable going to a restaurant that specializes in food he considers immoral than he would be going to another restaurant.

7. They ought to go where both of them will feel comfortable.

8. Alan will see that if there are only two choices and one of them is rejected, the other should be accepted.

Of course, all of these assumptions aren't usually stated every time someone gives an argument to someone else. In the first place, it's not usually necessary, especially when the parties know each other's beliefs and attitudes well. But if any of Diane's assumptions is incorrect, Alan might not be persuaded by her argument. For example, if assumption #2 is incorrect, he might reply, "Let's eat Chinese instead." Or if he rejects #4, he might ask, "What do you mean by 'good restaurant reviews'?"

Another example of what can go wrong when hidden assumptions are not shared is this example. Anne is an ardent pro-life advocate, and she's speaking to Joan, who takes a strong pro-choice position on abortion. Suppose Anne gives Joan the following argument:

> **Of course abortion is always immoral. Since every abortion always causes the murder of an unborn child, and murder is obviously immoral, it follows that abortion is immoral.**

It takes little imagination to guess that Joan will not be convinced by this argument, and not necessarily because she's bull-headed or irrational. The problem is that Anne and Joan do not share the same assumptions and that Anne's argument depends on some of the assumptions that Joan does not share.

OPERATIONAL VERSUS SUBSTANTIVE ASSUMPTIONS

What does Anne's argument assume? As in the case of Diane's argument, Anne's argument assumes a great deal of shared knowledge and experience. For example, in order to understand Anne's argument at all, Joan must share a similar working language and an approximately similar understanding of key terms. For example, if Anne had worded her argument in terms of "artificially induced therapeutic fetal expulsion," Joan simply might not have understood what she was talking about. As it is, Joan must know what an abortion is, she must have some idea of what murder is, and she must understand that by "unborn child" Anne means what Joan would probably call a "fetus." Also, Joan must be able to see that Anne intends her to recognize a connection of reasoning between Anne's premises ("every abortion causes a murder" and "murder is always immoral") and her conclusion ("abortion is always immoral"). That is, Anne assumes Joan will recognize that the sentences she is speaking are an argument. We can call the kind of assumptions needed to understand an argument **operational assumptions.** (Note: Precise interpretations of key concepts may become important beyond this operational sense. See below, as well as Chapter 3 on questions of concept and Chapter 5 on definitions.) When operational assumptions cause misunderstanding, it is usually easy to clear up the confusion. This can be done by rewording the argument, explaining further, or providing background information.

But even if Joan shares operational assumptions with Anne, she still may refuse to accept many of the beliefs that Anne's argument depends on. When people disagree about whether or not an argument's assumptions should be considered acceptable, they disagree about **substantive assumptions.** And when substantive assumptions cause people to disagree, the issue cannot usually be resolved without providing some argument for the assumptions that are causing the trouble. For example, Anne's argument presupposes that every abortion causes a murder. But this is a belief a rational person might question because she might believe that abortion causes only morally acceptable killing, not murder. In fact, in terms of the ideas we discussed in Chapter 3, the question "Should abortion be considered murder?" is a difficult question of concept. So the issue should be resolved by analyzing the concept of "murder" to see what the necessary and sufficient conditions for being an instance of murder are. Then it would be possible to see whether or not abortion fulfills them. (Again, how to do this is discussed in Chapter 5.)

A closely related problem is Anne's use of "unborn child" to mean "fetus." The problem here is a conceptual one as well as a matter of what she assumes: Anne is using emotionally charged language to influence Joan, while ignoring the question whether a fetus should have the same status and legal protections as a child. Anne's argument would be more rationally defensible if she avoided emotional language, a point we considered in Chapter 5. And since Joan would probably not accept the assumption that a fetus is a child (even an unborn child), if Anne wants to persuade Joan she will need to prove this, not assume it.

Finally, there is Anne's value judgment that murder is always immoral. This assumption is one that Joan would probably share, but only if she and Anne meant the same thing by "murder." That is, whether they share Anne's value judgment depends on how they resolve the question of concept about what murder is. To see why, suppose that *murder* is defined as "immoral killing." Then it would be obvious that every instance of murder (= immoral killing) is immoral. But since Anne is trying to convince Joan that the killing involved in abortion is immoral, she cannot rationally assume that it is, because Joan will simply deny that abortion is murder (= immoral killing).

But suppose that *murder* is defined as "the intentional killing of a human being." Then it will not be obvious that every instance of murder (= intentional killing) is immoral, because there may be some cases of self-defense, for example, that are not immoral but are intentional killing. And this is relevant to the abortion case because in some situations, such as abortions to save the life of the mother, abortion might be a kind of self-defense. (Besides, Joan might not accept the idea that a fetus is a human being.)

What all of this comes to is that Anne's argument will fail to convince Joan because Anne has too many hidden assumptions that are questionable. Specifically, she has oversimplified some very complicated questions of concept. Each questionable hidden assumption will undermine her argument. But Diane's argument concerning restaurants will probably succeed because her hidden assumptions are reliable ones. The general point this example illustrates is that if you want to persuade someone, you have to start with reliable assumptions of both operational and substantive kinds.

IDENTIFYING RELIABLE ASSUMPTIONS

There are two important tests for whether or not a hidden assumption should be considered reliable, regardless of whether the assumption is operational or substantive. They are:

- The assumption is shared or considered uncontroversial by the audience for the argument.

- The assumption is either known to be true or rationally justified on the basis of the best available information and valid reasoning.

It is important to remember that *both* of these tests need to be passed for an assumption to be reliable in the logical sense. Here's why.

As we considered in Chapter 2, arguments are never without an identifiable audience, and capable arguers need to keep the intended audience in mind when putting together an argument. Specifically, arguers need to imagine their audiences' attitudes, beliefs, and thoughts in order to decide whether their assumptions are reliable. In ordinary conversation, this is usually not difficult because we pick up cues from each other as we speak and listen. Facial expressions, gestures, and body language all provide information about whether people understand or agree with us. Besides, many of our conversations and arguments are directed to people we know reasonably well, in situations where shared goals can be assumed.

Sometimes, however, it can be difficult to anticipate what an audience is likely to believe or feel, especially if the audience is not present. When you're writing a persuasive paper, for example, there are no immediate cues about what your audience believes, so you have to imagine the people you're trying to persuade in order to decide what they're likely to accept and then go on to say the sorts of things likely to convince them. (Writing a persuasive paper is discussed in Chapter 10.) Because writing to a distant or impersonal audience requires so much imagination, it's a good rule to assume as little as possible in written argumentation. Instead, you should generally prove or justify any assumption you can possibly imagine a reasonable person questioning or even wondering about.

You should be especially careful about assuming four kinds of things:

ι technical information

ι value judgments

ι unsubstantiated facts

ι personal opinions

Most audiences will not necessarily know information that is familiar to people deeply involved in an issue or trained in a profession, so they will need to be informed. Any information that presupposes special interests, background, or training should be considered technical information, and you should provide it rather than assuming it. Next, as we saw in Chapter 3, value judgments almost always need to be argued for before you can assume people will share them. Although people sometimes overestimate the differences their audience has about values, it's usually most effective to persuade people to share your value judgments if your argument depends on them.

Any fact that you use to strengthen your argument should be verified by citing a reliable source for it (see Chapter 11). After all, unless your audience accepts your evidence as factual, they will see it as an opinion or value judgment and not give it the weight you want them to. And since people's opinions often differ, even about familiar issues, it's important to make sure yours are well founded and shared. After all, you don't want your audience to reply, "Well, that's just your opinion," when you're trying to give them an argument.

But the fact that your audience shares your assumptions is not enough to ensure that they are true. For example, if someone already believes that "all Communists are vampires," the argument "Smith is a Communist, so Smith must be a vampire," will convince him, even though the conclusion isn't true (since there are no real vampires). Besides, people have many prejudices, irrational fears, false beliefs, and other psychological influences that can be manipulated to influence their ideas. For this reason, the second test must also be passed. Assumptions must be either known to be true or justified by the best available information and valid reasoning.

Whether a hidden assumption is reliable is not an all or nothing matter. Some assumptions — the well-justified and widely shared ones — can be considered "safe." Anything else, including assumptions for which you think there are good reasons, should be considered "risky" (questionable) if there is some evidence on the other side or if a rational person might question them. The less risky your assumptions the stronger your argument. So even if you think an assumption is safe, if there is any doubt, you may need to provide an argument for it.

AVOID FALLACIES OF ASSUMPTION

Logically unacceptable arguments that depend on questionable assumptions are called **fallacies of assumption.** What all assumption fallacies have in common is that the reasons they provide depend on assumptions that are rationally unjustified on the basis of the best available information or the reasons depend on valid ways of understanding and applying that information. That is, fallacies of assumption are illogical arguments that violate the second condition for reasonable background assumptions.

People who give arguments that are fallacies of this kind assume what they need to prove, ignore or distort information that would tend to disprove their conclusion, or assume things that are false or highly questionable. Unfortunately, there is no simple, logical rule that will enable us to determine what assumptions are false or highly questionable; we must make this decision ourselves in real-life situations. So fallacies of assumption focus on types of arguments in which the question is whether the fact that something important is being assumed seriously undermines the argument. Some examples will help to clarify this point.

Begging the Question

Perhaps the simplest fallacy of assumption is to assume what you need to prove. This fallacy is called **begging the question,** and it occurs when a form of the conclusion is given as a reason or if the reason depends on assuming that the conclusion is true. The argument

> **We know that every other religion must be a false religion because none of them recognize the final and complete truth of our religion**

begs the question "Are all other religions false?" by assuming that ours is the one true religion — exactly what needs to be proved.

Similarly, the argument

> **We know that Ms. Yamamoto is the right candidate for the 6th District because she's right on the issues — she's a real voter's candidate**

begs the question "Is Ms. Yamamoto the right candidate for the 6th District?" by assuming that she's right on the issues and that she's a real voter's candidate, both of which are just different ways of saying "she's the right candidate." (Think of how unconvincing this argument would be to anyone not already on Yamamoto's side.)

But sometimes begging the question can be difficult to detect. In the example that follows, complicated language obscures the fact that the reason assumes the conclusion. In fact, the reason and the conclusion say the same thing, although you will have to think carefully to spot this.

> **Free market capitalism is the most socially beneficial economic system. This is because any governmentally unregulated structure of institutions permitting mutually beneficial and voluntary transactions to exchange and distribute goods and services obviously enhances the general welfare of society.**

Note that "any governmentally unregulated structure . . . " is the same thing as "free market capitalism" and that "obviously enhances

the general welfare of society" is the same as being "socially beneficial." Question-begging arguments such as this are also sometimes
called "circular" because they seem to go around in a circle, the conclusion coming out at the place the reason started.

Question-Begging Accusations

Another form of begging the question is **question-begging accusations.** This is a tactic much used by politicians and attorneys trying to
discredit people without supplying concrete proof. Here are two
examples:

> Ms. Berkowitz has so little financial skill she probably can't
> even balance a checkbook. Electing her comptroller would leave
> our finances in total chaos.

> Ladies and gentlemen of the jury, it would be a serious mistake
> to trust the testimony of a chronic liar like Jacobson. He lies so
> much that the man wouldn't know the truth if it jumped up and
> bit him!

In the first case, the question of Berkowitz's qualifications for comp-
troller is begged by accusing her of being unable to balance a check-
book. But notice that this is only assumed; no evidence or proof of
her financial problems is given. And in the second case, the proof
that Jacobson is a "chronic liar" is only the assumption that he "lies
so much . . . " But that assumption is exactly what needs to be
proved.

Complex Question

Yet another form of begging the question is called **complex question.**
In this assumption fallacy, the unjustified assumption is concealed in
the form of a question. Suppose a prosecutor hasn't proved the defendant broke into a gas station. If the prosecutor tries to create the
impression the defendant is guilty by asking the question "Exactly
when did you break into the gas station?" she is guilty of a complex
question because she assumes that the defendant did break into the
gas station in the first place, the assumption that the prosecutor
needs to prove. Similarly, imagine a student who says this:

> **Gee, professor, I'm sorry I missed the quiz—my alarm didn't go
> off. When do you want me to come in and make up the test?**

"If elected, would you try to fool some of the people all of the time, all of the people some of the time or go for the big one: all of the people all of the time?"

Figure 7.1

Reprinted with permission from TV GUIDE® Magazine.
Copyright © 1980 by News America Publications, Inc. Radnor, Pennsylvania.

This student will be guilty of complex question unless he or she knows in advance that the quiz can be made up, because as it stands the question "When do you want me to come in and make up the test?" substitutes for reasons why the professor should reschedule the quiz.

Finally, the reporter in the cartoon in Figure 7.1 is committing complex question by assuming that the candidate intends to fool his constituents at all (assuming he's trying to imply that the candidate cannot be trusted).

False Dilemma

False dilemma, which we discussed in Chapter 4, can be seen as an assumption fallacy, because it occurs when someone assumes that there is only a small number of choices when in fact there are other relevant possibilities. This is often done to promote a preferred choice by discrediting some other easy target. So if Diane had told Alan

> Look, we can go either to Giovanni's or to some cheesy burger joint. You can't call grabbing a burger a real dinner out. So we'd better go to Giovanni's

while in fact she knew all about O Solo Mio and many other Italian restaurants, she'd be guilty of false dilemma.

Remember that even though the name *dilemma* suggests this fallacy involves assuming there are only two options when there are actually more, the heart of the problem is unreasonably assuming that the number of options is smaller than it is, even if there are more than two choices presented. So this is also an example of a false dilemma:

> You can buy the fine, handcrafted $4,000 amplifier by Audio Perfection, or you can settle for something less, an expensive amp from someone else or a Japanese cheapie that will break down in no time. But you don't want to settle for less, and reliability is important. Go for the best: Audio Perfection.

What's being assumed here is that there are just three options. But the stereo salesman is overlooking some others, such as less expensive but equally good audiophile amplifiers, reliable but inexpensive products, and so on. (Note: If you're going to criticize an argument as a false dilemma, you'll need to be able to specify a relevant alternative that has been overlooked.) The cavemen in the cartoon in Figure 7.2 are committing false dilemma too: The man in the moon might just be a pattern of rocks!

Ignoring the Facts

Closely related to false dilemma is **ignoring the facts.** All cases of ignoring the facts involve disregarding relevant information that reasonably should have been taken into account. In effect, overlooking the facts is a kind of logical negligence, because the arguer is blameworthy through ignoring or not noticing what he ought to have recognized.

A very simple example might be Calvin's argument in the cartoon in Figure 7.3. He argues that since he has turned himself invisible, he can perpetrate any crime undetected. The fact he's overlooked, as revealed in the last panel, is that he has not turned himself invisible.

A more complicated example is this piece of reasoning by Sherlock Holmes, who concludes that Watson has been in Afghanistan by means of the following argument:

> The train of reasoning ran, "Here is a gentleman of a medical type, but with the air of a military man. Clearly an army

"Couldn't be a man. Must be a god!"

Figure 7.2

Drawing by Ross; © 1989 The New Yorker Magazine, Inc.

doctor, then. He has just come from the tropics, for his face is dark, and that is not the natural tint of his skin, for his wrists are fair. He has undergone hardship and sickness as his haggard face says clearly. His left arm has been injured. He holds it in a stiff and unnatural manner. Where in the tropics could an English army doctor have seen much hardship and got his arm wounded? Clearly in Afghanistan."[1]

Even though Watson considers Holmes the most nearly perfect logical reasoner, it is easy to see he is making a number of highly questionable assumptions here. Not all gentlemen of a medical type are doctors, for example, and not all people with the air of military men are in the army; in Holmes's day they might have been nurses or marines. You should be able to spot at least five other such questionable assumptions due to facts Holmes is ignoring.

However, this example illustrates two final points. First, note that Watson actually was in Afghanistan, so Holmes was right in his

---

1. From Arthur Conan Doyle, *A Study in Scarlet,* Beeton's Christmas Annual, 1887 (London: Ward, Lock, and Co.).

Figure 7.3
Calvin and Hobbes © 1986 Universal Press Syndicate. Reprinted with permission. All rights reserved.

conclusion. The fact that he was right about Watson, however, does not show that the argument he used to prove that conclusion is logically defensible. In fact, it shouldn't persuade a rational person because of all Holmes's questionable assumptions. The second point, one on Holmes's side, is this. It is *always* possible to question a person's assumptions if you are sufficiently disagreeable or if you interpret them unreasonably. But logic does not require nitpicking. On the contrary, if you object to someone's arguments because they involve questionable assumptions, it's up to you to show that the assumptions really *are* unreasonable, not just possible to doubt.

SUMMARY

In this section we have explored the role played by assumptions in offering persuasive arguments. Such assumptions can be either operational or substantive, and for an argument to be logically convincing, both kinds of assumptions must pass two tests. The first is that the assumptions your reasoning depends on must be shared by the audience for your argument. The second is that the assumptions must be either true or justifiable by the best available evidence and valid reasoning. To argue otherwise is to commit assumption fallacies, most of which violate the second restriction. We examined five examples of assumption fallacies: begging the question, question-begging accusations, complex question, false dilemma, and ignoring the facts. Effective reasoning involves not just avoiding these fallacies, however; it also involves making only reasonable assumptions.

EXERCISE I

For each of the following arguments, identify three or four of the most important substantive assumptions assumed by the arguer. Then decide how reliable those assumptions are. Be very specific, both about what assumptions you identify and about what, if anything, is wrong with those you object too. Remember to avoid nitpicking. Then see if you can give an argument for a similar conclusion that makes fewer questionable assumptions. (If you can't, explain why not.)

1. There won't be a serious recession for the next few years. There never is when a Republican is in the White House.

2. Even though we're only eighteen, Serena and I should get married as soon as possible. After all, she's rich and I'm good looking.

3. Anyone who majors in a traditional academic field in college must be crazy. Since the purpose of education is to get a good job, and there are hardly any jobs as historians or physicists, people ought to stick to practical majors such as business or engineering.

4. The only university resource that is really important to students is enough good faculty. So tuition should be increased only enough to pay for new faculty salaries.

5. It's obvious that Eastern European nations will continue to move toward an American-style democracy. Capitalism is the most efficient economic system, and everyone desires to be free.

6. Motorcycles are a good, economical alternative to automobiles. They're fun to ride, and if car drivers would just look out for them, motorcycles would be just as safe as cars. So I can't see why you don't want me to get a 'cycle.

7. Students shouldn't be required to get professors' signatures to drop or add their classes. After all, students are the ones paying for their educations, and they are responsible enough to make their own choices without somebody looking over their shoulders.

8. The death penalty is the only way to deal with serious crime in the United States. If you're going to face the electric chair

for dealing drugs or grand larceny, you'll think twice and change your mind. We should toughen up the sentencing guidelines as soon as possible.

9. Whether or not to eat veal is a matter of personal taste, since obviously veal calves don't have the same rights as people do. Animal rights advocates who think eating veal is immoral can eat something else if they want, but they shouldn't try to impose their ideas on others.

10. Abortion is a very personal matter that affects a woman profoundly. Nobody else is as directly involved. So abortion should be available to any woman on demand, and everyone else should stay out of the matter.

EXERCISE II

Carefully examine each of the following arguments, and determine whether or not it is or involves a fallacy of assumption. If so, explain why very specifically, and identify the fallacy by name if possible. Note: There may be more than one fallacy in an argument. Then give an argument for the same conclusion that would not be fallacious. If you can't, explain why not.

1. So, do you think you're too smart to spend time with your old friends from high school, or are you just stuck up now that you're in college? (Be sure to identify the conclusion here.)

2. You don't want to take English from that mean old Professor Curmudgeon. He's really nasty, and he never seems to be in a good mood.

3. If the drug problem in the United States is going to be solved, either the supply countries have to control the drug cartels or the U.S. military has to go in and clean up the mess. It's clear that the cocaine trafficking countries of South America cannot control the drug cartels. So the military should take care of the problem.

4. Professor, when can I make up the paper that was due last week? I wasn't able to get started on it until it was almost due, and I want to do a really good job on it.

5. The drug rehabilitation center should definitely not be built in this neighborhood. We don't want a bunch of drug-crazed losers, stoned out of their minds, wandering around, breaking into people's houses, and molesting children.

6. Which would you rather have, pollution or unemployment? OK, the chemical plant is going to produce toxic waste. But without it, there'll be even more people unemployed, and we can't afford that.

7. Trying to work more than twenty hours per week and go to college at the same time has to wreck a student's chances of doing well in school. After all, to do well in classes and homework you have to have more time than you'll have left if you work more than twenty hours.

8. People shouldn't put down newspapers like the *National Enquirer* just because they run sensational stories about aliens, reincarnation, and Elvis. After all, lots of people have seen aliens, and as Crosby, Stills, Nash, and Young said, "We have all been here before," even Elvis.

9. Either you can buy the boat you want now or you'll always be disappointed when you see somebody else doing what you can only wish you were doing. Go for it.

10.

Calvin and Hobbes © 1985 Universal Press Syndicate. Reprinted with permission. All rights reserved.

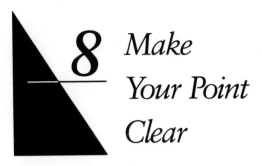

8 Make Your Point Clear

As we have seen, unless your audience shares your assumptions, they will not be easy to convince, no matter how relevant your reasons are to your conclusion. Similarly, unless your audience is able to follow your argument and is convinced that there is nothing tricky or obscure about it, they are unlikely to accept your conclusion. In this chapter, we will consider several steps which can help ensure that your argument is clear and straightforward. Among these are identifying reasons and conclusions precisely, presenting your ideas in a way that is easy to follow, using well-defined and specific language, and using key ideas fairly and consistently.

AVOID INFLATED LANGUAGE

Jack is looking to replace his old stereo equipment, since his tastes have matured and he's now interested in music that is less noisy and mindless. He's now trying to decide whether to buy a good, mid-priced receiver or to spend a bundle on separate electronics. Elena, the salesperson at Upscale Audio, offers Jack this argument:

> I notice you've been listening mainly to those bipolar planar speakers. If you think you might want to upgrade to them, you'd need high current, lots of power with pure class A biasing or maybe AB, and a quick slew rate. You can't get that in a receiver. Besides, you might want to biamp later on, which is a lot easier with separates.

Jack doesn't know what a bipolar planar speaker is, he doesn't know the difference between amps and watts, and he has no clue what biasing and slew rates are all about. But it's embarrassing to admit this. (Besides, Elena is extremely attractive.) So Jack nods his head wisely and wonders how he can get out of the store without embarrassing himself. Think, for example, about what the salesman is saying in the cartoon in Figure 8.1.

Now as it happens, Elena's advice is quite good, but Jack would not be acting rationally if he were convinced by it. Even though her reasons are relevant and reliable, Jack wasn't able to understand them because her language is inflated. What Elena should have done is kept her argument clear and understandable enough for Jack to make a rational decision.

PRESENT ARGUMENTS CONVINCINGLY

Elena might have given the following argument to Jack:

> If you're trying to decide between a midpriced receiver and separate electronics, it's good to remember that some electronics work much better with some speakers than with others. If you choose the receiver, you can't design your system to work together as well as you can with separates. So if you're mainly concerned with getting the best out of your speakers, you'll probably be happier with separates.

Now this argument may not make Elena sound as impressive as the earlier one with all the jargon. And if Jack had an advanced

"This CD player costs less than players selling for twice as much."

Figure 8.1

Drawing by Weber; © 1989 The New Yorker Magazine, Inc.

understanding of electronic technology, it might be too simple. But given Jack's actual level of understanding, this argument should be much more appropriate for him. That is because it offers true, relevant information in a clear and understandable way and the reasons bear a natural, supportive connection with the conclusion.

Elena's second argument has several other advantages. One is that her reasons and conclusion are clearly identified and presented in a logical order. As we know, conclusions can often be signaled by "indicator words," such as *therefore* and *accordingly. So* fulfills that function here. Moreover, the reasons are given first, which makes them appear to lead to the conclusion. And the structure of the argument is also very straightforward. Elena states her assumption that Jack is considering only two options and then provides information that tends to support one of the options and discredit the other. The conclusion then becomes that Jack should choose the option with the greatest support.

Starting with reasons and leading to the conclusion is one good way to set up an argument. The other is to start with the conclusion and then support it by giving your reasons. (Many of the examples in earlier chapters exhibit this order. So does the example that follows.) This pattern has the advantage of letting people know what you're trying to prove, so they can follow your reasoning more easily. But burying your conclusion in the middle of your reasons, or not making clear what it is you're trying to prove, will almost always leave your audience puzzled rather than convinced.

Make Connections Clear

In this example, Rachel is arguing for a change in the government's antidrug strategy.

> While reducing supply and better law enforcement may be helpful, the war on drugs cannot be won without much greater economic opportunity for disadvantaged Americans. This is because the main reason people turn to drugs is that they have no hope for a reasonable life in the American mainstream. And in today's society, a reasonable life requires a good job for all Americans.

Of course Rachael could say a lot more to support her conclusion. For example, she could give reasons why reducing supply and improving law enforcement won't be enough. But suppose she offered her original argument in this order:

> The government's policy of cutting off drug supplies won't be entirely successful as long as there is demand. Disadvantaged people turn to drugs because they have no hope for a reasonable life in the American mainstream. These people need greater economic opportunities. Better law enforcement won't deter people who don't have any better choices. And unless good jobs are available to all Americans, people will have no hope.

It's easy to see that the second argument will confuse more people than the first one will. In fact, even though the ideas of the first argument are all present in the second, most of Rachel's audience won't be able to identify them or see how they're supposed to support her conclusion (if they can figure out what her conclusion is!). The conclusion (that disadvantaged people need greater economic opportunities) is hidden in the middle of the paragraph, not clearly identified. And the relation between Rachel's reasons and her conclusion is also very confusing. The moral of this story is that if you want your arguments to be persuasive, you need to present them in a clear and logical order, either starting with the conclusion and supporting it with reasons or starting with reasons and leading to the conclusion.

Now suppose Dominic replies to Rachel's first argument with this:

> **It's foolish to suggest we should abandon law enforcement and reducing drug supplies and just assume that more opportunities for the disadvantaged will solve the drug problem. After all, not all disadvantaged people turn to drugs. Besides, everyone is disadvantaged in some respects. And even if we improve job opportunities for some disadvantaged people, we'll just wind up with other people being disadvantaged.**

Although the argument is presented in a natural order (conclusion first, followed by reasons), it shouldn't be persuasive. This is because Dominic's argument violates two more rules for good arguments — that arguments need to be fair and that they need to use key ideas in the same way throughout.

Dominic's argument is unfair to Rachel's in several respects. In the first place, Rachel did not conclude that we should abandon law enforcement and efforts to reduce drug supplies. She said only that those measures would not be enough and that improved economic opportunities were needed. And she didn't say or assume that all disadvantaged people turn to drugs, only that most people who turn to drugs are disadvantaged. (If Dominic intended to misrepresent Rachel's argument, he's guilty of a fallacy called "straw man," which we will discuss in Chapter 13.)

Notice, too, that Dominic is using the term *disadvantaged* in a way that is not the same as Rachel's way. When Rachel uses *disadvantaged*, she is referring to people whose educational, economic, and (perhaps) racial backgrounds make getting a good job unusually difficult. When Dominic uses *disadvantaged*, he means "having a little less of something valuable than somebody else has." And while everyone is disadvantaged in this sense, most of us are not disadvantaged in Rachel's sense. So even if it is true that boosting some disadvantaged person's job opportunities might make someone else disadvantaged relative to him, it doesn't follow that job programs make it unusually difficult for other people to get jobs. These are some of the reasons Dominic's argument should not be convincing.

AVOID FALLACIES OF CONFUSION

Fallacies of Confusion occur in arguments that make use of unclearly defined or inconsistent terms, obscure structure, or unfair interpretations to convince people to accept their conclusions. Although you might think that the most common reaction to such arguments would be to reject or ignore them just because they are puzzling, fallacies of confusion are surprisingly common. We will examine six of them.

Fallacy of Obscurity

The **Fallacy of Obscurity** occurs when reasons are given with such an air of authority that people accept them even though they don't understand them. Elena's first stereo argument was a fallacy of obscurity, and if it had worked, it would have been because Jack was too embarrassed to admit he didn't understand or because he was impressed by her apparent expertise (rather than by the cogency of her argument). When you identify something as an example of obscurity, be sure you can point out specifically what needs to be clarified or explained.

Fallacy of Unreasonable Definition

The **Fallacy of Unreasonable Definition** consists in reasoning by means of biased or questionable terms. Remember back to Chapter 5: The criteria for good definitions are accuracy, clarity, and lack of bias. If any of these requirements is not met, and the argument makes use of the inaccuracy, unclarity, or bias, the argument is fallacious. Dominic's argument involves a fallacy of unreasonable definition in that he used *disadvantaged* in a very unusual way and one which Rachel did not share. The following argument also involves an unreasonable definition.

> **It's wrong to condemn sensational grocery-counter newspapers as not serving the public interest. Since they sell out almost immediately, it's obvious that the public is very interested in stories about adulterous movie stars, aliens, and Elvis reincarnations.**

The problem here, of course, is the definition of "the public interest," which usually refers to what people ought to know to be responsible citizens and make reasonable decisions. Here, however, it is treated

Figure 8.2

as meaning what the public takes an interest in, and unfortunately that's not the same thing at all.

Another way in which unreasonable definition occurs is for a person to stick to the letter, rather than the spirit, of a term or an agreement. People do this when they rely on a strained interpretation or technicality to evade the meaning that would be more natural. In the cartoon in Figure 8.2, Calvin is doing exactly this, implicitly reasoning that he's obeying his mother even though he's not.

The way to avoid errors in reasoning due to unreasonable definition is to stick to the skills of good definition we developed in Chapter 5. There, you'll remember, we said a good definition is clear, accurate, and emotively neutral, and we explored several ways to achieve these goals. Among these were the methods of counterexamples and the test to determine whether all parties to a discussion would accept definitions that apply to them as accurate. By applying the criteria for adequate definitions in Chapter 5, you can be more confident of reasoning well.

Equivocation

A closely related definitional fallacy is called **Equivocation,** which occurs when an argument depends on using a single term, phrase, or idea in more than one way, to mean more than one thing. A Michigan sugar company commits equivocation in this advertisement:

> **Sugar is the body's storehouse of energy. And there's no more delicious, natural sugar than Michigan made, pure Homestead Sugar.**

The word *sugar* is being used in more than one way here. In the first sentence, *sugar* is used to mean glucose, which is (more or less) the "body's storehouse of energy." But in the second sentence, *sugar* means refined, granulated beet sugar, which is not at all the same thing as glucose. So the suggestion that Homestead Sugar is especially good for you as a source of energy is not supported by these reasons.

Another example of equivocation appears in this portion of an evangelist's sermon.

> My friends, there are those who will seek to deny the miracles wrought by God. The Scriptures say He fed thousands with a few loaves, healed the sick and called back the dead to life. Yet sinners say, "There were no miracles." But what of the miracles which surround us every day? The miracles of modern medicine which, with God's help, save lives in hospitals? The miracles of air travel and long-distance communication? No, sinners can't have it both ways, accepting the miracles of science and rejecting the miracles of God.

Here, of course, the equivocation is on the word *miracle,* which in one sense refers to divine interventions in the usual processes of nature and in the other sense refers to remarkable achievements that presuppose the usual processes of nature.

The best indication that equivocation may be going on is a feeling that some verbal trickery is involved in an argument or a feeling that the speaker is sliding around a topic. When you suspect equivocation, be sure you can accurately identify the term, phrase, or idea that is involved.

Fallacy of Misreading

The **Fallacy of Misreading** involves using a passage taken from another source in a way that would not have been consistent with its usual interpretation. The passage is misread by giving it an unintended or strained meaning, and that then serves as part of the reasoning supporting a fallacious conclusion. Here is an example from arch conservative Edward Verity.

> As Americans, we believe that all men are created equal. But notice that the Declaration of Independence refers only to men, recognizing the natural, subordinate role of women. And it only mentions men's condition at the moment of creation. Once we've left the womb, we're responsible for ourselves, and rightly

so. So people who complain about inequality are just plain unAmerican.

Verity's argument depends on at least two misreadings of the Declaration of Independence. The first is his interpretation of *men* to mean "males" rather than "people." The second is his reading of *created* to mean "conceived" or "at the moment of conception." The Declaration of Independence refers to the idea that all people deserve equal human rights just because they are human. So Verity's argument is a fallacy of misreading.

Misreading differs from unreasonable definition in that it involves twisting another source to support your own point of view. Misreading differs from equivocation in that the argument depends on only one meaning, but it's the wrong one—the one not intended by the original author, for example. To avoid misreading can be difficult unless you develop a feel for the importance of context in understanding what a person is saying. That is, to interpret someone's ideas accurately involves projecting yourself into that person's frame of reference, keeping that person's background information in mind, and the like.

Fallacy of False Context

The **Fallacy of False Context** is really a kind of misreading. It occurs when passages or excerpts that are used as reasons are taken out of the surroundings that point to one interpretation so that they can be used to mean something else. Senator Baggman, defending dishonesty in politics, commits false context in the following:

> **Why, even the most admired of American politicians recognized that sometimes you've got to shade the truth a little. As Abraham Lincoln said, "You can fool all of the people some of the time, and you can fool some of the people all of the time." The fact is, you can't avoid it.**

Of course the senator is ignoring the context of Lincoln's remark, which makes it clear that Lincoln was cautioning against dishonesty in politics, not condoning it. In the context, "but you can't fool all of the people all of the time" implies that dishonesty will eventually be found out and is therefore a bad policy.

Another fruitful place to look for false context fallacies is on the backs of novels and movie advertisements, where comments from reviewers are listed. Often it is only the most positive part of the review that is cited, while the context makes clear that the review is more neutral or even negative.

Hedging

The last confusion fallacy we'll consider here is called **Hedging,** and it's a fallacy that appears usually when someone's argument is criticized by others. When key terms in someone's argument are so vague or unclear that no matter how it's attacked the speaker can always say, "Oh, that's not what I meant at all!" the speaker is hedging. Suppose that Roger is running for a seat on the Middletown school board by urging reforms. He might argue this way:

> **I will make reforming our schools my top priority. Without major reforms, our schools are slipping farther and farther behind, turning out students who are less and less able to succeed in today's high-pressure environment.**

But what, exactly, does Roger mean by "reform"? If an audience member asked, "Do you mean you'll personally try to change the curriculum and tell our high school teachers what they will teach?" Roger could always say,

> **Oh no! Our teachers are dedicated, well-trained professionals, and they have the responsibility to design a responsible curriculum. I just want to reform the schools themselves.**

But if someone else asks, "Do you mean you'll work for tax increases to support more programs?" Roger could always say,

> **I'm opposed to further, pointless tax increases. Part of my platform is to reform the schools so that no such tax increases are needed.**

It's easy to see that the audience may never pin Roger down. And unfortunately, as in this example, one of the most common sources of hedging fallacies is the speeches of candidates for office, who often try to avoid offending anyone by not saying anything definite.

The only way to defend against hedging (or avoid committing it yourself) is to be very specific about identifying the reasons and conclusions of arguments. As long as people let themselves get away with using vague, sloppy language, the potential for vague, sloppy thinking is great.

SUMMARY

In this chapter we stressed the importance of keeping arguments clear and understandable. Among the important things to keep in mind are making sure the reasons and conclusion are obvious to the audience and presenting them in a straightforward, easy to follow way. The best ways to do this are either to present your reasons first and then show that your conclusion follows from them, or to present your conclusion first and then show that your reasons support it. It is also important to make sure your argument is framed in specific, well-defined language and that key ideas are used fairly and consistently. When any of these requirements breaks down, the result is fallacies of confusion. We examined six of these fallacies: obscurity, unreasonable definition, equivocation, misreading, false context, and hedging. Avoiding these fallacies won't guarantee a clear argument, but it will help.

EXERCISE I

You are a member of a committee set up to investigate and resolve problems in the campus class selection and registration system. Listed below is the information gathered by your committee. Now you need to organize all of this information into two or three main problems to be solved. Then use it to write up two or three recommendations your committee can make to solve each of the problems.

1. Students currently have to wait many hours in long lines to register for their courses. Some students even camp out overnight in the halls or skip classes to make sure they get into courses they need for graduation.

2. Student workers run the registration tables. They do not have the authority to override class size limits or change schedules approved by students' advisors. They are on campus for two weeks before classes start because they are almost all student athletes, and that's when their training begins.

3. The number of course sections to be given each semester is determined at the beginning of the previous semester, before enrollment figures are known. This is so the printing office can get the schedules printed early enough for students to decide what to take.

4. Faculty believe the main reason registration is such a problem is that not enough sections of popular courses are offered. The main reason for that is not enough faculty for the number of students, since class sizes are already too large.

5. Many students wait to do their schedules until registration has already begun. Since they often can't find their advisors at the last minute, they often don't think of good alternative courses and schedules. They often wind up getting in line too late to get the courses they originally thought of, and since those courses may be full, they have to go back, find an advisor, and start again.

6. Several off-campus printing shops have one-day turnaround time on materials set up by computer.

7. Because of chronic underfunding from the state legislature, it is unlikely more faculty can be hired anytime soon.

8. The academic vice president and deans believe enough courses exist for all students to get schedules that make sense for them if only they will consider less trendy, less popular courses.

9. Although a number of faculty have volunteered to help out at the registration table to advise students whose schedules have to be changed and to authorize changes, the athletic department wants to use student employees as part of their financial aid package. Also, there may not be enough faculty volunteers because they are given no recognition or pay for their assistance.

10. The registrar's office is willing to consider a registration-by-mail program, but this would require that the course schedule be issued much earlier and that more clerical workers be available to deal with the mail.

EXERCISE II

Revise each of the arguments below to make clear what their reasons and conclusions are. If crucial assumptions are not stated, identify those as well, but leave out unnecessary material. Then present the arguments in a logical order.

1. Fuji makes a great standard touring bicycle. Of course, some people prefer Schwinn or Univega, or, if they have the money, a bicycle that is assembled from special Italian parts. That's because Italian makers, like Campagniolo, have been into bicycle racing for longer than the Japanese or Americans. But if you're not into expensive custom bikes, Univega and Fuji offer about the same level of quality for the price, and Fuji has a better repair record. Schwinn's bikes tend to be a little heavy and expensive by comparison.

2. Many people who would like to go to college after five to ten years on the job feel trapped by their family and financial obligations. It's not easy trying to balance job, family, and academic responsibilities, especially if money is a problem. Many people who have jobs perceive them as dead ends, and others are required to get retraining by their employers. Better financial and family support is needed from businesses and universities if current employees are to be reeducated. After all, people will be much more productive and society will be better off with a more educated work force.

3. Problems have existed in the cafeteria for years, and nothing has been done about them. The manager only has a degree in business, so he should be fired. The only experience he has in food preparation or management was in the Army. In the student newspaper poll, 78 percent of students said the menu is boring, and the food is too expensive. Every year for five years now, the price of a bowl of soup has gone up 10 percent, and the size of the bowl has been reduced twice. The manager is ultimately responsible for customer satisfaction with the campus food service. We need action.

4. Many states have enacted laws requiring hospital personnel to ask the families of terminally ill patients to donate the patient's organs for transplantation. But "required request laws" are not enough. Although there was an initial increase in donations, the number has fallen off rapidly, and now even fewer families are donating than before. Many people don't understand that organ donation cannot harm their loved one and can help others. They're focused on their own grief. But if there were more effective public education on this topic before people got into the hospital, people could make better decisions. Many of them would probably choose to donate.

5. (Note: In this example, the speaker is trying to do too many things for his ideas to be clear. Identify as much of what's going on here as possible.)

According to a Harris Poll taken in September 1989, nearly 70 percent of Americans believe that the public schools are doing a poor or very poor job of preparing people for contemporary society. They recognize it's partly a matter of money and that the only realistic source of funding is tax revenue. But the same number believe what goes on in the classroom is the main problem, which might be a way of ducking parental responsibility. After all, most of the motivation and encouragement a student needs to achieve academic success has to come from the home. Besides, teachers have been told they have to make everyone succeed, which always leads to lower standards of success, namely the ones everyone can meet.

Eighty-seven percent of the public is willing to pay higher taxes to support higher teacher salaries, so that better teachers will be attracted into the profession, but only if teachers give up lifetime job security and become more accountable. Of course we do need to attract better teachers. In the past ten years, future teachers have had among the lowest grade-point averages overall. So if we want to address the problem, teachers will have to be more accountable. The tenure system has protected them from competency tests that would help identify weak teachers so they could be retrained or fired.

EXERCISE III

Carefully examine each of the following arguments and determine whether or not it is or involves a fallacy of confusion. If so, explain why very specifically, and identify the argument by name if possible. (Note: There may be more than one in an argument.) Then give an argument for the same conclusion that would not be fallacious. If you can't, explain why not.

1. "May I recommend this 1985 Pinot Gris wine? The 1985 cuvee has a firm structure with race and texture. I would describe it as sleek, noble, refined, with intense varietal character."

2. According to the state lottery, "Someone is a new millionaire every week." Well, I'm someone, and I've been waiting several weeks. I'd say I'm about due to win big.

3. Ladies and gentlemen of the jury, you've all heard Rossi testify he "saw Johannson leave Roberts's house and return in the afternoon." But since the crime was committed at 10:00 A.M., it's obvious that Johannson has an ironclad alibi.

4. Responding to a statement by the head of the teachers' union, Superintendent Blather remarked: "According to the story in this morning's *Bugle,* Ms. Jamison said, 'Since the Board of Education is unwilling even to meet with our negotiating team to discuss a contract, we feel no responsibility to the district to return to the classroom at this time.' Obviously, since the teachers feel no responsibility to this district, it would be pointless for us to try to bargain with them. Irresponsible people cannot bargain in good faith."

5. You can't be impartial if you take sides in a dispute. But the arbitrator decided on the free agents' salary figures rather than those offered by the baseball team owners. Since he's on the free agents' side, the arbitrator is not impartial. And since he's not impartial, management has no obligation to abide by his decision.

6. In industry, maintaining the equipment and machinery is the obligation of management and their right. Maintaining the health of workers is like maintaining the equipment, and so it's part of management's right and obligation. Since smoking interferes with workers' health, management has the right to fire workers who smoke.

7. When questioned by members of the student government about his proposed tuition increase of 10 percent for next year, President Marquez replied: "You'll undoubtedly remember that after the last increases, we agreed that 'there will be no further tuition increases unless they are deemed absolutely necessary by the affected parties.' Of course, I meant no further increases that year. Besides, I have examined the matter thoroughly, and I am convinced that they are necessary. And whereas the university is an affected party, many of you will be graduating, and therefore you are not affected parties."

8. (Alice in Wonderland, "There's 'glory' for you.")

> "I don't know what you mean by 'glory,'" Alice said.
>
> Humpty Dumpty smiled contemptuously. "Of course you don't—till I tell you. I meant 'there's a nice knockdown argument for you!'"
>
> "But 'glory' doesn't mean a 'nice knock-down argument,'" Alice objected.
>
> "When *I* use a word," Humpty Dumpty said, in a rather scornful tone, "it means just what I choose it to mean—neither more nor less."[1]

9. "Yes, I know you're supposed to be protected against water damage. But water backup in your basement from heavy rains doesn't really count as water damage unless you're in a flood, your house is located inside a flood plain, and you take out a flood rider on your policy. You have a flood rider? Oh, but this isn't a flood, because all you had was water backup in your basement."

EXERCISE IV

Compare the Euphonic Technology ad in Figure 8.3 with passages from the review referred to in the ad. Does the ad commit any fallacies?

---

1. Lewis Carroll, *Through the Looking Glass* (New York: Signet Classics, 1960), p. 186.

I had volunteered to bring the ET650PX Mk.II to one of the meetings of the NY Audiophile Society in order to round out the choice for input sources. Even though the guest speaker for that evening is not particularly enamored of CDs, he agreed.

You should have seen his response, as well as those of some of the members, when the first CD was played. As soon as a few bars had been heard, a buzz went up; a number of people in the audience wanted to know which player was being used, what CD had been played, and the guest manufacturer wrote down the title of the CD (*Tango*, a Concord Jazz release). And that's from a group traditionally inclined to prefer vinyl.

Tango demonstrates conclusively just how far digital has come; let me tell you, the ET throve on it.

The music had heft, impact, and attack. Transients are etched, and decays are marvelously detailed and delicate. Gone are glare, grain, and brightness.

This same CD also demonstrated that the ET was a standout in the transparency category. The veiling between listener and music was made vanishingly small, sonic imagery was very authentic, and instruments remained locked in their positions.

One of the characteristics I look for is a sense of the uninhibited and unbridled. My *Repercussion Unit* CD (CMP Records CMP CD 31) is just what's needed. On cut five, "It's Ridiculous," the sound of the Euphonic Technology player had fewer limitations as far as effusiveness is concerned. Its ability to properly proportion dynamic con-
continued on page 124

Figure 8.3

trasts along every point of the loudness scale was a definite plus. Soft, loud, louder—the ET took it all in stride, rendering all sounds crisp and clear. The soundstage suffered no distortions during climaxes, nor did fidelity. The sound was relaxed, containing fewer of the sonic aberrations usually associated with the digital nature of this recording.

Naturally, it helped to have the two other ingredients mentioned earlier: staging and extended frequency response. Handel's *Messiah* (L'Oiseau-Lyre 400 086-2) conveys considerable spaciousness and remarkably delineated performers. The sweep of choir and orchestra was depicted without diminishing the contribution of each voice or instrument. Of course, the soloists were more prominently displayed, just as intended. Here a bit of brightness intruded and some strain could be detected, but in this case I place more blame on the source than on the player.

Overall, the Euphonic Technology CD player was eminently coherent. It had an unlabored way about it, presenting music in a very tangible manner, digital vices appearing in gratifyingly reduced proportions. The main culprit, digital glare, had been tamed significantly to the point where it was only bothersome as an infrequent glistening effect.

As with many good components, the quality of the source material was very important. Some CDs are very hard to domesticate, and, while the ET performed no miracles, it fared very well. The ET650PX Mk.II readily exposed poor CDs, but fortunately this scrutiny worked both ways, allowing great CDs to provide significant sonic gratification.

Given a good CD, the Euphonic Technology player was capable of delightful performance. The sound was crisp and rendered with a relatively neutral spectral balance. Even through the pervading smoothness, the highs could be on the bright side. By no means was this a serious indiscretion, and some instruments even thrive on such added zest. Triangles, cymbals, and high hats, for example, took on an agreeable vividness, very reminiscent of the brightness perceived in live concerts. Still missing was the overt overtone structure and rapt ringing inherent in these instruments.

At the other end of the spectrum, I would like to have heard more deep-bass extension. Even though definition throughout the bass region was very good, the sense of having reached rock bottom was not convincing. Using CDs and DAT tapes from exactly the same source, Digital Music Products, playback on an Onkyo DAT player reproduced bass frequencies with more energy. It's true that the DAT machine could be the richer of two, but if that's true, then that's what I want.

The ET650PX Mk.II could not be characterized as a very warm-sounding product. It exhibited considerable richness and fullness, yet left a stark, analytical impression. I have little problems with its less than opulent balance, preferring it over something overtly rich. Gary Carr's double-bass rendition of Albinoni's *Adagio* (Firebird K33Y 236) brought this to my attention: While the obviously closely miked recording prominently displays vigorous

Figure 8.3 continued

bowing and woody cavity resonances, the sound was silky-smooth, though without a velvet cushion. Other than that, the presence of the double bass was stunning, especially when the very large recording space materialized. I've heard this recording many times, but the Euphonic Technology managed to give it some extra life.

But how does the 16-bit, 4x-oversampling ET650PX Mk.II stand up to a well-received component like the Tandberg TCP 3015A?

Favorably reviewed by JGH around 18 months ago, the '3015A also uses Philips components for the transport and the digital processing. Instead of modifying, however, Tandberg built their own chassis and designed their own direct-coupled, feedbackless audio circuitry. Not being helped by the present valuation of the dollar, the 3015A ends up costing $1895 *sans* remote control.

That omission, as well as other deficiencies in features (the shared display must be selected to display time *or* track, for example), puts it behind the ergonomic eightball.

The ET also had the sonic upper hand, exhibiting a more pristine and dynamic character, more transparency, and handling dynamic excesses with more control and less compression.

The Tandberg managed to capture more overall spaciousness, but with diminished airiness around each soloist. At least that's what I heard when I listened to the Handel *Messiah* CD. My notes indicate "more air and reverb" for the the 3015A, while the ET presented "more transparent" voices.

Tango was the tie-breaker. Here the impacts and dynamics were more impressive with the ET650PX Mk.II. The Tandberg had a slight tendency to bloat the sound, and transients sounded rounded off. The ET's tactile assertiveness was sorely missed.

Conclusion

Digital can only do so much — without analog it's nothing. The Euphonic Technology CD player is proof positive that carefully crafted analog circuits can do wonders to improve the sonic worth of a digital product. It acquitted itself admirably when surrounded by such established names as Apogee, ARC, Classe Audio, Krell, and Museatex (alphabetical listing plays no favorites). Michael Goldfield has produced a remarkably open-sounding CD player which impressed me most of all with its striking transparency. That's supported by refined dynamics, fine staging characteristics, and a smooth and extended frequency response. The ET650PX Mk.II's high-end aspirations should be taken seriously, especially at $1295. I recommend it wholeheartedly.

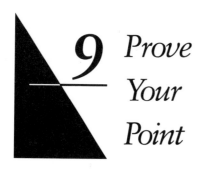

9 *Prove Your Point*

So far, we have discussed several aspects of good argument. We have seen that it is important to define terms accurately and without bias, to make sure your reasons are relevant to the conclusions you are trying to prove, and to start with reliable assumptions. In this chapter, we'll discuss what else you need to do to prove your point. That is, we'll examine several strategies for supplying enough information of the right kind to produce a logically convincing argument. Then we'll look at what happens when the proof appears sufficient, but isn't.

How Much Proof Is Enough?

Andrea, a criminal justice major, is concerned about the fact that many victims of crime are never compensated for their losses. She also thinks that criminals themselves should bear as much of the burden of restitution (paying back) as possible. So she makes this proposal:

> **Criminals guilty of property offenses should bear some responsibility for compensating the victims of their crimes. They should do this because the damage they do to their victims is part of the debt criminals owe for their crimes. They could at least begin to do this by sending any and all of the wages they earn through prison industries and work-release programs to their victims. They could also be held responsible for making support payments to their victims once they are released and employed, with levels set to avoid causing more hardship for the families of the criminals. These measures should be enacted as soon as possible.**

Antonio is also concerned about the widespread crime — much of it drug-related — that occurs in American cities, and he can't see why a simple solution shouldn't receive more attention than it usually gets. He argues:

> **Solving the problem of drug-related crime is very simple. We should simply execute those convicted of drug-related crimes. Capital punishment would eliminate the problem of repeat offenses, and it would deter potential criminals. Besides, it would be far less expensive than keeping criminals housed in prisons.**

Many people seem psychologically prepared to accept both Andrea's and Antonio's arguments, at least to some degree. But how logically convincing are they?

First, of course, we need to be sure we understand what their arguments are. Andrea's is very simple, even though it looks complicated, because most of her proposal spells out details rather than giving reasons. Her argument is:

> (Reason) The damage criminals do to their victims is part of the debt criminals owe for their crimes.

> (Reason, assumed) Criminals should repay the debt their crimes have created.

(Conclusion) Criminals guilty of property offenses should bear some responsibility for compensating the victims of their crimes.

Antonio's argument involves more reasons:

(Reason) Capital punishment would eliminate repeat offenses.

(Reason) Capital punishment would deter potential criminals.

(Reason) Capital punishment would be far less expensive than keeping criminals housed in prisons.

(Conclusion) Those convicted of drug-related crimes should be given capital punishment.

In evaluating these arguments, we need to turn to the criteria we've discussed in recent chapters. So far, we have five criteria for testing the logical quality of an argument. They are that (1) argument forms should be reliable, (2 key terms must be defined effectively, (3) the information provided must be relevant to the conclusion, (4) the assumptions on which the argument is based must be reliable, and (5) the argument must be clear. Applying these criteria to Andrea's argument, we find that it stands up pretty well. Her arguments rely on reasonable forms, her terms are not tricky, nothing irrelevant seems to have been brought in, her assumptions seem uncontroversial, and her argument is clear. Notice especially that her argument is strengthened by the fact that she's not trying to prove too much. She's saying only that criminals should accept *some* responsibility for compensating their victims, and she's willing to recognize that too great a burden might cause more harm than it solves. Besides, she's limiting her proposal to criminals guilty of property offenses, and that's a kind of crime that is fairly easy to decide how to compensate. So far, then, Andrea's argument seems logically convincing.

Looking at Antonio's argument, we find that some of his key terms pose definitional problems. What, for example, does he count as a "drug" or a "drug-related crime"? Antonio's reasons seem relevant to his conclusion, and the argument is very straightforward. But it is more difficult to determine how reliable Antonio's assumptions are. Capital punishment could certainly eliminate the problem of repeat offenses. But is it true that capital punishment deters potential criminals? The evidence regarding capital punishment for first-degree murder is decidedly mixed, some studies indicating that there is no clear correlation at all between the severity of a threatened punishment and reduced crime.[1] And is it true that capital punishment is less expensive than imprisonment? Again, the evidence is mixed. Executions typically involve long periods of imprisonment while very expensive and time-consuming court hearings are conducted appealing earlier findings and seeking stays of execution.[2]

There are other problems with Antonio's argument. Would it really be good public policy to execute anyone who commits a drug-related crime? "Anyone" covers a lot of people, including even children used to deliver drugs. And "drug-related crime" is also very broad, as we noted earlier. It's probably fair to say that Antonio's argument needs more work if it is to convince many people, whereas Andrea's argument seems much more acceptable. Why is this so?

QUALIFYING YOUR CONCLUSIONS

In addition to the five criteria for good arguments that we have already considered, (6) a good argument offers enough information and reasoning to prove its conclusion. That is, a good argument doesn't try to prove more than the available reasons can support. There are two ways to make sure your arguments are sufficient to prove your point. One is to limit your conclusions. The other is to support your conclusions so thoroughly that no reasonable person could disagree with them.

Now, the amount of proof that you need to establish your conclusions depends on many things. Here are the most important:

- The more certain the conclusion is supposed to be, the greater the burden of proof.

- The more controversial the conclusion (or the more skeptical the audience), the greater the burden of proof.

- The more universal or absolute the conclusion, the greater the burden of proof.

1. See, for example, "The Costs of Capital Punishment," *New York Times,* October 3, 1983, sec. 1, p. 15.
2. See, for example, Thorsten Sellin, *Capital Punishment* (New York: Harper & Row, 1967).

Deductive Arguments and Validity

As you will recall from Chapter 4, the only arguments that are able to establish their conclusions with certainty are *deductive arguments.* When a deductive argument is constructed so that its reasons cannot be true while the conclusion is false, it is called *valid.* Here are several examples of valid deductive arguments.

> If an NFL team wins its conference, it will make the playoffs. The Chicago Bears have a good chance to win their conference. So the Chicago Bears have a good chance to make the playoffs. (This is an example of "implication.")

> The only guys who might be willing to go out with Amy this weekend are Alex or Alan. But Alex has to work all weekend. So if Amy goes out this weekend, it will have to be with Alan. (This is an example of "dilemma.")

> If the next U.S. president is a Democrat, Bush will either have to lose or decide not to run. He's certain to run. And if he runs, he'll win. So the next president won't be a Democrat. (This is an example of "denying the consequent.")

What is true of all these arguments is that if these conditions are met, their conclusions cannot be false. This is because of the relation between the reasons and conclusions of these arguments, which we examined more carefully in Chapter 4. Once we have determined that the relation between the reasons and conclusions is deductively reliable, there are two problems that remain. One is to make sure that all of the premises on which the deduction depends are spelled out fully. Here's an example of a deductive argument where they're not:

Lady Greythorpe is a murderess. Therefore, she ought to be arrested.

What's missing from this deductive argument is a premise to the effect that all murderesses ought to be arrested; that premise together with the one given above do guarantee the conclusion. Another example is this argument:

Amy is going to be out with Alex this weekend, since Alan is busy.

Here, of course, what's missing is a premise that says Amy's only choices are Alex and Alan.

The other interesting question for people considering deductive arguments is determining whether or not the reasons are true or reliable. Do the Bears have a good chance to win their division? Are Alex and Alan really the only people who would date Amy? Will Bush run again? Will he win if he does? All of these questions need to be answered if the arguments in which they're involved are going to convince other people rationally. So, establishing that your reasons are true or reliable is a most important concern if you're using a deductive argument. You will need to support any questionable reasons in deductive arguments with proof that those reasons are true or reliable.

Strong Inductive Arguments

But, remember, there are other kinds of arguments that are not deductive. When the truth of the reasons increases the likelihood or probability that the conclusion is true by offering evidence, the argument is a *strong* inductive argument. As we discussed in Chapter 4, inductive arguments differ from deductive arguments in that it is possible for the reasons they offer to be true, yet the conclusion be false. This is because unlikely or improbable events do sometimes happen. So in addition to making sure the information offered in an inductive argument is true, it's vital to offer enough of it to raise the probability of the conclusion to a reasonable level. Here are some examples of inductive arguments.

> On each of the last three mornings, the fog burned off by 10:00 A.M. It's foggy again this morning. But the fog will probably burn off by 10:00 A.M.

> A baseball team that wins the World Series has to have first-class pitching. When the Yankees used to win the Series in the 60s and 70s, they had great pitching. So did Detroit in 1985. And when Toronto lost in 1988, it was because their pitching broke down.

> Diane told me that Professor Curmudgeon grades hard, and Inez said the same thing. I guess Curmudgeon is a tough grader.

Let's assume that all of the information given in each of these arguments is true — that the fog did burn off, that Detroit had great pitching, and that Diane and Inez did say Curmudgeon grades hard. Then how strongly the arguments support their conclusions depends on whether the reasons offer enough proof. Again remembering back to Chapter 4, the criteria for good inductive reasons are that they must be

▲ true/relevant,

▲ representative, and

▲ sufficient.

In the first argument, questions might be raised whether three mornings' observations are enough to support this conclusion and whether three mornings offer a representative sample. In the second, the questions are whether the Yankees, Detroit, and Toronto are a sufficiently large and representative sample. And in the third, again, the question is whether what Diane and Inez said is enough (a sufficiently large and representative sample) to establish the truth about Professor Curmudgeon.

Limiting the Scope of Conclusions

So part of what counts as enough of the right kind of proof depends on what kind of argument you're giving. But it's crucial to see that the answers to these questions depend on how controversial the conclusions are, as well as how representative and large the sample of evidence is. Of course, whether or not your conclusion is controversial depends on the attitude of the people you're trying to convince. People who already agree with you won't find your conclusion controversial. People who are gullible believe things without much proof, and for them there are few controversial conclusions. But people who are skeptical take a lot of convincing, usually because they don't start out by agreeing with you and because they care about what the truth really is. As a general practice, you should assume that your audience is skeptical, but reasonable, and present arguments that should persuade any reasonable but skeptical person.

Now whether the weather is likely to be foggy after 10:00 A.M. is not a question that most reasonable people would find particularly controversial. That's part of the reason most people would accept a small sample of evidence as sufficient to support a limited conclusion such as "The fog will probably burn off by 10:00 A.M." Besides, the consequences of being wrong about the fog aren't severe. But baseball fans care very much about whether pitching is the most important factor in winning a World Series, and they disagree strongly over this question. So probably a truly dedicated baseball fan would not accept this argument as sufficient proof of the claim "A baseball team that wins the World Series has to have first-class pitching." Finally, even though students are often influenced by rumors, if we really want to find out about Professor Curmudgeon's grading practices, it's obvious we'll need more than two samples. After all, we know nothing about Diane or Inez, nor whether their opinions are fair.

Finally, how much evidence you need depends on how sweeping or absolute your conclusion is. Where the weather is concerned, three day's experience is probably enough to establish that the fog will *probably* burn off, if "probably" just means "there's a good chance" or "there's a 60 percent likelihood." But if the conclusion were that "the fog will definitely burn off by 10:00 A.M.," there's no limit to the number of observations that would be needed. So the argument is best when the conclusion is limited; otherwise, the evidence needed would be impossibly large.

In the case of pitching and winning the World Series, notice that since the conclusion is that any winning baseball team *has to have great pitching*, only one example of a Series winner without great pitching would disprove the argument. So a few examples are not enough to be convincing in this case; you'd need to consider every single Series winner. Again, the argument would be stronger if the conclusion were less broad ("Most World Series winners have to have great pitching"); otherwise, the amount of support required is unmanageably large. And in the third example, the sample is definitely too small. We have no way of knowing whether Diane and Inez's experiences were representative of Curmudgeon's grading practices, for example, so two cases certainly do not establish that he's definitely a tough grader. The conclusion "Curmudgeon sounds like he might be a tough grader" would be more justified on the basis of this evidence.

So, to sum up, there are three things to keep in mind when you're deciding how much information you need to present to prove your point. They are:

- How universal or absolute is your conclusion?

- How controversial is your conclusion?

- What kind of argument are you giving?

Probably the easiest way to make your arguments stronger is to **qualify** your conclusions by not making them broad or sweeping. To avoid opening yourself up to criticism, then, don't claim more than your argument warrants. Here are two lists of English expressions; the ones on the left are unqualified and require strong proof, whereas the ones on the right are qualified and don't require so high a standard of evidence:

Unqualified (very broad)	Qualified (more limited)
Necessarily (couldn't be otherwise)	Possibly, May be
Definitely, Certainly, Obviously	Likely, Probably, Seems
Every, All, Each	Some, Most, Many

So, for example, the conclusion "Obviously, every NFL Superbowl winner has a great quarterback" will require much more proof than "It seems likely that most NFL Superbowl winners have great quarterbacks."

PROOF IN COMBINED DEDUCTIVE AND INDUCTIVE ARGUMENTS

Perhaps the most interesting arguments, as well as the most common, are combinations of inductive and deductive reasoning. In the most usual combination, the reasons that appear in the deductive part of the argument are themselves supported by induction. If the baseball fan gave this argument, his would be an example:

> To have a real chance to win the World Series, any team has to have great pitching. Look at the Yankees in the 60s and 70s, or Detroit more recently. The Chicago Cubs don't have great pitching; none of their starters have ERA's below 3.0 and no one in their bullpen has more than a few saves. So the Cubs don't stand a real chance to win the Series.

The deductive argument is that if a team is to have a chance, it must have great pitching; the Cubs don't have great pitching; so the Cubs don't have a chance. But are these reasons true? The proof of the deductive premises is inductive. In each case, some evidence is given that tends to support the reasons but is still consistent with the chance that they're false. So the strength of this argument depends both on the validity of the deductive argument and on the level of evidence provided for the proof that the deductive reasons are reliable.

Antonio's argument about capital punishment for drug criminals is even more complicated. The deductive structure of his argument is as follows:

> If executing drug criminals eliminates repeat offenses, deters potential criminals, and costs less than imprisonment, drug criminals should be executed. Executing them does eliminate repeat offenses, deters potential criminals, and costs less. Therefore, drug criminals should be executed.

But to make his argument logically compelling, he needs to say enough to convince his audience that his reasons are reliable, and that means providing some convincing proof that executing drug criminals deters potential criminals and costs less than imprisonment. To prove these things, Antonio (or someone) will need to study persons who might have committed drug crimes but didn't, to see whether they were deterred by the death penalty, and individuals who did commit drug crimes to see whether they would have been deterred by a death penalty, and so on. And he will have to study cases of imprisonment to see how much they cost versus cases of execution to see how much they cost, making sure that the cases he studies are really similar in relevant respects. This will be time consuming and difficult, which may be why people are so likely to express unsupported opinions on the issue of drug-related crime.

Of course, it is often not possible to gather the right sort of information to prove your reasons are reliable. Since the death penalty has not been imposed on drug criminals, Antonio will not be able to find cases in which people have been deterred from drug crimes by the death penalty. So he will have to find cases of crimes in which the death penalty was imposed and determine whether or not it had a deterrent effect, and then argue that the similarities between crimes and criminal motivations are so great that what is true in the case of, say, first-degree murder is also true in the case of drug-related crimes in general. This kind of argument, called argument from analogy, is a form of induction that we will examine in detail in Chapter 12.

So let's go back to a simpler case. Suppose Angie can take either Professor Curmudgeon's or Professor Sweetheart's English class. The argument that follows is deductive and valid.

> I have to take either Professor Curmudgeon or Professor Sweetheart for English. I shouldn't take Curmudgeon. So I should take Sweetheart.

But Angie's premises need support if her deductive argument is to be logically convincing. She could prove the first reason true by consulting the schedule and her course requirements. But the second premise depends on another deductive argument, which lurks in the background. That argument goes like this:

> **If I take a course from a hard grader, I am likely to do badly. I should not do badly. Professor Curmudgeon is a hard grader. So I shouldn't take a course from Curmudgeon.**

Again, this argument is valid, but whether it is logically persuasive depends on whether its premises are justified. Are they? Well, to prove the reliability of the first reason, Angie would have to offer evidence inductively correlating courses she has taken from hard graders and having done badly. And she'd need to establish that Curmudgeon is a hard grader.

We have already seen that the testimony of two friends is not enough from a logical point of view. To prove that Curmudgeon is a hard grader requires a representative sample of students who have taken his courses. To be fair, Angie would need to look at all of Curmudgeon's grades in comparison to those given by Sweetheart in the relevant English classes over the last several semesters, making sure that no other explanations existed for any differences she might find. (If she found out that Curmudgeon was assigned the least capable students in the university, spent hours and hours of extra time helping them, and bent over backwards to give them the highest possible grades, that would invalidate Angie's evidence.)

So giving reliable arguments involves supporting your reasons with enough proof that they're convincing. This can be time consuming and difficult, especially when you're giving an argument on a controversial topic. When you're using a deductive argument, make sure it's valid and that its premises are spelled out completely and are as true or reliable as possible. When you're using an inductive argument, make sure you offer enough representative evidence and don't claim more than your evidence warrants. Remember, you can always strengthen an inductive argument by offering more evidence or making your conclusion less broad.

AVOID FALLACIES OF INSUFFICIENCY

Arguments in which not enough evidence is given to support a conclusion are called **fallacies of insufficiency**. There are only two important fallacies of insufficiency. They are called hasty generalization and sweeping generalization. **Hasty generalization** occurs when a small, inappropriate, or unrepresentative sample is used as the basis for a broad or unlimited rule or claim. The reverse of this fallacy is **sweeping generalization,** which involves reasoning from a rule or general statement to a particular instance without proof that the application is appropriate. Angie's argument that Curmudgeon is a hard grader, based only on the comments of two friends, was a hasty generalization. If she had reasoned "Everybody at this place is a tough grader, so Curmudgeon must be really hard," she'd have committed a sweeping generalization, since she would have had no proof that Curmudgeon falls under the rule. (Besides, if the conclusion is that Curmudgeon is relatively tougher than others, that couldn't be proved by observing that everybody at this university is a tough grader.)

Here are some other examples of hasty and sweeping generalizations:

The two guys I met at freshman orientation were both immature and boring. I wonder why all the guys at this school are childish and dull? (This is a hasty generalization, because two freshmen at orientation are not a representative sample of guys at the university as a whole.)

Every guy I've met lately has been childish and boring, so I just don't have any interest in meeting Amy's brother. (This is a sweeping generalization, because there's no evidence showing that Amy's brother fits into the category of childish and boring guys, let alone guys the speaker has met lately.)

John Leong covers 47,000 miles per year on his postal route. It's tough weather because John's route is in rural Alaska. But he'll get through because he drives a Subaru. Subaru will get you through. (This is hasty because John's experience is not a sufficient basis for the conclusion that Subaru will get anyone through any weather conditions they might encounter.)

Hmm. Sweet-smelling aftershave. Must be a quarterback's locker. Real guys who get mud on their uniforms use Aqua Velva. (Two hulks go off with a sexy lady.) And you thought linemen were dumb? (This is a sweeping generalization about quarterbacks and their tastes in aftershave. It's also a sweeping generalization to assume that what's true of linemen is true of anyone who wears Aqua Velva. And it's also sweeping because the generalization that "all linemen are dumb" is assumed by the ad to apply to the linemen in question, even though the ad proves otherwise.)

Summary

In addition to defining key terms carefully, providing relevant information, starting with reliable assumptions, and keeping arguments clear, we need to give enough evidence to prove the conclusion. We distinguished between deductive and inductive arguments because what kind of argument you're giving determines how you go about proving your point. Deductive arguments offer reasons that purport to establish their conclusions with certainty. Valid deductive arguments are set up so that if the premises are true, the conclusion cannot be false. The main concerns about deductive arguments, then, are to make sure that the premises are fully spelled out, and true or reliable, and that the connection between the premises and conclusion is a valid one. Inductive arguments offer evidence that their conclusions are probably true. They are strongest when a sufficiently large and representative sample of evidence is provided to support a conclusion, especially if it involves a generalization. When too small or unrepresentative a sample is used, the result is the fallacy of hasty generalization. When a specific application is derived from a generalization without proof that it is applied correctly, the result is the fallacy of sweeping generalization. Inductive arguments can always be strengthened either by limiting the conclusion or by providing more evidence or proof.

Exercise I

For each of the following conclusions, discuss what kind of proof would be required to establish it convincingly. How could the conclusion be qualified to make supporting it easier?

1. All Germans love sausages.

2. Female weight lifters necessarily can't pump as much iron as men.

3. The most dangerous public health problem has to be AIDS.

4. We can definitely say that many other galaxies are inhabited by intelligent life forms.

5. Obviously, smoking in public places should be prohibited.

EXERCISE II

For each of the following arguments, decide whether it is deductive or inductive. Next, are there revisions you could suggest that would make the argument more persuasive? Is there additional information that would strengthen it?

1. No one who has to get along on a fast-food, minimum-wage job can afford luxuries. Since Joanne works at McDonalds, she can't afford a Mercedes-Benz.

2. Simpson works at Burger King, so he can't afford a Mercedes-Benz. Iacocca, who works at Hardee's, can't afford a Mercedes-Benz either. The same with Samuelson. So no one who has to get along on a fast-food job can afford a Mercedes-Benz.

3. No one who has to live on a minimum-wage job can afford luxuries. A Godiva chocolate is a luxury. So no one who lives on a minimum-wage job can afford a Godiva chocolate.

4. Unemployed people can still afford fine automobiles. Right after he won the lottery, James Earl quit his job and bought a Mercedes-Benz.

5. According to the *Guinness Book of World Records,* the longest running automobile is a 1957 Mercedes-Benz with over 4 million miles on it, which is about as long as anyone would want to drive a car. So if you buy a Mercedes-Benz, it will last as long as you want to drive it.

6. Of course the case worker will give you the runaround. All bureaucrats do.

7. When I tried to get help on my taxes from an IRS counselor, he couldn't answer my questions. Neither could the person who answered the IRS tax hotline. IRS regulations are so complicated nobody can understand them.

8. The Environmental Defense Fund successfully prevented an airport from being built in the Everglades. It also successfully sued a major oil company to clean up its drilling operation in the Gulf of Mexico. The EDF is the most successful advocate of environmental causes in America.

9. Faculty at Small State University are mostly underpaid. Bishop teaches at Small State. So she's probably underpaid.

10. Salaries for jobs in the services sector tend to be paid less well than other jobs. Many jobs traditionally done by women are in the services sector. So many women are not paid very well.

11. Most drug offenders start with marijuana and then move on to harder drugs. Therefore, if we can keep marijuana out of the neighborhood, our kids won't wind up on hard drugs.

12. South American governments are often repressive. Peru is a repressive South American government. So is Chile.

13. My neighbor quit smoking just before he died. So quitting doesn't do any good. Besides, my grandfather smokes, and he's almost ninety.

14. The only things that tend to prevent heart attacks are regular exercise and moderate diets. So you should get more exercise and eat less fat.

15. Horses normally seek out other horses. The only two stables in the area are King's Pyland and Mapleton. Silver Blaze is not at King's Pyland. Therefore, he is at Mapleton.

EXERCISE III

How representative is the evidence provided in each of the following arguments? What more would be needed to make the evidence convincing?

1. Three girls on my floor said biostatistics is almost impossible to pass. I'd better take something else.

2. Aram is the only other Armenian-American student on this campus. It's obvious we're being discriminated against in admissions.

3. Every guy in my physics class who isn't on the basketball team got a C or lower last semester. I guess you need to be an athlete to get a B in that class.

4. The average family income of Harvard Business School graduates is much higher than that of French literature majors at Central State University. Obviously, business is a better choice than French literature if you want a good income.

5. Every low-income family member under the age of nine had eaten a diet high in fats and carbohydrates. Most were also underweight. It follows that diets high in fats and carbohydrates tend to keep children from becoming overweight.

10 *Write Arguments Persuasively*

Students often find it easier to criticize other people's arguments than to write logically convincing arguments of their own. Part of the problem is in the logic: thinking up a reasonable position and defending it without falling back on fallacies and questionable support. But part of the problem is also in the writing: selecting a topic, brainstorming, identifying an audience, organizing and presenting ideas, and revising. These problems are closely related because writing is a way of learning, of discovering and working on (reasoning about) ideas. So, in this chapter, both aspects of writing a persuasive paper will be discussed. We will also work through writing a persuasive paper by following an outline that includes an introduction, thesis and main ideas, documentation and arguments, anticipated replies, and conclusion.

Persuasive Papers

An essay in which your main purpose is to influence someone to agree with your point of view can be called a **persuasive paper.** Persuasive papers often turn up as assignments in academic classes, even when they might be called something else. This is because in almost every piece of writing you do outside of English composition classes, you're trying to persuade someone, often your teacher, that your ideas are worth taking seriously. And persuasive papers are often required in business and other careers as well, when you're trying to get an OK on a project you want to work on, for example, or to convince a buyer to choose your product. So learning to write persuasive papers is a worthwhile skill to master.

Getting comfortable with writing persuasive papers involves two interrelated activities. One is the cluster of abilities we've been calling "reasoning." That is the business of seeing connections among ideas, formulating reasons to support a conclusion, avoiding fallacies and questionable arguments, and so on. The other is a cluster of abilities that go into writing. These include picking a suitable topic, coming up with good ideas on it, tailoring your writing to the audience for your paper, organizing your work logically, doing the actual writing, and revising your first drafts until you're completely satisfied with the result.

Writing Is Thinking

The first point to remember about writing persuasive papers is that these two clusters of activities are not separate when you're doing them. Writing is a way of discovering what you think and reasoning about it. That is, especially in the earliest stages of writing, you're exploring what you think, informing yourself, and seeing what your thoughts and information look like on paper (or on the computer screen).

Sometimes people say, "I know exactly what I want to say, but I just can't write it down." But this is almost never true. What is more likely is that if they can't write down what they think, they probably don't have a clear picture of what their ideas really are. Nobody starts writing by imagining their papers, worked out in all of the details, in their head, and then writing them down. In fact, most writers don't even have complete sentences, or even words, in mind that they then pause to write down. What they do is start with a general purpose or guiding direction and then experiment, writing things down, trying them out, seeing whether they work or "sound right."

Instead of trying to work things out in your head and then write them down, you might think of writing as being like painting a picture. You might have a general idea of what kind of thing you want to do—what kind of picture you want to paint, what kind of paper you want to write. An artist might want to paint a picture of the Maine shoreline, or a writer might want to write about high taxes. The artist will start out by drawing a general outline, putting down a few strokes, and then stepping back to look at how it's shaping up. The writer will start by jotting down a few ideas, then mentally stepping back to think them over. An artist will go on and dab a little paint here or there, then step back again and again to look at the effect. So do writers; they'll try this word or that sentence and then mentally step back to see how it works. And in the end, the painting may not look like any particular part of Maine, because the artist has followed her own creative impulses and made something that is her own. So with writers; by following their ideas as they take written shape on the page, people come up with a piece of writing that expresses their own, unique ideas.

CHOOSING A TOPIC

So you don't start writing by knowing in advance everything you want to say and how you're going to say it. Instead, you start with a general purpose or guiding idea. This might be your **topic**, the general area you're going to write about, or, maybe, your **thesis**, the specific point of view you want to take on an issue. Sometimes, of course, the topic is given to you. Your professor might assign a paper on a certain issue, or your boss might tell you to write a proposal on a certain project. If your topic is assigned, the crucial thing is to make sure that, as you work through the process of writing, you wind up fulfilling the assignment. A painter who is painting for personal fulfillment can let her creative impulses guide her work, but if she's assigned to paint a portrait of somebody's daughter, she'd better make sure the painting meets her customer's expectations. So with a writer. If you're asked to write on southern military strategy during the Civil War, you'd better not wind up talking about how immoral slavery is, no matter how strongly you feel about that.

But if you have to come up with your own topic, there are several rules of thumb to follow. They are:

1. Pick a topic that can be covered fully in the length of paper you're going to write.

2. Pick a topic you can handle with the available resources.

3. Pick a topic appropriate for the audience or for the course and professor requiring it.

4. Pick a topic of interest to you.

Usually, when professors assign papers, they'll give a page limit. The point of the first rule is that, if you have a limited number of pages, don't pick a topic that requires more space than you have. Instead, limit your topic so that you can cover it thoroughly in the number of pages you're assigned. "Abortion" is a topic that might be covered in a book, but it's far too broad a topic for a five-page paper. "Is Abortion Immoral?" is still too broad. Maybe "One Argument Against Abortion" would work, depending on what the argument is. On the other hand, you also need to pick a topic that is going to take up the number of pages you have to fill. Obviously, picking a topic that can be covered fully in two or three paragraphs won't be enough if your assignment is to write a five-page paper. "The Number of Abortions in Los Angeles, 1989," is too narrow a topic because you can cover it fully in just a few lines.

Second, pick a topic you know something about and can research in a nearby library. It's almost impossible to learn enough about a topic to write a good paper on it if you're starting from scratch. So if there's nothing in the card catalog or library computer on Sri Lankan separatist movements, you might want to write on something else.

Third, write on something related to your course and your professor's interests. If you're writing a paper for a business management course, you probably shouldn't pick "Why Basketball Should be America's True National Sport." And if your professor has spent much of the semester using examples from small businesses, writing about "Management Ideas for Neighborhood Groceries" would probably be a better choice than "Management at General Motors."

Last, pick a topic that is of interest to you. But notice, this is the least important of the rules of thumb. It is difficult to write a good paper on a topic that bores you, but we all have to do it sometimes.

Besides, once you get into writing about a topic, you might find it's a lot more interesting than you thought at the start.

Once you've decided on a topic, you can go on to think about it. Often, the fact that you choose a topic means you already have some ideas about it. But there are other ways to find some ideas to start with. You can talk with other students and your friends about the topic. You can jot down any ideas that come into your head. You can read up on the topic and react to what you read with your own ideas. You can ask yourself questions, such as "What's the problem with this issue?" and "What caused this and what's happening because of it?" and "Why should anybody care about this?" You can also ask, "Who am I writing this to?" which will help you identify what you're trying to say and make sure you say it. And if you're stuck, you can almost always talk with your professor.

As you get ideas, write them down. Think about how they're connected. Think about what you'd need to say to prove that the opinions you're coming up with are really true or convincing; make notes to yourself about any evidence you'd need to find. Think about what key terms might be unclear; then analyze the concepts and clean up the definitions. Think about whether any of the ideas you've come up with seem unrelated to the rest; set those aside. As you move toward your thesis, the specific viewpoint you want to argue for, make sure it's completely clear. Then say enough to make sure your point is proved. Let's look at an example of how to do all of this.

Kathy is concerned about pollution and wants to write about it for her biology class. First, she needs a topic. "Pollution"? Too broad. It's only a five- to seven-page paper. "Pollution in the Great Lakes"? Still too broad. "Pollution in Saginaw Bay"? What kind? "Chemical Pollution in Saginaw Bay"? That seems about right. But what about it? Well, it ought to be cleaned up. "Pollution Cleanup of Saginaw Bay." By whom? The people or companies responsible. Who are they? For that matter, what pollution is in Saginaw Bay? Once Kathy knows that, she may be able to find out how the pollution got into Saginaw Bay and who's responsible.

So far, Kathy is off to a good start. She's got a topic, she's moving toward a thesis, and she's begun to figure out what she'll need to do research on. What are the major pollutants in Saginaw Bay, and where did they come from? Well, who would know about pollution in Saginaw Bay? The Michigan Department of Natural Resources (DNR). Maybe some of their publications are in the library. If not, Kathy can write the DNR, assuming she started her paper early enough to wait for the DNR to get back to her. But what exactly is chemical pollution? Would farm runoff count as pollution? What about waste-water runoff? Kathy makes a note to herself: chemical pollution? And what, exactly, does she mean by "in Saginaw Bay"? All the way out to Lake Huron? Or just the area at the mouth of the Saginaw River? Maybe it's time to limit the topic again. How about restricting the paper to industrial chemical pollution in the mouth of the Saginaw River? Then the only issue is identifying the industrial polluters of the Saginaw River.

But would that be fair? Suppose there are four major sources of pollution in Saginaw Bay: chemical company discharge (dioxin, toxic metals), farm runoff (waste, fertilizer), inadequate municipal sewerage systems in communities along the Saginaw River and its tributaries (waste, fertilizer), and acid rain. If the chemical companies cause only a portion of the problem, would it be fair to make them shoulder the whole burden of cleaning up? If *pollution* is defined as "industrial pollution" alone, then it might look like farm runoff, city sewers, and acid rain are all innocent or don't exist.

Kathy originally had in mind a thesis such as "The chemical companies should pay for a complete cleanup of pollution in Saginaw Bay." Maybe that's too simple. Maybe the thesis should be "Major polluters of Saginaw Bay must work together to pay for a complete cleanup." (This is a pretty good thesis, in the sense that it's clear and fairly specific. But it could be better. How should the polluters work together? Kathy can explain this in the paragraph in which she presents her thesis.)

Now, what is Kathy assuming? She's relying on two value premises. One is that polluted lakes ought to be cleaned up. The other is that people responsible for pollution should pay for cleaning it up. Would her audience(s) accept these? Probably even the guilty parties would accept them, if they could pay for cleanup without serious consequences. But isn't Kathy assuming all of the guilty parties can pay for cleanup? Is this a good assumption? (Kathy writes herself a note: How much would it cost to clean up Saginaw Bay? Lots. Get this information from the DNR or library.) Maybe a big chemical company could afford it. (Another note: How much profit did the chemical companies make last year?) Can small farmers pay the costs of cleaning up farm runoff? Maybe not. If not, then the State? But that means the taxpayers. And who pays when cities are the guilty parties? Taxpayers again. And what about acid rain? It's often hard to find the parties responsible for that. Maybe the burden should be shared between taxpayers and companies in proportion to the extent of their responsibility. Kathy revises her thesis again; it's now "Taxpayers and polluting corporations should share the costs of cleaning up chemical pollution in Saginaw Bay."

ORGANIZING PERSUASIVE PAPERS

Kathy will need to spend some time doing research now. But once that's done, she can probably begin to write by taking all of the notes she's written to herself and putting them together in an organized way. Here is an outline for how to organize a persuasive paper:

Introduction

Presentation of Thesis and Main Ideas

Documentation and Arguments

Anticipated Replies

Conclusion

Introduction

In the introduction, you tell your audience what the topic is, why it's important, and anything else you think will capture their interest and set up your paper. But don't make the introduction too long. One good paragraph is usually enough in a short paper, unless the topic is complicated and you have to explain a lot of technical information to your audience.

Presentation of Thesis and Main Ideas

Kathy can then get on to her thesis and the main ideas she's going to rely on to support it. Her thesis, remember, is "Taxpayers and polluting corporations should share the costs of cleaning up chemical pollution in Saginaw Bay." She might need a paragraph to spell out her thesis clearly and to explain what she means by "chemical pollution" and "Saginaw Bay." In another paragraph or two, she might detail the extent of the pollution in the bay and then go on to talk about the consequences. (That would help support the idea that the pollution ought to be cleaned up.)

In another paragraph or two, she could talk about how the pollution got there, who's responsible, and to what extent they're responsible. Then she might elaborate on her idea that those responsible ought to pay the costs of cleanup, perhaps using examples of other cleanup projects funded by the parties who originally contributed to the pollution. (Kathy writes herself a note: What other cleanup projects have been successful? Who paid for them?)

Documentation and Arguments

Now Kathy needs to offer documentation and arguments for her position. In this section, the audience should be given all of the information they need to make an informed and intelligent evaluation of her position. Why should the polluters pay for cleanup? Two reasons: First, they caused the pollution and are therefore responsible for cleaning it up. (Maybe some other examples are in order here; what are some other situations in which it's generally accepted that those responsible for damages are obliged to pay for them?) Second, they—at least some of the polluters—have the money to do it. Here, Kathy needs to document how much cleanup costs, who has the money for it, and who doesn't. Then she should explain why it's appropriate to hold chemical companies responsible for their share and why those who can't afford to pay for cleanup should transfer their responsibility to the taxpayers generally.

Anticipated Replies

After Kathy has presented her documentation and arguments, she is ready to write the section of the persuasive paper called **anticipated replies.** In this section of her paper she tries to imagine how a member of her audience who is not convinced—maybe a member of a chemical company's board of directors or the leader of a taxpayers' rights group—might respond to her argument so far. Then she needs to address whatever concerns they might have that are not already dealt with in her paper. This step gives Kathy a chance to review her argument, take care of any weak spots it may have, and assure herself that she's treated her audience fairly.

This is also the most difficult step in a persuasive paper for most students. You need a vivid imagination to put yourself in the shoes of someone who doesn't agree with you. What would the chemical company's board member say? Is it fair that the company should have to pay when other polluters don't? If taxpayers are going to foot the bill for farmers and cities, why not foot the whole bill? Besides, the chemical companies have already spent millions to stop further pollution. Isn't that enough? What about a taxpayers' rights group? Why should all taxpayers chip in, when only those who use Saginaw Bay are affected directly? Maybe cleanup should be paid for only by the polluting corporations, recreational users of the bay, and property owners along the bay.

If Kathy's proposal is going to be accepted, she'll need to deal with these other alternatives too. So she might take a paragraph or two to anticipate how her audience might reply to her and deal with their concerns. Such a section of her paper might look like this:

> So far, I have shown that pollution in Saginaw Bay is a serious threat to health, recreation, and wildlife. I have also suggested that corporate polluters and taxpayers should share the burden of paying for a thorough cleanup. But polluting companies might object that singling them out is unfair, given that taxpayers foot the bill for other polluters. And taxpayers might object either that the problem, though serious, is only a regional one best handled by property owners and recreational users.
>
> I reply that the fairest way to fund the cleanup would be to have those guilty of polluting in the first place pay for it entirely. But the fact that it is impossible to identify the guilty parties in some cases should not relieve other polluters of their financial responsibility for cleanup costs. Further, the Great Lakes are a national—or even international—resource whose value is not limited to regional recreation. So it makes good sense to spread the costs for cleaning them up as broadly as possible, perhaps in a joint U.S.-Canadian effort.

Conclusion

Once the introduction, thesis and main ideas, documentation and argument, and anticipated replies are all complete, Kathy can go on to her conclusion. In the conclusion, she should remind her readers what her thesis was and, perhaps, the main reasons for it. She might go on to encourage her audience to act on her proposal. But the conclusion should not present much new information. And it shouldn't be too long, unless her paper itself is very long and complicated. In that case, her audience may need help putting the main ideas back together and seeing them in the proper perspective.

REVISING THE FIRST DRAFT

Now there's a draft version of Kathy's paper. It doesn't have a title yet, but it's usually best to wait until the draft is finished before coming up with one. The title can be the thesis, or it can be something catchy that's related to some of the main ideas of the paper. But once a title is chosen, the paper is still not done. It's crucial to remember that this is only a draft. Kathy owes it to herself—you owe it to yourself—and the audience to revise and rewrite any parts of the paper that could be improved. Here are some things to look for:

- Is the topic a good one? Has it been covered thoroughly?

- Is the introduction short and interesting?

- Is the thesis clear and specific?

- Are the criteria for good argument met? Clear, fair definitions? Strictly relevant reasons, with reliable documentation? Assumptions shared by the audience, or else argued for? Enough support for the main ideas? Valid reasoning, with no fallacies?

- Are opposing views stated without bias and given a fair response in the arguments and anticipated replies sections?

- Is the writing itself good? Are all of the mechanics taken care of: correct spelling, standard grammar, consistent and appropriate style? Do the sentences read easily? Is the meaning always clear? Is the tone appropriate? Is the organization obvious and effective? Do you deliver everything you promise?

You may find that, at the time you've just finished your writing, you're still too close to your paper to be able to answer all of these questions objectively. One way to deal with this is to read your paper to someone else, especially someone you haven't already talked to about this topic, and get that person's reaction. Don't try to talk him out of his reaction; just note any parts of your paper he finds confusing, objects to, doesn't agree with, and so on. Then go back and revise those parts of your paper. Another way to deal with being too close to your paper to revise it is to let some time go by before you reread it. If you read your paper too soon after you've written it, you'll see not only what's actually on the page but also what you had in mind while you were writing it. In this case, you miss spotting an important point that you meant to include but didn't. Here's one last point. If you read your paper out loud — to yourself or someone else — and you stumble over a word or sentence, that's something you should revise.

SUMMARY

In this chapter, the main issue has been how to develop and write a persuasive paper, which is an essay whose main goal is to influence an audience to agree with your point of view. Thinking through your ideas and writing them down are not separate activities. Instead, writing is a way of thinking, and doing so in a form that you can work on, revise, and develop. If you can pick your own topic, choose one that can be covered in the space allowed and handled with the available resources, and is relevant to your course and interesting to you and your audience. Brainstorm some ideas, write them down, think about the connections among them, and work toward a clear, specific thesis. Then, gradually, work your ideas into a clearly organized essay following the outline given here: introduction (keep it short and interesting), thesis and main ideas (tell your audience all they need to know), documentation and argument (prove your point with reliable information and valid reasoning), anticipated replies (think about how someone might react to your paper so far and deal with concerns), conclusion (again, keep it short). Then, following the checklist in this chapter, revise your work so that it is as successful as possible.

EXERCISE I

Think about each of the topics below. Then suggest a thesis statement that would be reasonably easy to support, clear, and specific.

1. American railroads

2. Something should be done about the growing trade deficit.

3. Western countries should send more aid to the countries of Eastern Europe.

4. College tuition should be free to all students.

5. The seasons of most professional sports are too long.

6. Many factors should influence students in their choices of academic majors.

7. Any use of drugs by athletes should be prohibited.

8. The death penalty should be handed down more often.

9. People should eat better.

10. Professors should have to work in the real world before they're able to teach.

EXERCISE II

For each of the thesis statements you developed in Exercise I, write down two or three of the main arguments and evidence you might give to support it.

EXERCISE III

For each of the passages below, think of two or three anticipated objections the author might expect. Then think about how the author might respond to them.

1. Since railroads can carry much more freight than trucks can and they do it more efficiently, trains should gradually replace trucks. By raising truck license fees substantially, we can rebuild American railroads while discouraging the use of trucks.

2. We should deal with the trade deficit by imposing high taxes on imported products. By making them much more expensive, foreign products won't seem as attractive and people will turn back to products built at home.

3. If Eastern Bloc countries such as Poland and Hungary are going to develop into stable democracies with market econo-

mies, they will require a large amount of financial aid. We should spend at least 4 percent of our national budget on helping Eastern Bloc countries make this transition.

4. In our fast-paced, technical job market, a college education is about as important as a high school degree was twenty years ago. Since everybody, rich or poor, deserves a chance at a good career, we ought to make tuition free for everybody.

5. Professional sports seasons are too long. We have basketball and hockey after baseball season has started, and baseball goes on long after football season. Each sport's season should be limited to three months.

6. Students should major in whatever they enjoy most because it's difficult to succeed in something that bores you.

7. Since all drugs potentially have an effect on an athlete's performance, any use of drugs by athletes within forty-eight hours of an event they participate in should be prohibited.

8. The death penalty should be given for all crimes in which a victim was killed or raped and for drug-related offenses.

9. Everyone should become a vegetarian. Animal protein is not necessary for good health, and raising animals for food is cruel.

10. Since most professors haven't had direct experience in making a living by doing what they're teaching, they often teach things that are either useless or outdated. Professors should have to work in the real world before they are able to teach.

EXERCISE IV

Write a four- to five-page persuasive paper on a topic drawn from these exercises or on a topic approved by your professor.

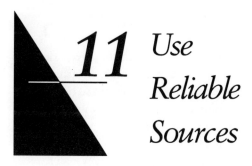

11 Use Reliable Sources

We're surrounded by experts, and given the complexity of the modern world, we must rely on them for much of our understanding and planning of things. For the most part, we do this without thinking about it, often trusting opinions without even knowing whose opinions they are. This can be a problem, because some supposed "authorities" have no right to be considered reliable. Since good reasoning requires sensitivity to appropriate uses of authorities, we need to learn how to distinguish reliable sources from unreliable ones and to use sources effectively. In this chapter, we will develop five criteria for determining whether a source is reliable, discuss how authorities can be used effectively, and describe some dangers to avoid.

Ramon is writing a short essay on how the harmful effects of stress can be reduced through attention to diet and other measures. Like most of us, he is neither a nutritionist nor a physician, so he will have to research his topic. At the library, he will find many articles about stress and diet, some of them in magazines whose titles he will recognize and others in more technical-sounding journals. He now faces the problem that is the main concern of this chapter: Which sources are reliable?

We have already seen that one of the most important parts of the persuasive paper is to document or argue for your main ideas. Remember that either all of the reasons in an argument are supported by evidence or other reasons, or they are assumed. Since we need to establish reliable starting places for our reasoning, we often can do this either directly, by citing facts, or indirectly, by basing our reasons on an authoritative source. Of course, for any source to support your reasoning, that source must be accepted by all of the parties to the discussion.

This is even more important when your conclusion is controversial. Using the opinions of the local Right to Life chairperson as expert testimony regarding abortion will not persuade people who are pro-choice because they do not consider such people to be experts at all. The testimony of a known criminal usually doesn't command much acceptance, even if he testifies on crime. And the smoker who tells her daughter not to smoke even though she herself makes no effort to quit is equally unconvincing.

Of course, most of the reasons such "authorities" are unconvincing are psychological rather than logical. People distrust the authority of those who appear biased or have a clear stake or interest in the results of the controversy they're expressing opinions about. People also tend to distrust what they see as hypocrisy and what they consider an unsavory source. Lawyers often use these tactics to discredit witnesses. So as a practical matter, if not a matter of logic, it's wise to avoid potentially biased, hypocritical, or unsavory sources. Logically, however, the personal attractiveness of an expert has no direct connection with the truth or falsity of what he or she says. What's required is only that sources be impartial, well qualified, and speaking within their areas of expertise. But how can we test for these features?

WHAT MAKES AN EXPERT TRUSTWORTHY

There are five rules of thumb for deciding how much confidence to place in an expert source.

Matters of Fact

Here is the first rule:

> **All other things being equal, expert testimony regarding matters of fact is more reliable than expert testimony on questions of value, concept, or interpretation.**

What makes someone an expert is special knowledge, so an appropriately qualified expert who provides facts from his or her own knowledge is generally reliable. Beyond their specialized knowledge, however, experts are not necessarily better qualified than informed ordinary people to analyze and interpret information, to judge an issue morally, or to analyze a key idea. While experts may have more actual experience in making judgments, the validity of their judgments rests on the strength of their arguments, not on their reputations. So if an expert offers a judgment that is not supported by arguments, it should be treated as a hypothesis rather than a reliable piece of evidence.

It is often tempting to violate this rule. People often assume that physicians and nurses are experts in matters of abortion or euthanasia, for example, or that physicists are experts in nuclear weapons policy. But there is no reason to suppose that their technical knowledge equips them especially well to make reasonable moral or policy judgments. Sometimes, people assume the opposite, that a person's technical knowledge *disqualifies* him or her from making responsible moral or interpretive judgments, as in the case of military officers regarding weapons policy or lawyers on almost any social question. Neither attitude is right. The only safe approach is to treat all matters of interpretation, value, and concept as requiring argument and to use expert sources primarily for facts.

Relevant, Documented Evidence

Here is the second rule of thumb:

> **All other things being equal, the testimony of experts who are identified by biographical evidence of their special knowledge is**

more reliable than any information that comes from an anonymous source.

Since expertise is special knowledge, documentation of how that knowledge was gained helps certify that the expert in question can be considered trustworthy. Such documentation can involve relevant experiences, research interests, academic degrees or training, and other forms of public recognition of accomplishments. Being an expert is not something you can claim for yourself. It's a status that has to be conferred on you by others. And it's the fact that someone's knowledge is documented by publicly accepted measures of achievement that entitles that person to be considered expert.

Original Sources

The third rule:

> **All other things being equal, experts who speak out of their own knowledge or clearly document their own sources are more reliable than those who merely allude to them.**

In a sense, everyone is an expert about his own experiences, at least if he understands them and expresses them clearly. So an eyewitness can be an expert in this sense. But often, experts rely on other sources to develop their knowledge. And when they do this, it's important for the expert to document the source. This is because when an expert uses someone else as a source, that source might be wrong or the expert might misinterpret the source. A critical reader needs to be able to verify an expert's use of sources, just as he or she needs to be able to verify your use of sources, which is part of the reason it's crucial to document your sources carefully and accurately. Suspicion is justified when a source says, for example, "As Freud demonstrated . . ." or "History suggests . . . " or "Most Marxists think . . ." and the like. In general, authors who use foot- or endnotes to indicate their sources are more likely to be reliable.

Not Outdated

The fourth rule:

> **All other things being equal, relatively recent expert testimony is more trustworthy than dated expert sources.**

It seems obvious that as new information is discovered and additional research yields new results, sources taking positions based on less complete knowledge become less useful than sources with a more complete knowledge. The problem, of course, is knowing when a source has been refuted or replaced. Time alone will not settle the question because some recent research is faulty and because some early work, especially in nontechnical areas, is especially influential. Ideally, you would read everything available on a topic before writing about it; that would tell you what the consensus is. But since you don't have unlimited time for research, your best bet is to use the most reliable articles you can find (we'll talk more about this later in the chapter) and trust that professional reviewers will screen out bad recent sources.

Consensus

The fifth rule:

> **All other things being equal, an expert source that expresses a consensus, is consistent with your experience, and makes sense is more reliable than an isolated source.**

If you find several sources on one side of an issue, and only one source taking a completely different point of view, you're generally better off trusting the consensus position to support your ideas. It's not that the one expert is necessarily wrong. Rather, it's only that when you're making use of sources you're not in a position to evaluate from your own knowledge, your best bet is to trust the testimony of other experts in the field. Of course, if you are in a position to evaluate a source from your own experience, by all means do that. The fact that you've found an expert source doesn't mean you can forget about testing whether what he or she says makes sense. Many students uncritically believe anything they see in books or articles, blindly assuming that anything in print must be true.

You can and should mention it when experts disagree about some issues. Also, there may be times when there is no expert consensus. An example might be when the prosecution and the defense in a trial both call expert witnesses to say that the defendant was or was not insane and these experts disagree without being able to resolve their differences. When that happens, you should report the fact that experts disagree and be very cautious about using one side or the other as support for your position.

If you follow these five rules of thumb, you will seldom go wrong with respect to the reliability of sources. You should remember, though, that these are only rules of thumb. There are some reliable experts who don't fulfill all of our criteria. For example, it's probably true that some film reviewers are experts, even though their judgments do not express facts. And sometimes people develop expertise in areas outside their formal training. There are some expert gardeners, for example, with no training in botany. But in general, these rules will ensure that your sources can be trusted.

One final but extremely important point about using sources is this. No matter how you use another person's ideas or where they come from, if an idea is taken from another source, you *must* document that source. Many ideas and much information have become "common knowledge" so that we've lost the original sources. But whenever it is possible to identify a source for an idea, if you don't cite the source you are guilty of *plagiarism,* which is pretending that someone else's ideas are your original ideas. At many institutions, plagiarism is grounds for failure or dismissal, and it always undermines a person's credibility. Besides, it's dishonest. So be sure to document your sources in a footnote, an endnote, or in parentheses following the citation, depending on the style accepted by your audience. Your English composition handbook will have many examples of how to document sources.

JUDGING WRITTEN SOURCES

Most of the time, when we are looking for expert sources, we need to find them in print. While there is nothing wrong with interviewing an expert, most of us don't have that opportunity and have to rely on what's readily available. And that's usually what's in your library. The question we started out with is how you judge a source. So how do you judge the reliability of an article?

In the following sections, we'll discuss some rules of thumb that apply specifically to articles as expert sources.

Informational Publications Versus Entertainment

All other things being equal, a publication whose purpose is to inform is more reliable than a publication whose purpose is to entertain.

This is because facts and carefully reasoned opinions are not always as interesting to the general public as are sensationalism and unwarranted claims. Many popular magazines and newspapers cross the line between fact and fiction without making it obvious that that's what they're doing. So if a publication carries any articles that seem sensational, or if it runs any fiction without clearly labeling it as fiction, that publication is probably unreliable as a source.

Professional Audience Versus Popular Interest

All other things being equal, a publication that is directed primarily to a professional audience is more reliable than a general interest magazine.

The easiest way to identify such journals is to see who publishes them. So, for example, since the *New England Journal of Medicine* is published by the New England Medical Society, you can be confident that the journal is very professional. The same goes for journals published by trade associations and academic institutions. But you should be careful not to confuse journals directed to a professional audience with journals directed to a special-interest group. Publications of the National Rifle Association or the Republican party or the timber industry will have a distinctive point of view where nonfactual information is presented. Moreover, since it is often difficult to separate facts from interpretations, it is best to avoid special-interest publications.

Peer Review

Probably the best way to tell how reliable a publication is, is to look at its criteria for selecting articles.

All other things being equal, the most reliable sources select their articles by means of blind peer review.

Blind peer review is a way of deciding which articles to print that ensures the highest standards of reliability. It works like this. When an author submits an article to an editor, he or she removes the author's name and sends the article to recognized experts in the article's subject. They check the article for factual errors and the quality of its reasoning and writing, and recommend that it be published, rejected, or corrected if necessary. The best professional journals reject many more articles than they print because they want to maintain a very high level of quality. But all you need to do is check the journal's editorial policy (usually it's located near the table of contents), and if it involves peer review, the journal is probably a reliable source.

WHO'S RELIABLE
AND WHO'S NOT—AND WHY

In light of all this, we are now in a position to name some names. The magazines listed below appear in order of general reliability as sources of expert information. If you're writing a term paper, and you're using sources as evidence to support your ideas, you should never rely on "least reliable" sources. Try instead to use sources that are "usually" or "most" reliable.

- Least reliable sources: sensationalistic publications. Examples include the *National Enquirer, Weekly World News,* the *Star Reporter.*

- Not always reliable sources: general interest publications. Examples include *Time, Newsweek, Vogue, Good Housekeeping, Sports Illustrated, Women's Day.*

- Usually reliable sources: reputable newspapers, public issue magazines. Examples include the *New York Times,* the *Wall Street Journal,* the *Christian Science Monitor,* the *Washington Post, Atlantic Monthly, Harpers,* the *New York Review of Books.*

- Most reliable sources: professional journals. Examples include the *Journal of the American Medical Association, Philosophy & Public Affairs,* and many others with blind review policies.

Consider first the example from *Weekly World News* in Figure 11.1. This article would be totally out of place as an expert source because its purpose is to provide sensational entertainment rather than information. Note that no editorial policy is available, no biographical information is presented regarding the qualifications of "Ed Anger" (probably a false name), and no documentation or argument is given for any of the claims made in the article.

Let's keep brain-boosting Big Macs out of Russia

By ED ANGER

The pesky Russkies are about to pull off their most diabolical plan ever for taking control of the world and it's got me madder than a python that swallowed a porcupine.

According to reports, the pesky Russkies are about to ink a pact to get a couple of McDonald's in boring Moscow and will follow that up with a string of Pizza Huts for their creepy cities.

At first this sounds like good business for America.

But it is really a sneaky commie plot to get beef burgers, cheese pizza and other "brain" food into the tummies of those Russkie dunderheads.

Let's face it, one of the biggest reasons we've been on top of the Reds all these years is food. I'm talking about junk food—the food that made America great. A lot of sissy scientists claim junk food is bad because it's loaded with fat. Well, burgers and pizza are also loaded with protein that beefs up tiny grey cells into mighty thinking machines. Meanwhile, the Russkies have been getting dumber wolfing down potatoes, onions and cabbage.

Let's face it, nobody dominates the world with a population of potato heads.

But if those greedy commies succeed in getting our restaurant chains to bring in beef burgers, milk shakes and cheese pizza to perk up their people, then the balance of power in the world could switch.

Suddenly, you'll see a whole new breed of clever Russian scientists and soldiers who were smartened up on American eats.

Yup, one generation of Russkie brats raised on Big Macs could tip the scales of the world's brain power. Soon Russkies will be so smart they'll be able to grow wheat!

Today McDonald's— tomorrow the world!

Figure 11.1

Now it may seem odd to place such publications as *Time* and *Newsweek* in the category of "not always reliable" because they are widely read sources of information. And in fact, all of these magazines are usually careful to get their facts right. As expert sources, however, they leave much to be desired. The qualifications of writers is generally unknown, and sources are usually undocumented. Little or no argument is presented to justify major claims. And coverage of controversial and complex issues tends to be simplistic and incomplete.

For example, on August 17, 1987, *Newsweek* reported the following:

Poll Test

Midwest backers of Sen. Bob Dole are upset with the ground rules for an informal presidential poll at a major Iowa Republican fund-raiser next month. Anyone willing to pony up $25 is welcome to attend, but only those with a driver's license—or other ID—proving they are Iowa residents will get ballots. Non-Iowans must vote in a separate poll. Organizers say they want to produce a geographically pure measure of the state's GOP voters. Their unstated goal: to keep busloads of Kansans supporting Dole from stuffing the ballot box. Just such an influx disrupted a Midwest GOP leadership conference in Des Moines last May.

Note, first, that the article is not attributed. Next, how was the information referred to in this article gathered? Finally, if the intentions of Iowa Republicans are "unstated," how would the unknown author know what they are?

Interestingly enough, "Your Diet: Anti-Aging Eating?" from *Vogue* magazine (see Figure 11.2) actually meets more of our criteria for reliable sources than many articles from *Newsweek* do. Although Dr. Stern does not document her references to other authorities in a way that would enable a reader to research them further, she both identifies her sources by their credentials and cites her own qualifications, which are, indeed, relevant to the subject matter of her article. Her treatment of this issue is still superficial, which we should expect from a magazine whose primary focus is fashion rather than science. But *Vogue's* efforts to ensure accuracy make the article suitable for persuasive writing where precise scholarship is not very important.

With *Atlantic Monthly,* we have made another step toward reliable expertise. Most contributors of essays are well qualified to write them, and their qualifications are readily available to readers. Coverage of controversial issues is thorough, and sources are usually documented. And this magazine provides an opportunity for critical readers to object in print to articles or ideas they dispute. All that keeps *Atlantic Monthly* and magazines like it from being among the most reliable is that research is usually not complete, especially in articles by staff writers, and that articles are often less balanced than opinionated. These problems, however, are minimized by the fact that readers often criticize errors, and the *Atlantic Monthly* does acknowledge errors when they occur.

Your Diet: Anti-Aging Eating?

BY JUDITH S. STERN, Sc.D.

In recent years, the search for a "cure" to aging has centered on nutrition, with hopes that eating the "right" diet will lead to a longer, healthier life. However, causes of aging are unknown, and there is little scientific agreement over what the "right" diet is.

Most "anti-aging" diets aim to prevent obesity, a condition that increases risk for heart disease, some cancers, diabetes, and hypertension. Yet there is debate as to the "best" weight associated with longevity.

Animal studies have shown that limiting the amount a rat eats throughout life will increase its life span by retarding age-related diseases and enhancing immune function (which normally declines with age).

Recently, Roy L. Walford, M.D., professor of pathology at the UCLA School of Medicine, restricted food intake in adult mice and found that they lived 10 to 20 percent longer and had fewer cancers than control mice. Based on this work, Dr. Walford, in his book *The 120 Year Diet* (Simon and Schuster), advises an adult to lose weight gradually, over four to six years until you are 10 percent (if you are already slender) to 25 percent (if you are obese) below "set point" (the weight you would be if you didn't diet). However, results from animal studies don't necessarily apply to people, and it is unwise to follow this advice if you are "normally" lean (weight loss may be hazardous), or if you are very overweight (a 25 percent weight loss may not be enough).

In contrast, epidemiological research by Reubin Andres, M.D., clinical director of the National Institute on Aging, suggests there is not any one "best" adult weight; for some older women it may be healthier to be slightly over their "goal" weight. He advises women in their twenties to be slightly leaner than weights in the Metropolitan Life Height and Weight Tables; around forty, "best weight" is about the same as in the tables; thereafter, it may be safe to gain about a pound a year through age sixty. "It is nonsense to advise a healthy middle-aged woman to gain weight; but if nature put you on the fatter side, or you gained a little weight as you aged, it is not necessarily bad," said Dr. Andres. "Excessive diet-

continued on page 166

Figure 11.2

166

ing may hurt you psychologically and physically." Many women smoke to control weight, but health dangers of smoking are far greater than those of being slightly overweight.

Lowering fat in your diet is another goal of many "anti-aging" plans. There's evidence that high-fat diets increase risks of breast and colon cancers. In one animal study, a diet typical of the American diet, with 40 percent calories from fat, promoted development of breast cancer; after ten weeks during which fat was reduced to 10 percent, tumor development was inhibited. There is debate whether fat itself or excess calories contributes to increased tumor development.

The issue becomes more complicated when one considers types of fat. While consuming more polyunsaturated—and less saturate—fats has been linked to decreased heart disease risks, animal studies indicate that polyunsaturated vegetable oils may promote development of cancer tumors.

This contradictory pattern may also be true for alcohol. In a study published recently in *The New England Journal of Medicine,* breast cancer risk was 60 percent higher in women who had one or more alcoholic drinks daily than in non-drinkers. In contrast, other studies have shown that drinking one or two alcoholic beverages per day may lower heart disease risks.

Some popular—but unproven—anti-aging strategies recommend supplements of "anti-oxidants" (e.g. vitamins E and C, selenium and beta carotene), elements thought to reverse effects of "free radicals" (byproducts of metabolism that may damage cells and possibly accelerate aging). Deficiencies of these nutrients may contribute to decreased life span, but taking large amounts of any of these nutrients can produce side effects and is not recommended.

Since the relationship between diet and longevity is complex, moderation is key; and it may be best to follow these guidelines . . .

• Maintain a lean but not extreme weight by eating a variety of foods high in nutrients and fiber but low in calories.

• Cut back fat to 30 percent of calories, divided evenly among saturated, polyunsaturated and monounsaturated fats.

• Discuss your family medical history with your doctor; and tailor your diet accordingly.

• Limit your intake of alcohol and salt.

Judith S. Stern, Sc.D., *is professor of nutrition, University of California, Davis.*

Figure 11.2 continued

Which newspapers are reliable is a matter of judgment. With regard to straight news, most large city papers are careful to get the facts right, and they, too, will correct errors when they are discovered. Be alert for sensationalism, however, and for bias, since some well-known papers (e.g., the *Detroit Free Press*) exhibit both.

The most reliable sources are professional journals. Not all professional journals are of equal quality, but for the purposes of term papers and general academic work not intended for scholarly publication, any peer-reviewed journal is satisfactory.

Avoid Fallacies of Improper Authority

Unfortunately, following all of the rules of thumb we've just discussed will not guarantee that the reasoning you do on the basis of your sources will be reliable. Fallacies that occur because of problems with sources are called **Fallacies of Improper Authority,** and we'll examine several of them. First, though, it's important to remember what sources can and cannot do for you. Except regarding questions of fact, sources don't prove anything. They provide information you can use to support your position, but you still have to make the argument yourself. Remember, too, that finding an expert who agrees with you doesn't prove that your conclusion is true. You have to make the argument that does that for yourself. And finally, remember that the fact that an expert gives an argument does not make it stronger than it would have been if you had thought it up yourself. How strong any argument is depends on how well it fulfills the criteria we discussed in Chapters 4 through 9.

Appeal to the Authority of the Many

People sometimes assume that if something is widely believed, it must be true or reasonable. This error in reasoning is an **Appeal to the Authority of the Many,** also called "mob appeal." In its simplest form, this appeal can appear in the argument of a child that she should be able to stay up late because "everybody else does." It also appears in much advertising, such as these examples:

Nine Out Of Ten Doctors Recommend Bayer . . .

To the Millions of People Who Should Not Take Aspirin . . .

Figure 11.3

Now in use at over 600 colleges and universities around the country, this lucid text offers your students . . .

The largest selling soft drink in the world just got better . . .

And you can see the same impulse working in Figure 11.3. The fact that so many (cartoon!) people are flocking (like sheep!) to Tourneau Corner doesn't provide any evidence that you, too, should buy a watch from them.

Appeal to the Authority of Unreal Experts

The fact that the "people" flocking to Tourneau Corner are cartoon characters raises another important point. We often forget that many of the characters whose opinions people are influenced by are not real experts at all but rather imaginary characters, cartoons, or models drawn or hired to express the opinions of others. The **Appeal to the Authority of Unreal Experts** is a fallacy of improper authority that assigns expert status to imaginary characters or performing actors. Such arguments work because people often find fictional characters—such as Bart Simpson—more real than ordinary people.

K-Mart, for example, has created an imaginary auto expert named "Will Start" to endorse their car batteries and an imaginary photography expert named "Dusty Lenscap" to endorse K-Mart photo finishing and film. But Will Start cannot have the expert knowledge of a real garage mechanic because he is a cartoon, and Dusty Lenscap lacks photographic knowledge for the same reason. Similarly, Fred Flintstone cannot be an expert on vitamins because he is a drawing, not a physician or nutritionist. Peanuts characters, such as Snoopy, cannot be experts on insurance because they will do and say whatever they are drawn and scripted to do and say. Even Morris the Cat cannot be an expert on cat food because, although the cats playing the role of Morris are real cats, their performances are the result of long training, and Morris's opinions are those an actor reads in voice-over.

We can avoid falling victim to appeals to unreal experts by being careful to distinguish what is real from what is fiction. Again, remembering to think about the actual qualifications of the supposed "expert" will keep us from being confused.

Appeal to the Authority of the Select Few

These days, Americans are less likely to want to conform than they once were. Another fallacy of improper authority is sometimes called **Appeal to the Authority of the Select Few** or, less kindly, "snob appeal." It works because people are sometimes willing to believe what stylish people tell them regardless of the evidence, perhaps because they want to identify themselves as having class. Many advertisers make use of this fallacy. For example, it is a natural, but mistaken, assumption that if Wild Turkey Bourbon or J&B Scotch is found in "finer nests" or among those who have "rare character" it must be a superior product, natural to assume that if "great Americans" stay at the Colonial Inn, or the Lygon Arms is one of "only 31 prestige hotels in Britain," that they must be great places to stay, and natural to suppose that the wealthy, stylish women who appear in ads must be authorities on perfumes. But it's possible, even likely, that Wild Turkey and J&B are drunk as much or more by cowards with bad livers, that ordinary Americans have stayed at the Colonial, that the designation "prestige hotel" is conferred on anyone who pays for the privilege, and that slinky looking models actually know little or nothing about perfumes.

Appeal to the Authority of Ordinary Folks

An interesting variation of snob appeal is *reverse* snob appeal, or **Appeal to the Authority of Ordinary Folks.** Each of the major American truck companies has used models representing "ordinary" farmers endorsing its trucks, but Chevrolet's "More People in Ford Country Drive Chevys" ads showing "down home folks" praising Chevy Trucks is a fine example of relying on ordinary folks as experts. Bartles & James Wine Cooler ads also substitute the appealing images of two "locals" (who are actually very successful business people representing one of America's largest wine producers) in place of the expert opinions of qualified wine connoisseurs. The idea of appeals to the authority of ordinary folks is that since most people can identify with an ordinary guy, he must be a reliable authority about whatever he's saying. But the point about experts that makes them especially reliable is that they're *not ordinary,* because they have special knowledge and experience that ordinary folks don't have. So, to avoid being taken in by reverse snob appeal, be sure to ask yourself what qualifications the supposed "expert" has that entitle his or her opinion to be considered especially authoritative.

Appeal to Tradition

Another form of appeal to authority occurs when the fact that something has "always" been done in a certain way, or has "always" been believed, is taken to support the idea that it should continue to be done that way or continue to be believed. This fallacy is called **Appeal to Tradition.** A familiar example is when your mother tells you the family has to spend Christmas at Aunt Betty's because "we've always gone there for Christmas." Bosses often reject unpopular suggestions on the grounds that "we've always done things this way, and we're not going to change now." This, too, is an appeal to tradition: "This family has been Catholic since there have been Sullivans in Ireland, so if you're going to get married, you'll do it at Saint Brendon's."

Appeal to Improper Authority

The most dangerous form of authority fallacy is one in which a person's genuine expertise in one area is used to support an opinion in an unrelated area. This is called **Appeal to Improper Authority,** and there are many examples. The fact that a number of well-known movie stars endorse a political candidate is not by itself a reason to consider the candidate worthy. The fact that Lauren Bacall endorses a certain coffee, Gloria Vanderbilt endorses clothes, Jim McMahon eats at Taco Bell, and Lyle Alzado prefers Hanes offers no evidence regarding the products' actual worth. The Rolex ad in Figure 11.4 is another example in which greatness in one field is carried over to another, here with a hint of "select few"; Kiri Te Kanawa's expertise is operatic singing, not watches, even though Queen Elizabeth II did name her Dame Commander.

SUMMARY

Since effective reasoning requires reliable information, it's important to be able to distinguish good sources and trustworthy experts from less useful ones. You can be most confident about using expert sources when you use them to establish facts rather than value judgments or other opinions. You should rely on clearly identified experts whose documented background makes them well qualified. And your sources should either speak out of their direct experience or document their sources. Recent sources are generally more reliable than outdated ones. And you should trust those that express a consensus more than those that express a controversial judgment. Regarding articles, the best are drawn from sources that are not primarily intended for entertainment, are written for professional audiences, and practice peer review in determining which articles to print. When authorities are misused, the result can be bad arguments, called fallacies of improper authority. Be careful not to engage in mob appeal, snob appeal, reverse snob appeal, appeal to the authority of unreal experts, or appeals to tradition or improper authority.

Rolex accompanies Te Kanawa.

Kiri Te Kanawa's voice has been called perfect by Sir Colin Davis of Covent Garden. She is so highly esteemed by the Metropolitan Opera that they chose her to star in the coveted new production of Strauss's *Arabella*.

In nineteen eighty-two, her rare talent was recognized when Queen Elizabeth II named her Dame Commander

of the British Empire.

Te Kanawa has won renown in film, recordings and television. She has gained international acclaim in recitals and orchestral concerts. Accomplishments foreseen from an early age for this storied New Zealand prodigy.

But for all her achievements, she remains a delightfully down-to-earth diva. As

energetic on a golf course as on a stage. As enthusiastic a wife and mother as a performer.

One of opera's most revered sopranos, Te Kanawa is accompanied by her equally celebrated Rolex. A duet well-matched for both commanding presence and consistently brilliant performance.

ROLEX

Lady Datejust Oyster Perpetual Chronometer in 18kt gold; bezel and dial set with diamonds.

Write for brochure. Rolex Watch U.S.A., Inc., Dept. 212, Rolex Building, 665 Fifth Avenue, New York, New York 10022-5383.
© 1986 Rolex Watch U.S.A., Inc.

Figure 11.4

EXERCISE I

Suppose you were assigned to write a paper on each of the following topics. Making use of the library, find four expert sources on the topic that would be considered reliable using the criteria in this chapter. Be sure both the individual and the publication could be considered at least usually reliable.

1. Are nuclear powered electric generators safe?

2. Effects of deregulation on the airline industry

3. Allied military strategy in the Persian Gulf conflict

4. Fetal injuries due to alcohol consumption during pregnancy

5. Are electric cars a practical answer to automobile pollution?

EXERCISE II

Identify any instances of improper authority in the following arguments. Explain exactly what the problem is, and identify what kind of expert would be more appropriate.

1. To enact reasonable drug legislation, we need to find out the facts about drugs. Accordingly, the League has invited several authorities on the subject: Dr. Hill, of the Obstetrics Department at County Hospital, and Roy Axel, pharmacist at Rexall Drugs.

2. Shouldn't you be using the pain medication used in more hospitals than any other?

3. Is Glenlivet's high price justified? You can get a good Scotch for less. But The Glenlivet is Scotland's oldest distillery, and it produces only a few precious casks each day, just as it always has. Glenlivet. If you want the best, you have to expect to pay for it.

4. Any Miller Lite ad.

5. The social and economic problems of ghetto dwellers have their origins in the weak family structure that occurs when one or more parents is absent. According to Dr. Harold Hill, Medical Director of the Central City Hospital, the average minority family will make little economic progress until the family unit is strengthened.

6. You work hard for your money. So do I. I'm Bob Blackman, at Blackman's Insurance, and you should come on in for a free insurance review, like so many of your neighbors here in Littleton have done.

7. The fastest growing segment of the automobile market in the 1980s is not cars at all, but trucks and vans. And who's sold more trucks and vans than anybody else? Chrysler, that's who.

8. The Union of Concerned Scientists is joining with a majority of the members of the National Academy of Sciences—our nation's most prestigious scientific body—to lobby Congress to cut off funds for testing and deployment of antisatellite weapons, such as Star Wars. It's not just bad foreign policy. It's potentially the end of the human race. Join us, and help reduce the threat of nuclear war.

9. Find and bring to class at least one example of an appeal to an unreal authoity. Then discuss what sort of expertise might be appropriate to your example.

12 *Make Effective Comparisons*

Many arguments, like most thinking, involve making comparisons between similar situations or ideas and then reasoning that what is true of one must be true of the other. Such reasoning, which depends on seeing relevant similarities, is called reasoning by analogy. In this chapter, we will examine several kinds of analogical arguments, determine what makes them effective, and then consider several ways in which such arguments can break down.

ARGUMENTS USING ANALOGIES

Tanya is preparing her editorial against the proposed tuition hike for the student newspaper. Among the many reasons she can think of to oppose a tuition hike, she offers the following argument:

> **From the point of view of students and their families, tuition is exactly like a tax. Just as taxation without representation has been considered a perfect example of injustice, so the proposed tuition increase, which was decided without any student input, is equally unjust. We therefore urge that the proposal be withdrawn.**

In this example, whether Tanya's argument that the increase is unjust is convincing will depend on whether she's right that tuition is exactly like a tax. Specifically, taxes and tuition need to be similar in the respect that increases are unjust if they're decided without the consent of those who must pay them. The logical strength of Tanya's argument depends on the degree of similarity between tuition and taxes.

Tanya's argument, which is called an **analogy,** works this way. She begins by identifying two things, tuition and taxes, as being similar. The two things being compared are called **analogues.** Then she points out that something is true of one of the analogues, in this case that taxation without representation is unjust. She goes on to reason that if the two analogues are exactly similar, then what's true of one of them must be true of the other. So, given that taxation without representation is unjust, and that taxation is exactly like tuition, then tuition increases without student input must be unjust as well. Put formally, her argument would look like this:

Premise 1: X (taxes) is like Y (tuition).

Premise 2: Something (an increase without representation is unjust) is true of X (taxes).

Conclusion: So that something (an increase without representation is unjust) is also true of Y (tuition).

Of course, the university administration might reply with an analogical argument of its own, such as the following:

> **Tuition is merely one of the ways in which a university meets its expenses. Just as any business or service must increase its costs in proportion to increased expenses, the university must**

increase tuition when its expenses exceed its income. This decision, though difficult, is not one the consumer has a right to make; it is the responsibility of management to establish reasonable increases in costs when they become necessary. Since such management decisions involve no injustice, neither does an administrative decision regarding tuition increases involve injustice.

In this argument, the analogues are universities and businesses, students and customers. The administration is claiming that businesses have the right to increase prices without consulting consumers. And since businesses and universities are supposedly similar in the relevant respects, and businesses commit no injustices if they raise prices without consulting consumers, the administration concludes that if the university raises tuition without consulting students, it commits no injustice.

APT COMPARISONS

Whether Tanya's argument or the administration's argument is more logically convincing depends on which comparison is more apt. To decide whether or not a comparison is apt, look for these things:

- Are all of the claims made in the reasons true?

- Are the analogues similar in relevant respects?

- Are there differences between the analogues that outweigh their similarities?

In the cases of the two tuition arguments, determining which is more logically persuasive depends on whether tuition increases are more like taxes or more like rising prices. Such judgments can be hard to make, which points to another fact about analogical arguments: They're almost never conclusive. That is, *there can be good analogical arguments on all sides of an issue.*

Are All of the Claims True?

Let's look at some other examples. Suppose twelve-year-old Randi wants to stay out after 10:00 P.M. on school nights, and he gives his mother the following argument:

Aw c'mon Mom. Everybody else's mothers let them stay out after 10:00.

Even though this may not look like an analogical argument on first glance, it is. Randi's conclusion is that he ought to be permitted to stay out after 10:00 P.M. His reason is that he and his mother are relevantly similar to "everybody else" and their mothers. Then he's claiming that what's true of everybody else's mothers—that they let their children stay out after 10:00—is (or ought to be) true of his mother too. So she should let him stay out after 10:00 P.M.

How apt is this argument? Not very, because at least one of the premises is not true. It's false that everybody else's mothers let them stay out, even if Randi is implicitly restricting "everybody else" to people relevantly similar to himself and his mother. Some mothers, perhaps those who care most about the well-being of their children, do not let them stay out. So Randi's argument fails to be logically convincing because a crucial premise is untrue.

Are the Analogues Relevantly Similar?

Suppose that Randi goes on to point out that his mother does let his sixteen-year-old sister, Jennie, stay out until 1:00 A.M. on weekends, even though she, too, is expected to be at home by 10:00 P.M. on school nights. He might say:

You're not being fair. You let Jennie stay out until 1:00, and she comes in late a lot of times on school nights.

Does this strengthen his argument?

To see that it doesn't, we need only to spell out the analogy that Randi is trying to draw between himself and his sister. Here, he's saying that the relevant analogy is between himself and how his mother treats him, and his sister and how his mother treats her. Again reasoning that what's true of one analogue is (or ought to be) true of the other, and pointing out that their mother permits Jennie to stay out until 1:00 and often come in late, Randi concludes that in fairness, he should be able to stay out until 1:00 and come in late too.

But the aptness of this argument depends on there being more relevant similarities between the analogues than there are important differences. In this case, there are several important differences. Among them are that their mother's curfews on *weekends* are not relevant to Randi's argument regarding curfews on school nights, because students typically have different obligations on school nights than on weekends. And while Randi might not wish to admit this, sixteen-year-old girls are typically much more mature and reliable than twelve-year-old boys, so their differing ages are relevant differences.

Do Differences Outweigh the Similarities?

Perhaps the weakest analogical arguments are those in which the connections between the analogues are very far fetched or unreasonable. An example is this argument, given by Mr. Blocker, the football coach, in reply to parents' concerns about practice injuries among football team members:

> **Hey, you can't make an omelette without breakin' a few eggs. Ya gotta expect a few sprains and strains.**

The analogues here are high school football players and eggs, football teams and omelettes. The coach is saying that since football players are like eggs, and teams are like omelettes, what's true of eggs must be true of football players. And since it's impossible to avoid breaking eggs when you make omelettes out of them, parents are supposed to conclude that it's impossible to avoid injuring football players when you make a team out of them.

But how apt is this analogy? Not very, because there are hardly any relevant similarities between high school football players and eggs or between teams and omelettes. For example, whereas football players suffer pain when they are injured, eggs don't. Whereas making omelettes does unavoidably involve breaking eggs, building football teams can be done without injuring players. So Blocker's analogy breaks down and fails to offer reasonable logical support.

AVOID FALSE ANALOGIES

Arguments like Coach Blocker's are fallacies of false analogy. **False analogies** make use of analogues that are not apt—where the comparison depends on false or questionable similarities, where the similarities are not relevant, or where there are differences between the analogues that outweigh their similarities. Here are two false analogies:

Permitting student participation in decisions about tuition increases would be a disaster. Just think about what happens in families where children are allowed to run the household.

Human history is a cycle of excessive population growth followed by wars and natural disasters. Just as plants and bushes actually benefit from an occasional pruning, so the human race is actually better off because of wars, earthquakes, and famines.

The first analogy is between students participating in tuition decisions and children running a household. What makes the analogy false is that there are many important and relevant differences between children and college students, such as the relative maturity of college students and the fact that most students pay tuition while most children do not pay household expenses. The second analogy is between people and plants, and between wars and natural disasters and pruning. What makes the analogy false is, again, that the comparison is not apt: People suffer when they are victimized by wars and natural disasters, whereas plants do not suffer when they are pruned.

Is a Fetus Like a Concert Violinist?

A more interesting example is this one, from the philosopher Judith Jarvis Thomson, who is arguing that a fetus's right to life does not necessarily outweigh a mother's right to decide what happens in and to her body:

> You wake up in the morning and find yourself back to back in bed with an unconscious violinist. A famous unconscious violinist. He has been found to have a fatal kidney ailment, and the Society of Music Lovers has canvassed all the available medical records and found that you alone have the right blood type to help. They have therefore kidnapped you, and last night the violinist's circulatory system was plugged into yours, so that your kidneys can be used to extract poisons from his blood as well as your own. The director of the hospital now tells you, "Look, we're sorry the Society of Music Lovers did this to you—we would never have permitted it if we had known. But still, they did it, and the violinist now is plugged into you. To unplug you would be to kill him. But never mind, it's only for nine months. By then he will have recovered from his ailment, and can safely be unplugged from you." Is it morally incumbent

**on you to accede to this situation? . . . I imagine you would
regard this as outrageous, which suggests that something really
is wrong with that plausible sounding argument I mentioned a
moment ago.**[1]

Thomson's analogy is between a fetus and a concert violinist, and
between a mother and the person being kidnapped and hooked up so
that the violinist can survive nine months until he can be "born" (live
on his own). And she argues that just as you wouldn't have a moral
obligation to stay hooked up to the violinist, a mother wouldn't have
a moral obligation to stay hooked up to a fetus. In each case, she says,
it would be morally acceptable to ask a doctor to perform a "disconnect" (an abortion).

Whether this analogy is false is much more controversial than our
earlier examples, but it still depends on whether there are relevant
dissimilarities that outweigh the similarities. In her article, Thomson
notes that this analogy would hold only if the mother became pregnant against her will, as in rape, because in the violinist case the subject is kidnapped. But we might also ask whether it's really true that
a mother has no responsibility *at all* for her fetus, even if it was conceived involuntarily, the way you would have *no* responsibility for
this violinist who is a total stranger, unrelated to you. If you think the
mother might well have some responsibility for the fetus, the analogy
would be false.

Is the Universe Like a Watch?

It is often true that interesting analogical arguments are difficult to
test. Here are two more arguments from analogy, both of which have
interested philosophers for a long time. One of these is an argument
that God exists. The other is an argument for the claim that we know
that other people have thoughts, feelings, and sensations.

The eighteenth-century theologian William Paley used an analogical argument to persuade skeptics to believe in God as He is usually
thought of by Christians. A version of his argument follows.

**If you were to find a watch, you would not doubt that it had
a maker, because "when we come to inspect the watch, we**

---

1. Judith Jarvis Thomson, "A Defense of Abortion," *Philosophy and Public
Affairs* 1, no. 1 (1971): .

perceive . . . that its several parts are framed and put together for a purpose . . . to point out the hour of the day," and the fact that the watch exhibits purposeful construction justifies us in concluding there must have been a watchmaker "who formed it for the purpose." Now if you "look around the world, contemplate the whole and every part of it: you will find it to be nothing but one great (watchlike) machine, subdivided into an infinite number of lesser machines . . . adjusted to each other with an accuracy which ravishes into admiration all men who have ever contemplated them. The curious adapting of means to ends throughout all nature resembles exactly, though it much exceeds, the productions of human contrivance, of human design, thought, wisdom, and intelligence. Since, therefore, the effects resemble each other, we are led to infer, by all the rules of analogy, that the causes also resemble, and that the Author of Nature is somewhat similar to the mind of man, though possessed of much larger faculties, proportioned to the grandeur of the work which he has executed. By this argument . . . do we prove at once the existence of a Deity and his similarity to human mind and intelligence."[2]

Once you have worked through the flowery writing style of the time, you will probably be able to identify the analogues of this argument without much trouble. Paley is saying that the world, or the universe, is very much like a watch, or a machine. Specifically, they are like each other in being complicated, profoundly interrelated and "adjusted to each other" in amazing ways, most of which imply purposeful interaction. What is true of watches and machines (which have these characteristics) is that they have makers who design their complicated structures, adjustments, and purposes. So, since the world is very much like a watch, and what's true of the watch must be true of what's very much like it (analogous to it), the world, like the watch, must have had a maker (God). Only God must be far more wise and great than any human designer, since his creation "far exceeds" anything humans are capable of.

To determine how logically convincing this argument is, we need to return to our three criteria for evaluating analogical arguments. First, are the premises true? Well, it probably is true that no one who

---

2. From William Paley, *Natural Theology* (1802), and David Hume, *Dialogues Concerning Natural Religion* (1779).

knew anything about watches would find one and think it probably grew there like a mushroom. Things that really do exhibit design (as opposed to pattern, for example) do have designers. And the more we know about ecology, the more we realize how intricately everything in nature is interdependent. But some of the other aspects of Paley's argument are more questionable. Is it really true that when you look around, you see anything very much like a watch, or "one great machine, subdivided into an infinite number of lesser machines"? (Not all of these words are Paley's; perhaps we shouldn't blame him.) Perhaps not—perhaps what most of us see are stones, trees, cars, and people, not all of which are very much like watches or machines at all.

But that brings us to the next two tests, whether the similarities are relevant and whether there are differences that outweigh the similarities. Is the universe relevantly like a watch? Well, it would be only if the universe, like a watch, has a purpose or a design. But whether the universe has a purpose or design seems to depend more on whether it has a creator than whether it is intricate or complicated, or interactive. After all, it might have only a pattern rather than a design, and whereas a design seems to require a designer, a pattern requires only someone to recognize the pattern, not someone to design it. In short, the relevance of the similarities seems to depend on begging the question and assuming that the universe has a creator.

But there's another problem, first noticed by David Hume. That is, even if we assume the analogy holds, and the universe has a designer, the analogical argument that compares abilities to designs would not prove the existence of the kind of God Christians worship, because the world contains great evil, suffering, ugliness, and waste as well as some instances of goodness, well-being, beauty, and perfect adaptation. So perhaps this analogical argument is not one Paley should have used. Of course, that doesn't mean Hume has proved God doesn't exist. Our criticisms show only that this analogical argument doesn't prove He does.

Knowledge of Others' Sensations

Another analogical argument is this one, used to prove that we can sometimes know that other people's sensations, emotions, and experiences are like ours. (Perhaps you can't see why it would be necessary to try to prove this. You might start by asking yourself *how* you know what another person is feeling and why you are so often unable to tell.) A particular application of this kind of argument can be put very simply:

> **Whenever I fall off my bicycle and skin my elbows, I feel pain. That person over there has just fallen off her bicycle and skinned her elbows. So she's probably feeling pain too.**

This kind of argument is what underlies most of our judgments about other people's feelings, attitudes, and sensations. That is, we reason that we are exactly similar to another person, and whenever we are in a certain situation we typically feel a certain kind of sensation. The other person is in that situation. So, we conclude, the other person is feeling the relevant kind of sensation. But how good is this argument?

Again, the logical quality of this argument from analogy depends on whether or not it fulfills our criteria. Of course, the premises might not be true. That is, instead of falling off her bicycle in the usual way, the woman you saw might be a stunt person practicing falling off her bicycle painlessly while simulating scraped elbows with make-up. Or the woman might have had her elbows anesthetized, so that she would not be relevantly like you in having a fully functioning nervous system. But let's assume that the situation is as it appears.

Our attention then turns to whether the similarities we're counting on between the analogues are relevant and whether there are dissimilarities that outweigh them. Many philosophers have pointed out that there is no way to tell whether the comparison between yourself and someone else is valid because there's no way to get inside someone else's self and check to see whether her nervous system works like yours. Maybe, they suggest, situations in which you feel pain are situations in which others feel something else, but they have just learned to respond to that other feeling the way you respond to pain. Or maybe, like robots, they don't feel anything at all; they just exhibit behavior.

But the criteria we have developed for acceptable arguments from analogy permit us to continue to use the analogical approach to justify our belief that others experience pain and other feelings. We can, after all, check for similar nervous systems, the presence or absence of anesthetic, and the like. And we can often tell whether our initial assumptions about similarity between ourselves and others hold true by looking for inconsistencies between their behavior and ours in other situations. But if there are no outweighing dissimilarities, our criteria permit us to count an analogical argument as logically acceptable. So this argument about skinned elbows and feeling pain should be counted as rationally acceptable, and we should conclude that other beings relevantly similar to ourselves in having similar nervous systems and exhibiting pain behavior probably experience painful sensations much like ours.

Of course, not all analogies are arguments. Metaphors and similes are analogies that are used to call attention to features of similarity in a memorable or striking way, rather than to support a conclusion. "Your smile is like a summer's day" and "The fog came in on little cat feet" are both analogies that are not used as arguments, since they support no conclusions. But such analogies also illustrate two other crucial points about good analogies. One is that if the analogy is to mean anything, your audience must understand the comparison. In these cases, people must understand what a summer's day and cat's feet are like for the analogies to mean anything to them, just as they need to understand something about watches and injuries for some of our other examples to work. The other point is that the more vivid or striking an analogy is, the better, so long as it isn't misleading. It's difficult to be interesting when you're using sports analogies. And if your analogies are pointlessly vague, people generally won't find anything exciting about them. Stylistically, then, it's useful to avoid confusing or vague analogies.

SUMMARY

In this chapter, we examined arguments based on comparisons, called analogical arguments. The heart of an analogical argument is a comparison between two things or ideas, called analogues, together with the assertion that something is true of one of them. The reasoning of an analogy is that if two analogues are relevantly similar and something is true of one of them, it's true of the other as well. Although no analogical argument is ever logically conclusive, some are much better than others. The quality of an analogical argument depends on three things: Are all of the claims true? Are the similarities relevant? Are there differences that outweigh the similarities? If any of these tests is failed, the analogical argument breaks down and loses its logical force. Finally, the most effective analogies are not confusing or vague, but clear and vivid.

EXERCISE I

For each of the following pairs of objects or ideas, find at least two respects in which they are similar (analogous) and two respects in which they are different (not analogous).

1. Animals and people

2. American Revolutionary War participants and the Viet Cong

3. The electrical system in your car and the nervous system in your body

4. Athletics and academic study

5. The college's curriculum and a grocery store

EXERCISE II

Identify any analogies that occur in the following examples. Pick out the similarities on which the analogy is based, and evaluate the analogies in terms of the criteria in this chapter.

1. Warning labels should appear on all records, cassettes, and compact discs that include objectionable lyrics. Just like the warning labels on cigarette packs, people need to know before they buy something if it is potentially harmful to them and others.

2. Computers perform many operations, such as mathematical computations, that require people to think. Moreover, computers have an electronic "nervous system" that can be functionally equivalent to the human brain. So it would be reasonable to say that computers think just as people do.

3. Blaming violent television shows and movies for violent behavior in children and adults is like blaming sale prices in department stores when shoppers get a little carried away or like blaming subways because some people get mugged in them.

4. Teaching is like pouring your students' heads full of ideas the way we pour a pitcher full of water. Some pitchers are bigger than others, and when they reach capacity, they just can't contain any more. When you see people's eyes starting to glaze

over, all of the knowledge you're trying to pass on will be wasted, just like the water that runs down the drain.

5. Suppose you find yourself trapped in a tiny house with a growing child. I mean a very tiny house, and a rapidly growing child—you are already up against the wall of the house and in a few minutes you'll be crushed to death; if nothing is done to stop him from growing he'll be hurt, but in the end he'll simply burst open the house and walk out a free man. . . . However innocent the child may be, you do not have to wait passively while it crushes you to death. Perhaps a pregnant woman is vaguely felt to have the status of a house, to which we don't allow the right of self-defense. But if the woman houses the child, it should be remembered that she is a person who houses it.[3]

EXERCISE III

Write a short (two- or three-page) persuasive paper based on an analogy. You might use the taxation/tuition increase analogy, but if you do, be sure to address the costs of doing business/tuition increase analogy in your anticipated replies section. Or you can use one of the analogies you developed in Exercise I. Again, though, be sure to deal with the features limiting the analogy when you anticipate objections, and make sure your thesis is clear.

---

3. Thomson, *A Defense of Abortion.*

13 Criticize Arguments Fairly

While you'll often have to argue effectively for your own point of view, you will also have to criticize others on many occasions. When you do this, it's important to be fair about it. Being fair starts with making sure you understand others' ideas accurately and can summarize them without bias. Then you need to single out important concerns for criticism having to do with the thesis, the arguments for it, and the assumptions it rests on, or the consequences of putting it into practice. Finally, we'll look at several forms of unfair criticism to avoid.

BEFORE YOU CRITICIZE

People usually have little trouble spotting errors in other people's arguments. Even when it isn't obvious which fallacy is being committed, people can often sense that something is wrong. It's harder to spot the errors in our own reasoning, of course. And it's also harder to explain what's wrong with others' arguments in a way that will convince our audience. But that's just what we're often required to do, not only in academic situations but also in public discussions of important issues. Since there are almost always other seemingly worthwhile ideas besides ours, we often need to explain why those alternatives are not satisfactory in order to prepare the ground for our ideas or to just warn people not to be taken in by unwise proposals. At the same time, we are more convincing if our comments are fair and constructive, not aggressive or biased. Being critical is not the same thing as attacking a person or discrediting his or her ideas. We can disagree without being disagreeable.

Julia is in a situation like this. A member of the Business and Economics Club, she is scheduled to debate Emilio on the issue of comparable worth. Julia believes in comparable worth, which is the idea that jobs which require roughly similar levels of education, effort, and responsibility should be paid similar wages. Emilio, however, thinks comparable worth is a "can of worms" and that wages should be set by the free market. Emilio has given Julia a copy of his main ideas so she can prepare her response. Here they are:

> **Comparable worth is both a bad idea and bad public policy. Its main purpose is to improve women's salaries by passing laws to force employers to raise wages in traditionally female occupations, such as nursing and teaching. But there are many good reasons men are paid more than women. Men's jobs tend to be more stressful, physically exhausting, and responsible than women's jobs. Men traditionally have to support families on their incomes, whereas women's incomes have helped improve the family's situation. And the free market determines the salary paid to workers; people regardless of sex who work in high-demand areas are paid more than people who work in low-demand areas. If women want higher wages, the best way to get them is to train themselves to go into high-demand areas.**

Julia disagrees with almost everything Emilio is saying here. But if she is going to convince the other members of the Business and

Economics Club, she will have to explain what's wrong with Emilio's position in a way they will be likely to accept. Stamping her feet and accusing Emilio of gross insensitivity and male chauvinism doesn't do this, even if Emilio is insensitive and chauvinistic. It's important to limit yourself to criticizing someone's ideas, not his personality or character, because even if someone is a bad person in some respect or other, his ideas might still be well justified or true. So how should Julia go about criticizing Emilio's ideas in a fair and persuasive way?

Summarize Accurately

First, she needs to make sure she *understands the position she is criticizing.* If she is emotionally involved in the issue under discussion, as she may be here, she may have a hard time understanding Emilio's position accurately. This is because intense emotions block accurate thinking, and her certainty that Emilio is wrong may prevent her from seeing aspects of his position that should convince a rational person. So Julia needs to make sure she doesn't let her feelings interfere with her ability to understand. She might begin by stating the issue in a neutral way. In this case, it's whether or not comparable worth is a good idea. And in general, stating the issue as "Whether or not . . . " can help create some emotional distance.

Another important point is that Julia should be careful not to mix this step with criticizing the position she's trying to understand. This is because if anyone tries to criticize while spelling out what the idea is, the desire to find things to criticize may bias her interpretation. So it's important for Julia (or anyone) to put her feelings and desire to criticize aside for a while, to get Emilio's position straight in her own mind.

Ordinarily, this step will be very time consuming, because people are not always as helpful as Emilio in providing a good summary of their ideas. Most of the time it will be necessary to summarize an article or speech in which the ideas to be criticized are presented, boiling it down to a paragraph or two, so that the audience can follow exactly what the issues and criticisms are. In Chapter 14, we will discuss how to summarize accurately from original material. But even though Emilio has provided a summary for Julia, there are several steps Julia will need to go through in getting started.

Identify the Thesis

She'll need to begin by *identifying the thesis,* which is the conclusion Emilio will try to persuade people to accept. It's in the first line: "Comparable worth is a bad idea and bad public policy." Of course, this is really two conclusions, namely that "comparable worth is a bad idea" and "comparable worth is bad public policy." This means Emilio will need to prove both parts of his thesis, something Julia will decide after she's looked at Emilio's arguments.

Next, she should *identify the main arguments for the thesis.* This will involve figuring out what arguments go with which part of the thesis. However, it's clear that Emilio is making use of basically three claims as his reasons:

1. Men's jobs tend to be more stressful, physically exhausting, and responsible than women's jobs.

2. Men have to support families on their incomes, whereas women's incomes are mainly supplemental.

3. The free market determines salaries on the basis of demand, with high salaries going to people in high-demand areas.

So Julia's next step is to figure out what he's using these claims to try to prove. It's not obvious that any of these reasons are directly connected to Emilio's thesis. But two of them, #1 and #2, seem to be tied up with showing that "there are many good reasons men are paid more than women." (Whether Emilio is right in thinking his reasons are true or "good" is beside the point right now. Remember, Julia is only trying to understand his argument, not criticize it, at this stage.) And the third, the "free market" idea, seems connected to the last sentence, that the best way for women to get higher wages "is to train themselves to go into high-demand areas."

One way to see the structure of Emilio's arguments so far is this:

Argument #1

1. Men's jobs tend to be more stressful, physically exhausting, and responsible than women's jobs.

2. Whereas men have to support families on their salaries, women don't.
   Therefore (there are good reasons why), men should be paid more than women.

Argument #2

3. The free market assigns high salaries to high-demand jobs
    regardless of the sex of the worker.
    Therefore, the best way for women to get high salaries is to
    train themselves for high-demand jobs.

But how do these arguments connect up with Emilio's thesis? To
explain the connection, Julia will have to go on to the next step in
understanding Emilio's positions.

Identify the Assumptions

The third step is to *identify all assumptions on which the arguments
rest* and explain their function in the argument. One way for Julia to
spell out Emilio's assumptions might be the following:

4. (Stated Assumption A) The main purpose of comparable
    worth is to pass laws to force employers to raise women's
    salaries.

5. (Unstated Assumption B) It's a bad idea/bad public policy to
    force employers to raise salaries if there are good reasons for
    differences and/or if the free market provides other ways for
    people to get high salaries.

Now, if these assumptions are combined with the arguments identified earlier, we can begin to see how Emilio's thesis is supposed to
be proved. Keeping #4 and #5 in mind, we can add #6:

6. There are good reasons for differences, and the free market
    does provide other ways for people to get high salaries. (These
    are the conclusions of arguments #1 and #2 above.)

And #4, #5, and #6 then lead to the conclusion, #7:

7. So comparable worth is a bad idea and bad public policy. (This
    is the thesis and the ultimate conclusion of Emilio's argument.)

It is important that Julia reconstruct Emilio's argument as
reasonably as possible. That is, whenever possible, she should set up
Emilio's reasons and conclusions so that they make sense and fulfill
the requirements for good arguments that we have been studying.
She might, for example, just assume that Emilio's ideas amount to a
bunch of unrelated prejudices and deny that there is any connection

between them. But if she does, she will appear unreasonable and biased, and her credibility will be completely undermined. So it is also important for anyone criticizing someone else's ideas to make sure those ideas are presented as reasonably as possible. The more fair and reasonable you are, the more convincing you are likely to be.

MAKE FAIR CRITICISMS

So far, Julia has been trying to make sure she understands Emilio's position. This has required her to

- identify the thesis,

- identify the arguments (reasons, conclusions),

- identify the assumptions and claims the arguments rest on, and explain how they go together.

Now she can go on to the next stage of criticizing an argument, which is the actual criticism itself. What's important in criticizing an argument is that she must *criticize the argument fairly.* And there are three approaches that can be used to ensure fair criticism. She can

- question the argument's premises,

- question the argument's assumptions, and

- question the conclusion's consequences.

We'll now look at each of these approaches.

Question the Argument's Premises

Questioning the argument's form involves two kinds of criticisms. First,

Are the premises true or reliable?

And second,

Does the conclusion follow from the premises?

Under the general category of questioning the premises, Julia should ask herself whether they violate any of the rules of good argument that we have studied so far. Are any factual claims true, documented, and reasonable? Are key terms well defined? Are the reasons relevant to the conclusion? Are the reasons sufficient to establish the point in question? Does the conclusion follow from the premises clearly and rationally? Do the reasons make use of questionable analogies or generalizations? Are the reasons based on reliable sources? If any of the reasons are false or unreliable in any of these respects, it is fair and constructive criticism to point this out.

Question the Argument's Assumptions

Next, Julia should examine the argument's assumptions. Many of the questions she should raise here are the same as the questions regarding the premises. Are they true or uncontroversial? Are they well defined? Are they used relevantly? Are they clear? And so on. But she must be very careful in criticizing assumptions she has identified in Emilio's argument. This is because Emilio did not actually state some of his assumptions, nor did he indicate how they worked in his argument. Julia did this. So if Julia misstated Emilio's assumptions, it's not fair to criticize him for her misunderstanding.

Julia's interpretation of Emilio's argument begins with assumption #4, Emilio's stated claim that the main purpose of comparable worth is to pass laws to force employers to raise women's salaries. But is this really true? At this point, if she weren't already well informed about comparable worth, Julia would have to do some research. But let's assume that she has already done enough research and has kept good enough notes to document her knowledge if necessary. Then she might go on to question this premise, because although low women's salaries are one target of comparable worth, they're far from the only one. The point of comparable worth — that any two people doing similar jobs should be paid similarly — applies as much to discrimination on the basis of race, religion, or age as it does sex, and it would apply to cases in which women's jobs are paid better than men's if there are any. Still, Emilio may be saying that the main purpose of comparable worth is to address apparent differences between women's and men's salaries, and so far, that's been pretty much true. So perhaps her objection to #4 is worth mentioning, but Julia's objection is not powerful enough to call #4 into serious question.

Assumption #5 is a question of value, concerning whether or not it's bad to force people to raise salaries under certain circumstances. Reasonable people may differ on questions of value, and as we saw in Chapter 3, it's usually important to provide some support for judgments of value. Emilio doesn't do that here, so it's possible his argument is vulnerable. On the other hand, this may not be a particularly controversial value premise if the conditional it involves is true. That is, if there are good reasons for differences and the free market provides other avenues to better salaries, most people might accept the value claim here. And it's not at all obvious that Julia herself would necessarily disagree about this. So, again, assumption #5 is probably not the best target for Julia's criticisms, even though it does involve a value judgment that hasn't been argued for.

The most questionable claims in Emilio's argument appear in #6. But that premise comes from arguments 1 and 2. So Julia should look at those arguments. Is it true that men's jobs tend to be more stressful, exhausting, and responsible than women's jobs? How would anyone be able to prove this? Surely it depends partly on what is meant by "men's" and "women's" jobs, "stressful," "exhausting," and "responsible." To do a complete survey of all jobs, workers, and the stress, exhaustion, and responsibility they feel (and decide if they're right to feel what they do) would be an impossible task. Besides, Emilio might not agree with Julia's definition of *stress* or *responsibility,* for example. So what can we do?

One possibility is to look at one or more typical examples. After all, Emilio's claim is very general, so one good counterexample should disprove it. Of course, the examples should be specific and uncontroversial. And if Julia can use one she knows Emilio would accept, she'll be in a stronger position. Now, Emilio himself suggested nursing and teaching as typical women's jobs. But a Washington State study found that registered nurses had substantially higher levels of stress, exhaustion, and responsibility than do computer systems analysts (who are mostly men), but their starting salary is $7,600 less a year.[1] So that might be a good counterexample, because it shows that Emilio is wrong in thinking that all men's jobs tend to be more stressful, exhausting, and responsible.

Emilio is even farther off base in thinking that his second premise is true—that men have to support families on their salaries whereas women don't. In 1986, 69 percent of U.S. families were headed by men, but 31 percent—27,420,000 families—lived on a woman's income alone.[2] Besides, the median income for households headed by men with jobs was $27,093 in 1985, whereas the median income for

---

1. See Helen Remick, *Comparable Worth & Wage Discrimination* (Philadelphia: Temple University Press, 1984).
2. *Census Population Reports,* United States Government Printing Office, 1986.

households headed by women with jobs was only $13,660 in that same year.[3] But Julia must be careful not to claim too much here. She's in a position to prove that Emilio hasn't proved there are good reasons for men to enjoy higher salaries than women for comparable jobs. But she is not in a position (yet) to prove there are no good reasons why men should be paid more than women. This is a subtle but very important distinction. If she wants to go on to prove that there are no good reasons . . . , she'll have to make that argument separately.

Now, is it true that the main influence on salaries is demand for the type of work—that people in high-demand areas always make (relatively) high salaries? Again, Emilio is making a broad generalization, so only one good example is necessary to disprove it. And again, nursing provides such an example. In 1988 there were over 300,000 vacant nursing positions—positions that couldn't be filled because there were no qualified applicants—while the total number of *employed* computer analysts was only 308,000 and the number of vacancies was under 30,000.[4] But if high salaries followed high demand, it would follow that nursing salaries should be far higher than computer analyst salaries. They're not. So Emilio's general claim must be wrong.

What does this prove? Again, Julia has not proved that it's a good idea to force employers to raise salaries. She's proved only that the reasons Emilio gave why it would be a bad idea should not convince a rational person. That is, she might well question at least one of Emilio's assumptions, but she's in a position to prove that premise #6 is false. And that means she is in a position to prove that a rational person need not accept Emilio's conclusion, #7. Again, this is not the same as proving that comparable worth is a good idea. Julia would need to argue for that separately. But now she's in a good position to frame her criticism of Emilio's position in a way that should be convincing to an unbiased audience.

Question the Conclusion's Consequences

Now there is one more critical approach that Julia might use that is also fair and constructive. It is to point out any consequences that Emilio's position has that are not desirable or acceptable. In this

---

3. "Median Money Income of Families and Unrelated Individuals, in Current and Constant (1985) Dollars: 1960 to 1985," *Statistical Abstract*, No. 705, 1988.
4. Newscaps, *American Journal of Nursing* 88 (July 1988): 1028. *Occupational Outlook Handbook*, U.S. Department of Labor, Bureau of Labor Statistics, 1986–87 ed., Washington, D.C., April 1986.

example, she might point out that continuing to disregard unfair differences between salaries causes low morale, leaves some high-demand jobs requiring very good people without enough applicants (such as nursing and teaching), and allows an obvious injustice to continue. But this strategy also involves going beyond what Emilio actually said, and whenever you do that, you have to argue for your claims. So, even though Julia could criticize the consequences of Emilio's position, it's probably not her best move in this case.

In the next chapter, we'll look further at criticizing the consequences and discuss how to present criticisms convincingly. Meanwhile, Julia might drop Emilio a note summarizing her position as follows:

> I intend to show that comparable worth is not necessarily a bad idea or bad public policy. Comparable worth has many goals besides improving women's salaries. And even if we agree that employers shouldn't be forced by law to increase salaries when there are good reasons for inequities or when the market will make the adjustments without legislation, it's still possible that comparable worth legislation should be passed. This is because evidence I shall cite shows that men's jobs are not necessarily more stressful, physically exhausting, or responsible than women's jobs, that many women also have to support families, and that the market does not ensure high salaries for high-demand fields when the fields in question are staffed mainly by women.

If Julia criticizes Emilio's ideas for these reasons, she has been both fair and constructive, and her argument should carry lots of weight.

AVOID CRITICAL FALLACIES

As we've seen, it's important to criticize the ideas of others in a fair and constructive way. There are five common tactics people sometimes use in criticizing others that are not fair or constructive, and that we need to avoid. These are called **Critical Fallacies,** and they include criticizing the person rather than his or her ideas, attacking a false or biased version of another person's ideas rather than his or her true position, and offering trivial objections.

"*Let's talk comparable worth.*"

Drawing by P. Steiner; © 1989 The New Yorker Magazine, Inc.

Personal Attack

The first of these critical fallacies is **Personal Attack,** which means trying to discredit the person giving an argument rather than criticizing his ideas fairly. You commit this fallacy if you try to show that the person you're criticizing is a bad person in certain respects and then assume that shows his or her ideas are not true. Probably the simplest form of personal attack is simple name calling. So if Julia had responded to Emilio's ideas by this kind of personal attack, she might have given a reply like this one:

> Emilio is saying that comparable worth is a bad idea and bad public policy. But you'd expect a totally insensitive male chauvinist like him to say something as crude as that. Emilio, like most men, simply doesn't care about the unfair treatment of women. So there's no good reason to take him seriously either.

Here, Julia is name calling; she's calling Emilio a "totally insensitive male chauvinist" rather than discussing his arguments.

Attacking the Motive

Personal attacks aren't limited to name calling. Another form of personal attack is **Attacking the Motive,** in which you criticize a person's possible motivation for saying something rather than criticizing what he or she actually said. Usually, when people attack others' motives, they try to show that their real reason for saying what they do is to benefit them in some way, assuming that somehow discredits people's arguments. Julia would be guilty of attacking the motive if she replied to Emilio this way:

> Emilio is saying comparable worth is a bad idea. But being a male computer science major, Emilio himself would likely face lower salaries if comparable worth were put into effect. He obviously is just protecting his own interests by criticizing comparable worth, so he can't be taken seriously.

Sometimes name calling and attacking the motive are combined. If Julia had claimed that Emilio's ideas shouldn't be taken seriously because he is a hypocrite who benefits from social programs for some minorities and then rejects those that benefit others, she'd be guilty of both name calling ("Emilio is a hypocrite") and attacking the motive (she's assuming his motivation is self-interest).

"You're Just As Bad"

Another common form of personal attack consists in accusing the person with whom you're arguing of being just as bad as you are, or of offering an argument just as bad as yours, and assuming that shows your argument ought to be accepted. This form of unfair

Figure 13.1
By permission of Doug Marlette and Creators Syndicate.

criticism is called **You're Just As Bad.** Julia could commit this kind of fallacy by arguing as follows:

> Emilio has said that comparable worth is a bad idea because it mainly benefits women. But Emilio doesn't seem to mind social programs that benefit him. I don't see why women shouldn't benefit from social programs if other groups do.

Obviously, the problem here is that Julia isn't criticizing Emilio's argument. She's claiming he's just as bad as she is in wanting to benefit from social programs. But whether or not that's true, it has no bearing on the quality of Emilio's actual arguments. So it's an unfair criticism.

And of course, critical fallacies can be combined. In the cartoon in Figure 13.1, Rev. Will B. Dunn answers Sam's personal attack with a you're just as bad reply.

Straw Man

A fourth form of unfair criticism is a fallacy called **Straw Man.** You commit straw man by changing someone's ideas in order to make them easier to criticize. It's called "straw man" because instead of confronting the ideas that fight for themselves, you're confronting a wispy substitute that's easy to blow away. Here's how Julia could have committed a straw man fallacy on Emilio's arguments.

> Emilio is saying that comparable worth is a bad idea because it enables women to be paid a fair wage. Men, he says, always deserve higher salaries just because they're men. But Emilio cannot turn back the clock and deny women the right to earn a

fair wage in the American work place. He's just trying to keep
discriminating against women.

But Emilio didn't say comparable worth is a bad idea because it
enables women to be paid a fair wage, and he didn't say men deserve
higher salaries because they're men. Instead, he claimed the differences between men's and women's salaries are not unfair because
there are good reasons for them and that these reasons favor men's
jobs, not because they're done by men but because they're more
stressful, physically exhausting, and responsible. Of course, Julia
can show he's wrong about that. But to distort his argument like this
to make it easy to attack is an example of straw man reasoning.

Trivial Objections

The last form of unfair criticism we'll look at here is called **Trivial
Objections.** You commit this fallacy when the aspects of someone's
position you pick out to criticize really don't make much difference or
don't influence whether or not the person's ideas are true. Also, if
your criticism could easily be accepted by your opponent without
having to change his or her position much, your objection is probably trivial. Here are some objections Julia might have made that
would be trivial:

> Emilio says that higher salaries in men's jobs are not unfair
> because they're more physically exhausting and responsible and
> because men traditionally have to support families. If men were
> in better physical shape, they wouldn't be exhausted at the end
> of the day, so their jobs wouldn't be so exhausting. Besides,
> some men don't have families to support.

What makes these objections trivial is that even if they're true,
they don't affect Emilio's argument very much. That is, even if some
men are not in good physical shape, that doesn't prove that being a
secretary, for example, is generally as physically exhausting as working in heavy construction. Besides, Emilio's point is that *most* men
traditionally supported families on their salaries, not that *all* of them
did. Pointing out that *some* men don't have families doesn't affect his
point. So it's important to stick to worthwhile objections and not
lose credibility by bringing up points that don't carry much weight.
Even if there is a problem with one or more examples, that might not
be important to bring up.

SUMMARY

In this chapter, we've discussed fair and constructive criticism of other people's arguments. Fair criticism begins with making sure you understand other people's ideas accurately and without bias. Usually you'll need to summarize them carefully. Then you identify (1) the thesis, (2) the main arguments and supporting material for them, and, finally, (3) the assumptions the arguments rest on. There are four legitimate things to criticize about arguments. You can criticize reasons or premises if they aren't true or if they violate any of the criteria for good reasoning we have learned in Chapters 4 through 9. You can criticize the assumptions the argument rests on. You can show that the reasons don't prove the conclusion. Or you can show that the consequences of the position you're criticizing would be unacceptable. But there are also forms of criticism you should avoid. These critical fallacies include personal attack, attacking the motive, you're just as bad, straw man, and trivial objections.

EXERCISE I

For each of the following examples, identify the thesis (or conclusion) and main arguments (or reasons) for it. Then determine what would be some fair and constructive criticisms of the argument. Be sure you can explain which criteria for good argument the example violates.

1. All whales are fish, and all fish have lungs. Therefore, all whales have lungs.

2. It's important to take effective steps to reduce organized crime. Wiretapping suspected criminals would provide police with an additional tool that would help. Most members of the Mafia have Italian surnames. So it would be reasonable to wiretap the telephones of people with Italian surnames.

3. The Soviet Union is an evil empire seeking world domination through the repression of its people. Hundreds of thousands of Soviet citizens were massacred by Stalin. It would be crazy to trust Gorbachev and lay ourselves wide open to total destruction through disarmament.

4. Everyone has a right to equal opportunity for a successful career, but in today's complex world it's hard to succeed

without a college education. Therefore, college should be treated like high school, and it should be made available to everyone without any charge.

5. NFL teams that fail to get into the playoffs for ten years or more disappoint their fans and lower the level of play in the league. When a team has sunk to the point where it's just not competitive anymore, the team ought to be dropped from the league. When a player can't perform, he's cut from the team. So, once a team has failed to qualify for the playoffs for ten years it's proven that it can't perform, and it should be cut.

6. A college education is just like any other service or product. A student picks out what he wants to study, just as a shopper picks out what he wants to buy. And just as nobody forces a shopper to buy what he doesn't want, nobody should force a student to take courses he doesn't want either. So required courses should be eliminated.

7. General Products Corporation is considering passing a rule prohibiting smoking on the premises. This is a terrible idea. Not only does it discriminate against people who are not doing anything illegal, but it also will force people who want to smoke to stand around outside, regardless of the weather, wasting company time and their own. People should be more tolerant of others. After all, nonsmokers have annoying habits too, and nobody's perfect.

8. Although originally well intentioned, welfare has become a cause of poverty rather than a way out of poverty. Giving people money for sitting around at home all day only encourages them to be even more lazy than they already are. Besides, people often use welfare payments to buy expensive luxury cars and clothes or even drugs. When children are raised to see their parents getting a fat check for doing nothing, they learn that they don't have to try to make it on their own. So we should abolish welfare completely. Then maybe people would take some responsibility for themselves.

9. From an environmental point of view, the most ideal forms of outdoor recreation are such activities as sailing and cross-country skiing, which do not pollute or injure the land or water. Big power boats and snowmobiles not only spread oil

and gas residues into the water and air, but they also use up valuable resources, all for the pointless enjoyment of running around aimlessly. Besides, they're noisy. And many speedboat drivers, not to mention snowmobilers, drive recklessly. If we radically increased the license fees for speedboats and snow-mobiles, people would be less likely to turn to them as recreational outlets. So we should raise the fees on those licenses at least 100 percent.

10. People are very worried about drugs in today's society. But most problems about drugs are due to the fact that drugs are illegal, which is what keeps prices high and causes people to commit crimes to support their habits. If drugs were legalized and distributed at low cost by prescription, under carefully monitored conditions, people would have no reason to commit crimes to support their habits, and fewer people would be killed through overdoses. Besides, the immense profits made by drug dealers now could be taxed, which would be a big boost to the economy, and the jobs created by legalizing drugs would employ as many people as the beer and wine industry does now. It seems obvious, once you think about it, that drugs should be legalized.

EXERCISE II

Identify any critical fallacies committed in the following exercises. Be sure you can explain exactly why the example illustrates an unfair criticism.

1. Senator Adams has accused me of misusing campaign funds by spending them on gambling debts. This is a serious charge. To answer it, I need only point out that Adams wasted a fortune on risky investments and worthless stocks.

2. Ms. Jones says that the Exxon Oil Company has already done all it can to clean up the coast of Alaska after the oil spill from its tanker. Of course, Jones is a major stockholder in Exxon, so she'd naturally take Exxon's side, ignoring all of the devastating effects of the spill on marine life.

3. "Maybe I am an Exxon stockholder," Jones replied, "But at least I'm not a mindless tree-hugger like Smith. You can't seriously expect Exxon to spend billions and billions more dollars to make sure every sea otter gets a manicure and every rock is polished."

4. The spokesperson for the Alliance for Progress has suggested this city offer new businesses a five-year tax break. That would be a terrible precedent to set. If we keep giving tax breaks to new businesses over a period of time, it will become harder and harder to keep track of who owes what, and the city's bookkeeping will be a mess.

5. The proposal to provide every citizen a minimum standard of medical care is just one more example of creeping socialism that will gradually strangle our economy and destroy individual initiative.

6. Dean Blowhard has turned down my request to graduate early so I can take a job I've been offered. He's such a fascist — so totally bound up in his stupid rules he can't see that there's a time for exceptions.

7. I can't understand how Professor Curmudgeon can penalize me for skipping a few classes. He missed two classes this semester himself, and besides, whenever I've gone past his office during office hours, he's never there.

8. The vice president for Business Services has proposed a 9 percent dues increase for next year, together with some program cuts, in order to balance the club's budget. I don't understand why the membership should always have to shoulder the whole cost of keeping this club solvent. Of course there'll be another whopping increase next year and the year after. How long can this go on? I think we should vote down the increase.

9. I can't understand why I got turned down for promotion to associate professor. They said I had poor student evaluations, and hadn't done any scholarly work. But not everybody can be popular with students, especially if they've got high standards like mine. Besides, when you're teaching as many classes as I am, you can't be expected to turn out a book every few weeks.

10. Professor, I deserve a much better grade than you gave me on this paper. I read two other students' papers, and they weren't any better than mine. And I don't see how you can count me down for spelling when you put misspelled words on the board all the time. I know you hate it when I read comics in class, but you shouldn't take it out on my grades. That's really mean.

14 *Write Criticisms Effectively*

In the previous chapter, we discussed fair and constructive criticisms and also talked about criticisms that are not rationally convincing. In this chapter, the main topic is how to present your criticisms in an effective critical paper. Since all good criticism starts with accurate summary, we'll talk about how to summarize. We'll briefly review criticizing arguments and assumptions and then talk more about criticizing consequences. And, finally, we'll discuss how to put together short critical essays. Specifically, we'll look at three types: the critical paper, the counterproposal paper, and the judgment paper.

THE CRITICAL PAPER

Imagine that, instead of making a spoken presentation to the Economics Club criticizing Emilio's ideas on comparable worth, Julia was asked to write a short paper criticizing an article Emilio had written in which he presented his ideas on comparable worth.[1] Then she'd be in a very common situation. Although some situations in which people have to criticize other people's arguments formally involve making spoken presentations, many others, especially in college, involve writing essays. We'll call an essay in which your main purpose is to criticize someone else's ideas a **critical paper** or essay.

Sometimes even students who have mastered many of the skills of logical reasoning presented in this book still have trouble writing essays that present their ideas in a clear and convincing way. Sometimes this is because students may not be familiar with the kind of standard English that's expected by most college-level teachers. Since most of us sense that our English is correct when it "sounds right" to us, if we are used to hearing English spoken in ways that aren't standard, we wind up making mistakes, at least until we begin to understand what really makes English grammar work.

Other students have trouble writing well because inventing or organizing their ideas is difficult. In most English writing courses today, students are taught that writing is a process involving several steps or stages. This is partly because if writing can be broken down into smaller, more manageable tasks, it's easier to deal with any problems that might come up. Some of the tasks involved in the process of writing include prewriting strategies, audience identification, essay organizational planning, writing, and revision.

Writing critical papers is like writing other papers in that all of these steps are involved. The main thing that makes a critical paper different from narrative papers, persuasive papers, and others, is that its main purpose is to subject someone's ideas to fair and constructive criticism. Remember, in persuasive papers, your purpose is to convince people to agree with your ideas. Since we spent much of our time in the previous chapter on how to come up with reasonable criticisms, which is one of the main things you'd do in prewriting a critical paper, we'll spend most of our time in this chapter on the rest of the writing process as it relates to writing a critical paper.

---

1. You might want to review pages 189–92 in Chapter 13, and other parts of that chapter, to remind yourself what Julia's and Emilio's ideas are.

Throughout this book, we've referred to the audience for your arguments. Basically, your audience is a group of reasonable people, many of whom, you should assume, don't already agree with you but are willing to be convinced if you give them good reasons. Part of what you're doing when you look for good reasons to support your opinions is trying to put yourself into the frame of mind of people who don't already agree with you so that you can say the kinds of things that will change their minds. And this imagining yourself into their ways of thinking is especially important when you're writing a critical paper, just as it was in the anticipated objections and replies section of the persuasive paper. It can also be difficult, as we saw in Chapter 13 (and in Chapter 10). This is because, if you disagree with someone, it may be hard for you to understand that person fully. But, again, you will need to do everything possible to be fair when you're criticizing someone else's arguments. And if you want to convince other people, you will need to meet them on their ground, starting from assumptions and reasons they already accept.

AN OUTLINE FOR A CRITICAL PAPER

When you're writing a critical paper, you'll probably find it useful to plan out what you're going to say and how you're going to organize it. One standard form of organization that most people find useful is this:

Introduction

Summary of Ideas to be Criticized

Strengths and Weaknesses of the Ideas Discussed

Evaluation of Ideas and Justification

Anticipated Objections or Replies

Conclusion

We'll explain each of these steps individually.

Good Summaries Again

In the *introduction,* your main purpose is to tell your audience what you're writing about, why the audience should be interested, how the issue got to be a problem, and what your *thesis* is. In a critical paper, your **thesis** is what you're going to prove. For example, Julia's thesis, from Chapter 13, would be that Emilio's ideas on comparable worth are not justified. And because you're giving your thesis as well as getting your audience interested in the issue, the introduction is a good place to make clear who your audience is and to make sure that what you say is addressed to them. Remember, though, that introductions should be short and to the point—usually not more than one or two paragraphs (unless the issue is extremely complicated and your paper is very long). Long introductions usually lose people's attention and occupy space that would be better used for the body of the paper.

The next step is to present a *summary* of the ideas you're going to criticize. These ideas should include not only the conclusions you disagree with, but also the main arguments for them. In fact, *everything* you're eventually going to criticize *must* be mentioned in the summary. Now, in Chapter 13, Julia had no problem with this because Emilio provided her with a summary that was not only accurate (because he wrote it himself) but also complete. But most of the time, we have to do our own summaries, and as we've already mentioned, that can be a difficult task.

A good summary meets four criteria. It should be

1. accurate,

2. complete,

3. clear, and

4. brief.

These criteria are listed in the order of their importance. That is, it's more important that your summary be an exact and fair description of the ideas you're criticizing than it is for your summary to be short, for example. Remember, if you distort someone's ideas, whether intentionally or not, your criticisms are no longer fair, and you're guilty of the fallacy of *straw man*. But in addition to being accurate, your summary should be complete, in that you mention everything you'll later criticize. It should be clear, in that your summary should present what you'll be criticizing so that it can be easily (and accurately) understood. And it should be brief, mainly so that you can save the body of your paper for the criticisms you're going to be making.

Here is an example. Suppose Carlos is assigned to criticize the following proposal by Marie, as part of a debate in a political science class. Here is Marie's position:

Voter participation among all Americans is very low. One reason is that many potential voters do not understand the issues, and another is that many voters do not know how or where to vote. However, the vast majority of Americans watch television shows, such as Oprah Winfrey or one of the afternoon soaps. So I propose to improve voter participation by making it possible to vote by calling a televised telephone number, just as people can now buy things by telephone. On election day, ads would run on all television channels explaining the issues and giving a telephone number people could call to register their votes. The telephone calls could be toll free so that even more people could afford to participate. I believe this would effectively increase voter participation.

First, Carlos will need to summarize Marie's position. Here is one possible summary:

Marie proposes to increase voter participation by letting people vote by telephone.

This summary is certainly brief and clear. But even if the only thing Carlos is going to comment on is problems about voting by telephone, there is not enough information here about the actual proposal Marie is making for Carlos's criticisms to be understood. So this summary is not complete enough. Also, this summary leaves out many important aspects of Marie's position, such as why she thinks there is a problem and how her proposal specifically addresses it. And leaving this out may create the misunderstanding that the only thing Marie is proposing is voting by telephone, ignoring the television ads. That would not be an accurate understanding of her idea. Since this summary fails both the accuracy and the completeness requirements, Carlos will need to try again.

So suppose Carlos tries this summary:

Marie's position is that voter participation among Americans is very low. She thinks this is because many potential voters do not understand the issues and do not know how or where to vote. Since, she says, most voters watch television shows, such as Oprah Winfrey and afternoon soap operas, she proposes to run ads on election day on all television channels like the ones used to get people to buy items by calling toll-free numbers. However, these ads would explain the issues and give a different kind of toll-free telephone number that people could call to register their vote. **Marie thinks this will increase voter participation.**

This summary is both accurate and complete: All of the details of Marie's original proposal are presented here. But, unfortunately, this summary basically repeats Marie's words, so it is neither more clear nor more brief than the original proposal. What Carlos needs to do is **paraphrase** Marie's proposal, which means to put it into his own words, while making it shorter and clearer.

While it is very important not to leave out anything that might lead to misunderstanding Marie's ideas, there are many things in her proposal that can be skipped without any loss. For example, it doesn't matter to Marie's proposal which television shows people watch, so her mention of Oprah Winfrey and afternoon soaps can be left out. It also doesn't seem to matter that people buy things through television ads, so this, too, can be left out. In general, examples, illustrations, instances, and other irrelevant details can be left out of your summaries, which will help shorten them.

However, it is also often possible to restate an idea more simply and clearly. So suppose Carlos tries this:

> **Since many potential voters in America do not understand either the issues or how or where to vote, Marie is proposing to run ads on all television channels. These ads would explain what the issues are and give a toll-free telephone number people could call to record their votes.**

This version seems to pass all of the criteria for a good summary. It tells exactly what Marie's proposal is, so it is accurate, and it gives enough details, so it is complete. It is also briefer than the original, and it is just as clear. (There is a more complicated example at the end of this chapter; you might wish to look carefully at the summary illustrated there.)

Discuss Strengths and Weaknesses

Once the ideas you're criticizing are well summarized, you should go ahead and *discuss* their *strengths and weaknesses*. By discussing their strengths—what's right about the ideas you're criticizing—as well as their weaknesses—what's wrong with them—you further demonstrate that you're giving the other person's ideas the fairest, most accurate consideration possible. You're also pinpointing exactly what the problems are by contrasting them with aspects of the position that aren't problems. At the same time, the main emphasis in this section should be on the weaknesses of the ideas you're criticizing. This is a critical paper, after all!

Evaluate and Justify

Once the strengths and weaknesses of the idea you're criticizing are clear, you can go on to the criticism itself. That's the main point of *evaluation and justification*. In this section, you're evaluating the idea in question by subjecting it to criticism, and you're justifying your evaluation by documenting and arguing for the objections you make. Of course, critical objections can be of many kinds. In Chapter 13, we discussed fair criticism and identified four types: criticism of the arguments, either because of false or otherwise unsatisfactory reasons or because of conclusions not adequately proved by them; criticism of the assumptions the arguments depend on; criticism citing problems or information overlooked in the argument; and criticism of the consequences of accepting the conclusion as true and acting on it. Violation of any of the criteria for good arguments that we've developed in this book is a legitimate objection. But you should bear in mind that your audience is not likely to know the terminology that we've used here, so you will need to explain what you find troubling about the arguments you're criticizing without simply labeling the problem as, for example, a fallacy. Moreover, you will need to document your criticism by pointing out exactly where and how the fault is committed.

Now, since Marie didn't give much support to her proposal about telephone voting, it will not be possible for Carlos to criticize the logic of her arguments directly. Instead, Marie's position is most vulnerable because of problems she doesn't seem to see and because of potential unwanted consequences of putting her proposal into effect. So, Carlos might point out, there are many practical and theoretical problems with Marie's idea. Two practical problems might be how to prevent unqualified people (children, for example) from voting and how to prevent people from voting more than once. A theoretical problem might be how to explain the issues—which are almost always very complicated—in a simple way that all political parties would accept. Both of these could be legitimate criticisms.

Other kinds of criticisms will depend on what kind of arguments and ideas you're attacking. Generally, some kinds of criticism are more suited to factual claims, whereas others are more relevant to questions of value, concept, or interpretation.[2] In matters of fact, since they are usually supported by an appeal to some source, the most likely criticism is that the source is unreliable. You can show this either by proving the source is not trustworthy (biased, a small or hasty sample, factually incorrect, etc.) or by finding other, equally reliable sources that give different results. Remember not to attack the source personally, however; that's the fallacy of personal attack.

Often it's not so much the facts themselves that are questionable as the interpretation that is given to them. It's a reasonable criticism to point out that facts which are used one way can have an entirely different meaning when seen from a different perspective. But you will need to supply this other meaning and perspective and show why it's reasonable. Don't just say that there is one and assume that's enough to undermine the original interpretation.

Where questions of value are concerned, it's often reasonable to question the value premise. If the conclusion of an argument is a judgment of value, one or more of the reasons used to support that conclusion will also involve a statement of value as well. And often the value premise will need to be given more support than it gets. Suppose, for example, that Edward, who strongly opposes the death penalty, argues that it should be abolished because "any civilized person should view the death penalty as cruel and unjustifiable torture." His conclusion, a moral value judgment, can't be proved without some value premise, such as this one, which says that the death penalty is wrong (cruel, unjustifiable, etc.). But often, as in this case, the value premise is questionable; there are many civilized people who do not view the death penalty as unjustifiable. So, in general, criticism of value conclusions often starts with value premises.

Of course, Edward might reply that such people are not "civilized." This would be quibbling about the definition of *civilized,* and you would be justified in pointing that out, just as you would be justified in objecting to any strange or unfair definition that an argument depends on. More generally, where matters of concept are concerned, the usual criticisms consist in finding counterexamples to the conceptual claims that are made or demonstrating that the conceptual claims are themselves doubtful. And, finally, where questions of interpretation are involved, the most common objection is to argue

---

2. See Chapter 3 if you need to review this material.

that some other interpretation is preferable to the one you are criticizing, in that it explains things better or more simply, is clearer, and so on.

Anticipate Objections and Replies

When you have thoroughly discussed the strengths and weaknesses of the idea you're criticizing and have said all you intend to about what you see as the problems with it, you next need to consider how someone might reply to your criticisms. That is, you need to *anticipate objections and replies* to your criticisms. This is partially to ensure fairness—to ensure that you're giving your opponent every possible consideration. But it also helps to ensure that none of your objections is trivial. Remember, a trivial objection is a complaint about something that doesn't affect the basic point or that could easily be given up without affecting whether the main idea should be accepted or rejected. In this section of your paper, you should try to determine what might be said in reply to your most important criticisms and then say what more might be required to be convincing.

Suppose Carlos had arrived at this point in his critical evaluation of Marie's idea for telephone voting. But suppose, in addition to criticizing her proposal because it risks voter fraud and biased or incomplete presentation of the issues, he had also objected that Marie's proposal is unfair to people who don't have televisions or telephones. At this stage, Carlos should ask himself whether Marie might have a good reply to his criticisms. And it seems obvious Marie could answer some of them easily. After all, her proposal is to *increase existing options* so that it becomes easier for people to vote. Therefore, even if it is true that some people might not benefit from her proposal, others will, and that was her point. Besides, she might say, the potential for voter fraud might be dealt with by requiring callers to identify themselves by their Social Security numbers, which would then have to be matched to voter registration lists before the vote would be counted. And summaries of the issues could be done by respected network news organizations, including the "CBS Nightly News," the "MacNeil-Lehrer Newshour," and others.

Now, how well would these replies deal with Carlos's objections? Carlos might point out that increasing voter participation is a good thing only if that participation is well informed and honest. So even if more people get access by Marie's proposal, that may not be beneficial, unless his other objections can be met. Can they? Well, what's to stop people from giving other people's Social Security numbers so that they could vote twice or perhaps dozens of times? And Marie is assuming that the summaries of issues done by news organizations will be complete and unbiased. But many people feel that the news reports of major news networks are too short, too sensational, and too biased. How can we be sure that the news reports will be entirely fair?

Now it's hard to see how Marie could reply to these objections. But it's important to consider what she might say, because it contributes to the fairness of Carlos's criticisms by giving her ideas every possible consideration. Besides, thinking about how she might reply to Carlos's "unfairness" objection helps make clear what the real problem is: that unless increased voter participation is well informed, it may not be desirable. So Carlos might well decide to skip the "unfairness" objection entirely and instead focus on the value of increased participation. At this point, he's ready to present his conclusion or, in fact, to write all of this up in the form of a critical paper.

What would such a critical paper look like? It might look like this, except that in its final draft, the sections and their function would not be listed, even in parentheses, as we've done here.

(Title) Voting By Telephone?

(Introduction) Voter participation in American elections is very low, which is a source of concern to many people. One proposal to increase voter involvement, recently suggested by Ms. Marie Roberts, involves voting by telephone. While I agree that better voting participation is generally a good thing, I am opposed to her proposal. In this short paper, I will explain why.

(Summary) Briefly, Ms. Roberts believes that since many potential voters in America do not understand either the issues or how or where to vote, ads should be run on all television channels. These ads would explain what the issues are and give a toll-free telephone number that people could call to record their votes.

(Strengths and weaknesses) As Ms. Roberts realizes, many Americans do use television as their main source of information about the issues. So television ads might reach people who are not well informed now. And people are mostly familiar with how to order over the telephone, so they might easily adapt to voting by telephone as well.

On the other hand, Ms. Roberts does not spell out a number of important details about her proposal. How, for example, can voting privileges be limited to registered voters? Can the ads explaining the issues be complete and unbiased enough?

(Evaluation and justification) I believe that the potential for fraud and uninformed voting outweighs any possible benefit from Ms. Roberts's proposal. The two main weaknesses of her proposal are serious. Increasing voter participation may not be a good thing if uninformed voting and voter fraud are also increased. But the potential for fraud in telephone voting is very serious, since unqualified voters might vote, perhaps more than once. Besides, Ms. Roberts does not discuss who would write the television ads discussing the issues or how the ads would be kept unbiased as well as interesting.

(Anticipated replies) Of course, Ms. Roberts might suggest that voters be given an identification number, such as their Social Security number, which would be checked before their vote was counted. But even a system like this would not ensure that unqualified voters wouldn't give someone else's number, or several people's numbers. Perhaps the job of writing ads could be given to television news departments. But many people feel that nightly news presentations are already biased. So they might well think that the ads would be biased as well.

(Conclusion) While inadequate voter turnouts are a problem, I conclude that Ms. Roberts's proposal is not the solution. Telephone voting is simply too risky to put into effect.

Of course, it's possible that Marie might have something else to say in reply to Carlos's critical paper. But at least she would have to feel she was treated fairly.

VARIATIONS ON THE CRITICAL PAPER

Now, one of the things that Marie—or the political science class— might say to Carlos is, "OK, you agree that there's a problem, but you don't like Marie's solution. Can you do any better? What do you suggest?" This is a natural reaction to a critical paper. But it's important to note that *criticizing another idea doesn't mean you're obliged to come up with a better alternative.* It only means you can identify problems with a proposal that's already been made. That's something worthwhile in itself, but it's different from developing a new proposal of your own. So if Carlos—or you—choose to do more, you're going beyond what's required for a critical paper.

Variation 1: The Counterproposal Paper

A paper in which you *both* criticize an existing idea and present an alternative you think is better can be called a **counterproposal paper,** because a **counterproposal** is a suggestion made after having rejected an earlier idea. A minor modification of the outline for a critical paper will allow for this:

> *Introduction*
>
> *Summary of Ideas to Be Criticized*
>
> *Strengths and Weaknesses of the Ideas Discussed*
>
> *Evaluation of Ideas and Justification*
>
> *Presentation of Alternative*
>
> *Arguments Supporting Alternative*
>
> *Anticipated Objections or Replies*
>
> *Conclusion*

Because we've already explored how to argue effectively for your own ideas in Chapter 10, and the counterproposal paper is just a combination of a persuasive and a critical paper, we will not discuss this outline extensively here. Two quick observations are in order, however. One is that your arguments in support of your alternative will need to show that it doesn't suffer (or doesn't suffer as much) from the weaknesses and criticisms you've leveled at the original proposal. The other is that anticipating objections now includes responding not only to what the supporters of the original idea might say in reply to your criticisms but also to what critics of your idea might say. This requires considerable imagination, and it is vital if your ideas are going to be taken seriously.

For example, suppose that Carlos went on to propose this:

> **(Presentation of alternative) I propose that informed voter participation be increased by a three-step plan. First, both political parties would participate in nationally televised debates in which their political ideas would be fully discussed and presented. Second, members of the political parties would visit**

eligible voters who were not registered, register them to vote, and offer them free transportation to the polls on election day. Then, on election day, voters would be transported to the polls so that they can participate.

(Arguments for alternative) These suggestions will solve many problems. First, both parties would have the chance to present their own ideas so that the chances for bias are less. Second, unregistered voters would become registered. And third, the problem of getting voters to the polls would be solved.

But if Carlos stops here, without thinking about objections, his proposals will be vulnerable. Political parties already stage televised debates, but that doesn't seem to have increased voter participation. And isn't the potential for abuse very great? Do we want political party leaders to know who votes and who doesn't? Do we want people coming to our doors, demanding to come in and talk about politics? Wouldn't members of the parties who visit unregistered voters use the opportunity to manipulate the voters' opinions unfairly? What's to stop members of one party from registering and transporting to the polls only people who agree with them? Couldn't they register people who aren't qualified to vote, or even invent totally imaginary people and register them and then vote for them on election day? Maybe Carlos has answers to all of these questions, but his proposal won't be taken seriously unless he recognizes that they need some attention.

Variation 2: The Judgment Paper

The other variation on a critical paper that is needed sometimes might be called a **judgment paper,** because you're critically examining two or more possible alternatives and then judging between them. The outline for a judgment paper is just a more complicated version of the critical and counterproposal papers:

Introduction

Summaries of Alternatives

Strengths and Weaknesses of Alternatives

Evaluation of Alternatives and Justifications

Judgment in Favor of One of the Alternatives

Arguments in Favor of the Preferred Choice

Anticipated Objections and Replies

Conclusion

There are several aspects of a judgment paper that call for special attention. It's always important for summaries to be fair, but it's especially important in a judgment paper, because anyone who agrees with one or the other position will reject your judgment if he doesn't feel his position has been presented fairly. Strengths and weaknesses can often be presented in a series of comparisons and contrasts. (Comparisons show similarities between two ideas; contrasts show differences.)

But the most common problem for students writing a judgment paper is leaving out the judgment in favor of one of the choices. That is, it's often tempting to do something like this. Emil, assigned a judgment paper on Marie's and Carlos's proposals, concludes:

Obviously, both Marie and Carlos have given the problem of low voter turnout a lot of thought. Each has made proposals that have different advantages and disadvantages. Who's to say which is the better choice? Perhaps this is a question best left up to each one of us.

But this is a total flop as a judgment paper, because Emil *doesn't give a judgment*! Difficult as it may be to decide among alternatives, if you're assigned to make a decision, you can't avoid your responsibility—you must give a judgment. Emil might go ahead and argue that in spite of its problems, Marie's proposal has real promise, and give his reasons. Or he might argue that because of the problems Carlos has identified, Marie's position can't be accepted, and give his reasons. But stopping short of a judgment will not be good enough in a judgment paper.

SUMMARY

In this chapter, we've looked at ways to apply the fair critical strategies we discussed in the previous chapter. First, after arranging your ideas in an effective order, give an introduction, in which you present the issue as well as why it's important. Then give a summary, which should be accurate, complete, clear, and brief. This will usually involve paraphrasing the original material, which is restating it clearly and briefly. Next, go on to the strengths and weaknesses of the ideas you're discussing and provide evaluation and justification. Avoid trivial objections—make sure your comments go right to the heart of the issue. Then anticipate objections and replies, which involves thinking through your paper from the perspective of the people you're trying to convince—people who don't already agree with you. And, finally, offer a conclusion. Remember, too, you're not obliged to provide an alternative, but if you want to, you can use the counterproposal paper outline. Or, if you are asked to decide between two or more choices, use the outline for a judgment paper.

EXERCISE I

This exercise involves four steps. For each of the following examples, (1) write a good summary and (2) identify one or two good criticisms you might make of the main idea(s). Then (3) write down one or two replies or objections the original speaker might make to your criticisms. (4) How would you respond to them?

1. Although there are three sources for additional funding for college programs—increased state appropriations, gifts from businesses and alumni, and raising tuition and fees—the only practical way to meet the current financial crisis is to increase tuition. The state legislature has shown no willingness to consider increasing appropriations, and the state is already running a deficit. Gifts from businesses and alumni are down because of the current recession. So we should raise tuition.

2. Marriage is an increasingly outmoded concept in the late twentieth century. After all, it's unreasonable to expect that two people can stay together for a lifetime. People will not always change at the same rate and in ways that are compatible. Besides, it assumes that men and women can't settle differences or disagreements without the courts stepping in. So people should have the freedom to enter and leave relationships without the legal and religious baggage of marriage.

3. People who engage in behavior that risks their health should have to pay the full costs of any medical care they may need. Nobody forces people to smoke, dive out of airplanes or climb mountains for fun, or have unsafe sex. So if people come down

with lung cancer, physical injuries, or AIDS, they should have to pay for treatment out of their own pockets. Why should the rest of us who make sensible choices help pay for others through our health insurance premiums, Medicare, or Medicaid?

4. Many of the most serious problems in today's society can be traced back to poor parenting and bad home situations. We already investigate families seeking to adopt children to determine whether they will be good parents and whether they will be able to provide a secure and stable home situation. Why not require the same thing of prospective biological parents? Once the prospective parent is identified as pregnant, why not evaluate the situation using the same criteria as adoptive parents have to meet? If the parents fail to meet those criteria, they could be counseled and educated if possible, or if not, the child could be aborted.

5. In some neighborhoods, crime is so common that people don't feel able to go out at night or even during the day. And even in the safest big cities, people are often at risk of violent crime. Since police have to wait until crimes are committed to act, they can't protect people adequately. Besides, criminals are often back on the streets within hours, many times seeking revenge from their victims.

   While some liberals propose gun control as a way to stop violent crime, that will never work. After all, when guns become criminal, only criminals will have guns. Instead, I propose a gun distribution and training program. Give everyone a handgun, and teach people how to use their handguns as a routine part of high school physical-education classes. Then, and only then, nobody will be helpless in the face of rising crime.

6. More and more middle-class taxpayers are becoming unwilling to see their tax dollars going to support people unwilling to support themselves. Welfare has created a huge number of people willing to sit at home and watch television, letting society pay for their children and themselves. Sometimes this goes on for generations and spreads to whole neighborhoods. For example, in several areas of Detroit, Chicago, and Los Angeles, social services workers have found that every family was on welfare.

To deal with this problem, Aid to Dependent Children should be provided only on a limited time basis and should include both child care and educational benefits. Up to four years of educational benefits would be provided so that parents could train themselves for jobs in areas of high demand, such as computers and health care. Child-care benefits would also be provided so that parents could free up the time necessary to learn job skills. Job-placement services might also be provided for graduates.

After four years, however, all benefits would stop permanently. This would provide strong incentive for people to make something of themselves and contribute positively to society. Once parents were off welfare, living productive lives, they would be in a position to influence their children to become productive citizens as well. And there would finally be a limit to how much we, as a society, have to pay for welfare.

7. The student government is sponsoring a curriculum proposal, which will be brought before the curriculum committee once the necessary number of signatures appears on petitions now being circulated among the students. The proposal would eliminate all general education requirements, leaving requirements only for a student's major and minor. All other courses would be elective.

This proposal has many advantages. First, although 84 percent of students in a recent survey said that their first concern in attending college was to be able to get a good job after graduation, most of the courses in general education are not connected with a student's vocational goals. What does a nurse need Western civilization for? Why would a computer programmer need a course in music or art? Why would an elementary-school teacher need a course in a foreign language that he or she will never teach? What does a criminal justice major care about Victorian literature? Of course, students who want to take these courses can do so. But no one would be required to take them unless they chose to do so.

Second, with the hours freed up by eliminating the general education requirement, students could prepare for their careers by taking more courses in their majors. Or students could take courses in more than one vocational area, giving them extra options in the job market.

Of course, professors might object, if it looked as if they would be out of a job. But if they're not teaching anything relevant, money could be saved by letting them go. We conclude that this is one student government proposal that deserves your support.

8. My thesis is that there are many planets in our galaxy that are inhabited by intelligent beings and advanced civilizations. It is only people blinded by their prejudices who believe that in the vastness of this universe, we are the only intelligent life. In spite of many probes into the distant reaches of space, no evidence has been discovered that there aren't other civilizations out there, waiting just beyond the reach of our puny technology.

   Well, you might ask, if there are other civilizations out in our galaxy, why haven't they tried to contact us? The answer, of course, is that they have. Many of the gods worshipped by ancient human societies, such as those of prehistoric Central America, may well have been visitors from another planet. And how could early civilizations have mastered the engineering needed to build the pyramids and erect huge stone statues without the assistance of more sophisticated visitors from space? Besides, efforts to contact us might have gone unnoticed because we were too primitive to receive them.

   The situation is exactly similar to Africa's relationship to Europe before the nineteenth century. Until explorers from Europe arrived in Africa, people in Europe didn't believe in African civilizations, and people in Africa knew nothing about European civilizations. Now, since people don't recognize explorers from space, they don't believe in civilizations out in the galaxy. But just as people were proved wrong in the past, they'll be proved wrong again. The existence of other civilizations in space is a reality.

9. So-called clean air legislation that prohibits smoking in public buildings, such as the university campus, except in tiny, crowded smoking areas, is just another form of unjust discrimination, like racism and sexism. Just because intolerant, puritanical antismokers are irrationally sensitive to smoking, that is no reason to infringe on the rights of smokers. These restrictions should be repealed.

   First, everybody knows that smoking poses some health risks for the smoker. Of course, lots of things besides smoking pose some health risks, but that doesn't mean they get out-lawed or shoved off into back rooms. Sky diving poses health risks, but nobody says people can't do it except in tiny, crowded rooms. Second, there's never been absolutely convincing proof that second-hand smoke is harmful. But if it is, that still doesn't mean smoking should be prohibited. Parents who serve large portions of high-cholesterol meats are endangering their families' health, but they're not discriminated against.

Third, a lot of people who don't smoke don't mind it if other people do. So people who whine when somebody else lights up are just being unreasonable and intolerant. If someone is bothered by other people smoking, why should smokers be locked away in tiny, crowded rooms? Why doesn't the person who's bothered just leave instead?

Of course, antismokers might say that sometimes they can't leave, for example, if people are smoking in the work place or in the university cafeteria. But that applies just as much to smokers too; they can't leave their work place every time they want a cigarette, and if there's only one cafeteria for non-smokers, there's only one for smokers too.

Most women wear perfume. Suppose people didn't like the smell of perfume or were irritated by it. Would we then be justified in putting women in tiny, crowded rooms to wear their perfume? If we did, we'd be guilty of sex discrimination, just as we'd be guilty of racial discrimination if we restricted people to special rooms because of their race. I conclude that people who discriminate against others because they're smokers are guilty of discrimination too, and we shouldn't tolerate that either.

EXERCISE II

Write a critical paper on one of the arguments in Exercise I, numbers 6, 7, 8, or 9, or another topic of interest to you. (If you don't write on numbers 6, 7, 8, or 9, clear your topic with your professor first.) Be sure you follow the outline in this chapter.

15 *More Controversial Arguments*

Now that you've become more comfortable arguing for your own beliefs and criticizing other people's arguments fairly, we can begin to consider issues where consensus is harder to achieve. In this chapter, we will discuss the issue of animal rights. Looking at two arguments, one on each extreme, we will discover some fallacies. But we will also find interesting arguments without one side being clearly more justified than the other. Accordingly, we will move toward recognizing that when there are good arguments on different sides, the situation is more like an ongoing conversation than like a problem to be solved once and for all. In these circumstances, the most rational approach is to work out the most justified position you can and act on it, while recognizing that there's still room for reasonable people to disagree.

Many issues of public interest seem to be debated endlessly. Issues such as abortion and the environment arouse strong feelings on all sides, and arguments for various positions rage in the public media. Somehow we might expect that more progress would be made on such issues as these, or even that they might be settled once and for all. But in real life, efforts to settle issues where there are good arguments on different sides often amount to giving up on reasoning and turning to the coercive powers of courts and legislatures. And this tendency is reinforced when intense emotions cloud people's rational judgment. As we look at the arguments in this chapter, keep in mind that the main issue we're concerned with is the quality of those arguments. Be sure not to let your unconsidered opinions bias your judgment.

AN EXAMPLE: ANIMAL EXPERIMENTATION

In this chapter, we will analyze an issue where there are interesting arguments on different sides. The issue concerns animal rights and, more specifically, the morality of using animals in experiments. To some people, it seems obvious that there are profound differences between people and animals and that these differences justify us in using animals for research. To others, it seems just as obvious that the similarities between animals and people are so great that using animals for research is as immoral as it would be to use people for the same purposes. Perhaps most people adopt a standpoint between these extremes.

This issue has received much attention from writers on each side who have offered interesting arguments to support their beliefs. The "animal rights" side argues that animals, like people, have moral rights similar to those which protect people from abuse. While these moral rights are not all recognized by law, some of them are; we have laws prohibiting cruelty to animals, for example. Those arguing for animal rights often suggest that we should go much further in recognizing the moral rights of animals and should prohibit their use not only for research but also for sport, food, furs, and pets.

Those who oppose the animal rights position sometimes suggest that rights are a matter of implicit agreement, or "social contract" among (human) members of society—which does not include animals. Others emphasize the far-reaching consequences of taking animal rights seriously. These consequences are not only matters of

Figure 15.1
Reprinted with permission from the American Society
for the Prevention of Cruelty to Animals.

taste and fashion; they also include serious economic effects, perhaps even the elimination of most traditional farms. Moreover, virtually every important medical development, as well as many scientific advances, has depended on using animals for research purposes. To prohibit the use of animals in research might well mean the end of humanity's chances to conquer AIDS, cancer, and a host of other sources of human suffering.

Most people can feel some sympathy with each side in this debate. Hardly anyone is insensitive to animal suffering, which is why pictures like the one in Figure 15.1 inspire many people to join such groups as the American Society for the Prevention of Cruelty to Animals or People for the Ethical Treatment of Animals. At the same time, the need for continued medical research is also important. And most people don't seem to think that a concern for animals means they should become vegetarians or stop using mascara. Can a rational basis be found for concluding that some uses of animals are unethical whereas others are morally justified? A rational decision about all of this should depend on the arguments each side can give.

Because the issues surrounding animal rights are so complicated, we'll focus on only one: animal experimentation.

ANIMAL RIGHTS ARGUMENTS

One of the most persuasive cases for animal rights has been made by Peter Singer in "All Animals Are Equal."[1] His thesis is "that we [should] extend to other species the basic principle of equality that most of us recognize should be extended to all members of our own species." And the heart of his argument is that refusing to grant animal rights is like racism and sexism in being an immoral and irrational preference for members of one's own kind. Singer says:

> The racist violates the principle of equality by giving greater weight to the interests of members of his own race, when there is a clash between their interests and the interests of those of another race. Similarly the speciesist allows the interests of his own species to override the greater interests of members of other species. The pattern is the same in each case.

Singer lists a number of practices that demonstrate human speciesism. Among these are using animals for food (merely to "gratify our tastes"), raising animals in "cramped, unsuitable conditions for the entire durations of their lives," and "experimenting on other species in order to see if certain substances are safe for human beings, or to test some psychological theory about the effects of severe punishment on learning, or to try out various new compounds just in case something turns up." Here Singer argues that eating meat, raising animals in the way many farmers usually do, and doing medical and psychological experiments and product testing on animals are all morally wrong, just as racism and sexism are morally wrong. And, of course, he could add many other practices, such as hunting, wearing fur coats, and keeping animals in zoos.

It's important to see that Singer's argument depends on two assumptions. They are, first, that there are no important differences between speciesism, racism, and sexism and, second, that speciesism, like racism and sexism, is morally wrong. Most people now

---

1. Peter Singer, "All Animals Are Equal," *New York Review of Books,* April 5, 1973. Singer's views are more fully developed in *Animal Liberation* (New York: Avon Books, 1975).

recognize that it is immoral to maltreat people just because of their skin color or sex. So they would agree that racism and sexism are morally wrong. But probably most people think that there are enough important differences between people and animals to justify treating animals differently—using them for food and experimentation, for example. So most people probably think that their preference for human good over animal good is *not* irrational speciesism but rather that it is reasonable recognition of relevant differences.

Singer anticipates this objection. He says:

> One way in which [critics] might reply to [my] argument is by saying that the case for equality between men and women cannot validly be extended to nonhuman animals. Women have a right to vote, for instance, because they are just as capable of making rational decisions as men are; dogs, on the other hand, are incapable of understanding the significance of voting, so they cannot have the right to vote. There are many other obvious ways in which men and women resemble each other closely, while humans and other animals differ greatly. So, it might be said, men and women are similar beings and should have equal rights, while humans and nonhumans are different and should not have equal rights.

He also replies to this objection. His reply is that while there are many differences between people and nonhuman animals, and they do affect which rights animals have, those differences are not *relevant* to whether or not animals should be used for food, experimented on, and the like. "There are," he says,

> important differences between humans and other animals, and these differences must give rise to *some* differences in the rights that each have. Recognizing this obvious fact, however, is no barrier to the case for extending the basic principle of equality to nonhuman animals. The differences that exist between men and women are equally undeniable, and the supporters of Women's Liberation are aware that these differences may give rise to different rights. Many feminists hold that women have the right to an abortion on request. It does not follow that since these same people are campaigning for equality between men and women they must support the right to men to have abortions too. Since a man cannot have an abortion, it is meaningless to talk of his right to have one. Since a pig can't vote, it is

> meaningless to talk of its right to vote. There is no reason why either Women's Liberation or Animal Liberation should get involved in such nonsense.

So Singer agrees that it is not immoral to deprive animals of *some* rights, such as the right to vote, because they cannot have an interest in voting. But he thinks animals do have rights to equal protection of the interests they do have. And the most important of these is their interest in not suffering. So he thinks animals have a right not to be subjected to unnecessary suffering, just as people do. This right *might* be outweighed by other, even more important interests. For example, Singer would not think it immoral to cause an animal to suffer if that were the only way to save its life. But raising animals for food and experimenting on them are not interests more important than avoiding animal suffering, according to Singer.

Again, someone might object that Singer is overlooking how much more intelligent people are than animals; perhaps that is what gives people rights that animals don't have. Besides, animals don't respect others' rights; why should they enjoy rights they don't respect? And don't human beings have a kind of intrinsic worth, or human dignity, that animals don't have? Singer anticipates these objections too, pointing out that some people, such as babies and people with serious brain damage, are *not* more intelligent than some animals, such as some dogs and chimpanzees. Still, we don't think it would be morally acceptable to eat such people or do experiments on them. The same goes for not respecting others' rights: Babies and the mentally defective do not do this either, yet they don't forfeit their rights. And what is this idea of intrinsic worth based on? Is it really obvious that "all humans—including infants, mental defectives, psychopaths, Hitler, Stalin, and the rest—have some kind of dignity or worth that no elephant, pig or chimpanzee can ever achieve"? Singer thinks not.

The point, Singer says, is that

> our concern for others ought not to depend on what they are like, or what abilities they possess. . . . It is on this basis that the case against racism and the case against sexism must both ultimately rest; and it is in accordance with this principle that speciesism is also to be condemned. If possessing a higher degree of intelligence does not entitle one human to use another for his own ends, how can it entitle humans to exploit non-humans?

Instead, Singer suggests that having rights depends on the capacity to suffer and enjoy happiness:

> The capacity for suffering and enjoying things is a prerequisite for having interests at all, a condition that must be satisfied before we can speak of interests in any meaningful way. . . . If a being suffers, there can be no moral justification for refusing to take that suffering into consideration. No matter what the nature of the being the principle of equality requires that its suffering be counted equally with the like suffering—insofar as rough comparisons can be made—of any other being. . . . Since, as I have said, none of these practices [raising and eating animals for food] cater for anything more than our pleasures of taste, our practice of rearing and killing other animals in order to eat them is a clear instance of the sacrifice of the most important interests of other beings in order to satisfy trivial interests of our own. To avoid speciesism we must stop this practice, and each of us has a moral obligation to cease supporting the practice.

Singer makes the same point about experimentation:

> The same form of discrimination may be observed in the widespread practice of experimenting on other species. If the experimenter is not prepared to use an orphaned human infant, then his readiness to use nonhumans is simple discrimination, since adult apes, cats, mice, and other mammals are more aware of what is happening to them, more self-directing and, so far as we can tell, at least as sensitive to pain, as any human infant. . . . The experimenter, then, shows a bias in favor of his own species whenever he carries out an experiment on a nonhuman for a purpose that he would not think justified him in using a human being at an equal or lower level of sentience, awareness, ability to be self-directing, etc.

Since there are very few product-reliability tests or medical experiments that people would feel comfortable doing on babies or people with brain damage, Singer concludes that most animal experimentation is also immoral.

Singer concludes that animals have moral rights not to be subjected to unnecessary suffering because they are relevantly similar to people and people have such rights. Refusing to recognize this and change our ways—stop eating meat, stop experimenting on animals—is immoral in the same way that racism and sexism are immoral. So if Singer is right about all of this, either we each must stop doing things that cause animals unnecessary suffering or we each will be behaving immorally.

FIRST REPLIES TO THE ANIMAL RIGHTS CASE

Singer's position has not gone unchallenged. One approach has been to emphasize how dependent medical advances have been on animal experimentation. In "Some Thoughts on the Value of Life," Dr. John A. Krasney documents this point with Tables 1 and 2, which illustrate "some of the discoveries that had to be made before modern open-heart surgery, the coronary bypass procedure, and the heart transplant could be achieved" (Table 1).[2] Table 2 offers further "selected examples of major biomedical advances that depended on animal research (other than cardiology). Clearly the list is an impressive one. And animals, too, have benefited from biomedical research through the development of vaccines and genetic research.

Another reply is to point out that by the standards of regulatory agencies, there have been very few instances of animal cruelty in laboratories. Krasney points out:

> The animals at UB are cared for according to the Guiding Principles of Animal Care as promulgated by the American Physiological Society, and the NIH Guide for Care of Laboratory Animals (Institute of Laboratory Resources). The humane standards required by state regulations and the Federal Animal Welfare Act are adhered to as well. The Laboratory Animal Facilities are certified by the American Association for Accreditation of Laboratory Animal Care, an accreditation body formed by scientists which has higher standards than those required by the Animal Welfare Act. In addition, experimental protocols are reviewed, and investigations are monitored by an Institutional Animal Care Committee. This committee consists of a veterinarian, experienced laboratory animal investigators, and non-scientist representatives who ensure that high standards of human care are maintained on a local basis. Animals are killed at the end of experiments by euthanasia techniques promulgated by the Veterinary Medical Association.

---

2. John A. Krasney, Ph.D., "Some Thoughts on the Value of Life," *Buffalo Physician* 18 (September 1984): 6–13.

TABLE 1. The Heart Transplant and Other Cardiology Advances That Depended on Animal Research: A Chronology

WORK INITIATED OR CULMINATED DURING	MEDICAL ADVANCE	SPECIES STUDIED
Pre-1900	Management of Heart Failure	
	Asepsis	dogs
	Blood pressure, heart rate	many species
	Fluid & electrolytes, acid-base balance	many species
	Surgical instruments & materials	dogs
	Relief of Pain	many species
	Wound healing	many species
Early 1900s	Electrocardiography	dogs
	Cardiac catheterization	dogs, rabbits, cats
	Components of blood & plasma	monkeys, dogs
	Nutrition	many species
	Surgical techniques	dogs
1920s	Intravenous feeding	dogs, rabbits, rodents
	Ventilation of open thorax	dogs
1930s	Transfusion, blood groups & typing	many species
	Monitoring EEG	many species
	Modern anesthesia & neuromuscular blocking agents	rats, mice, rabbits, dogs, monkeys
	Anticoagulants	cats
	Pump oxygenator	cats, dogs
1940s	Antibiotics	many species
1950s	Blood preservation	many species
	Blood O_2, CO_2, pH	many species
	Chemotherapy	many species
	Cardiac pacemaker	dogs, developed at UB
	Floating cardiac catheter	dogs, developed at UB
	Open heart surgery	dogs
1960s	Selective coronary angiography, ventriculography	dogs
	Assessment of cardiac, pulmonary, renal, hepatic, brain function	many species
	Hypothermia & survival of ischemic organs	dogs
	Defibrillation	dogs
	Coronary collateral circulation	dogs, pigs, primates
	Coronary bypass	dogs
	Modern CPR	dogs
1970s	Elective cardiac arrest	dogs
	Vascular anastamosis	dogs
	Principles of intensive care	dogs
	Measurement of coronary blood flow in humans	dogs, developed at UB
	Myocardial preservation techniques	dogs
	Beneficial effects of exercise on heart (cardiac rehabilitation)	dogs
	Heart transplant	dogs
1980s	Cyclosporin & antirejection drugs	monkeys
	Artificial heart	dogs, cattle, porpoise

235

TABLE 2. Selected Examples of Major Biomedical Advances That Depended on Animal Research (Other Than Cardiology)

WHEN INITIATED OR CULMINATED	MEDICAL ADVANCE	SPECIES STUDIED
Pre-1900	Treatment of rabies	dogs, rabbits
	Treatment of anthrax	sheep
	Treatment of beriberi	chickens
	Treatment of smallpox	cows
Early 1900s	Treatment of histamine shock	dogs
	Treatment of pellagra	rhesus monkeys, dogs
	Treatment of rickets	dogs
1920s	Discovery of penicillin	Therapeutic use established in 1939
	Discovery of Thyroxin	many species
	Insulin & control of diabetes	dogs
1930s	Therapeutic use of sulfa drugs	mice, rabbits
	Prevention of tetanus	many species
1940s	Treatment of rheumatoid arthritis	rabbits, monkeys
	Therapeutic use of aureomycin	dogs, cats, pigs, rodents
	Therapeutic use of streptomycin	chickens, guinea pigs
	Discovery of Rh factor	rhesus monkeys
	Prevention of diphtheria	horses
	Whooping cough (pertussis) treatment	guinea pigs, rabbits
1950s	Prevention of poliomyelitis	rabbits, monkeys, rodents
	Discovery of DNA	rats, mice
	Chlorpromazine & its tranquilizing derivatives	rats, rabbits, monkeys
	Hypertension oral diuretics (thiazides)	dogs, other species
	Cancer chemotherapy	monkeys, rabbits, rodents
1960s	Prevention of rubella	monkeys
	Radioimmunoassay	many species
	Prevention of surgical post-operative adhesions	dogs
	Therapeutic use of cortisone	rabbits, monkeys
	Corneal transplant	rabbits, monkeys
1970s	Cimetidine (tagamet) treatment of gastric ulcer	rabbits, rats, other species
	Prevention of measles	many species
	Modern treatment of coronary insufficiency	dogs
	Viral origin of cancer	cats
	Treatment of leprosy	monkeys, armadillos
	Immunotherapy technology	many species
	Cerebral revascularization procedures	monkeys
1980s	Monoclonal antibodies	mice, rabbits

Moreover, Krasney observes, it is of interest that, over the past 80 years, no scientists have been convicted of animal cruelty.

A temporary exception was Dr. Edward Taub, whose Maryland Laboratory was invaded by police after a staged antivivisectionist raid, and was initially convicted of animal cruelty by a Maryland court, but all of the convictions were subsequently overruled on the grounds that Maryland anti-cruelty laws did not apply to federally funded laboratories.

A third approach has been to point out that many of those who aggressively advocate animal rights do so hypocritically or out of unworthy or suspect motives. In "Who Will Live, Who Will Die?" Katie McCabe paints a picture of cynical animal rights activists "who oppose all use of animals for human benefit," twisting evidence of animal cruelty to attract the well-meaning support of sentimental animal lovers.[3] Moreover, she says, "Over the last five years, the ALF (Animal Liberation Front) has taken credit for dozens of lab break-ins, bombings, and threats to animal researchers."

Krasney, too, questions the motivation of animal rights advocates, which he thinks "is based on a kind of Disneyish anthropomorphism, or the imparting of human characteristics to animal creatures." Such sentimentalism is equivalent to condoning human suffering and "usually devolves to outright hatred and personal attack of the researcher and even to physical threats." Moreover, animal rights advocates are hypocrites. Krasney points out that since "the number of animals killed for food in the country is vastly greater (134 million cattle, hogs and sheep annually) than the number of animals killed in research laboratories," activists "should focus their activities on the much larger numbers of abused and potentially suffering animals used by the food industry." Further,

If killing animals for medical research is wrong, it is also wrong to have medicines which were developed through animal research. It is inconsistent for antivivisectionists to go to the doctor and accept modern diagnosis and therapeutic medicine, most of it derived from animal research.

Animal rights activists are pet lovers, Krasney charges. They make use of veterinarians, much of whose skill depends on animal

---

3. Katie McCabe, "Who Will Live, Who Will Die?" *The Washingtonian,* August 1986, pp. 112–15, 153–57.

research. And to feed their pets, "we have to kill off other animals for their food." Yet "no priority" is placed on "pet care programs that would reduce the tremendous number of animals abandoned by irresponsible owners." A final hypocrisy is the emphasis on stopping experiments on "cats, dogs, rabbits and monkeys" rather than those on "rats, mice and other rodents which comprise 87 percent of all experiments."

Both Krasney and McCabe cite Peter Singer as the philosophical source of the excesses of the animal rights movement. Krasney quotes Singer's remark that "an experiment cannot be justified unless the experiment is so important that the use of a retarded human being would also be justifiable" as proof that "this 'speciesism' argument makes no distinction between the value of human life and that of animal life." McCabe summarizes Singer's position as follows: He "argues that all sentient beings have equal moral status and regards humans' use of animals for food, sport, or research as 'speciesism'—the moral equivalent of racism." Following Singer, McCabe says, "the movement" has come to regard "'the right to life as a perversion,' meat eating as 'primitive, barbaric, and arrogant,' and pet ownership as 'an absolutely abysmal situation brought about by human manipulation.'"

EVALUATING THESE FIRST REPLIES

Careful readers of this summary of Krasney's and McCabe's articles will have noticed several interesting points. First, their summaries of Singer's position are inaccurate and misleading. Indeed, some of them amount to instances of straw man fallacies. Singer did not deny that there are important distinctions between animal and human life, nor did he ever say "all sentient beings have equal moral status." What he said was that the differences between people and animals do not justify us in using animals for "food, sport or research" unless we would be prepared to use people *at the same stage of consciousness* for the same purposes, or unless there are overridingly important interests at stake. He certainly does not think that "gratifying our tastes" for meat or hunting count as "overridingly important interests." But the way may still be open to argue that at least some medical experimentation might involve interests that override animal interests in not suffering.

Second, neither Singer nor any other animal rights activist has denied that some animal experiments have produced important medical and other breakthroughs. (Many other experiments, of course, did not, producing only animal suffering.) The point is, some of these experiments may have been immoral, even though they produced beneficial results. So showing that some animal experiments "paid off" does not show that those experiments were morally acceptable.

This is a very important point. Some (very few) experiments conducted on Jewish prisoners by Nazis during World War II may have produced some medical knowledge. But it would not follow from this that abuse of Jewish prisoners by Nazis for medical research was morally acceptable. Similarly, some well-known psychological experiments have involved placing subjects under conditions of severe stress, anxiety, and pain without fully informing them. But many now feel that whatever knowledge may have come out of these experiments, using subjects this way without their informed consent was not morally acceptable. So it's not obvious that the benefits of some animal research by itself prove that animal research is not immoral.

Singer's critics are on even shakier ground when they attack the motives and character of animal rights advocates rather than his arguments. The general point is, even if all of McCabe's and Krasney's personal attacks are true, they would have no effect on the truth of Singer's position. Suppose it's true that some animal rights groups have emphasized rare abuses of appealing animals in order to generate broad support. That wouldn't prove the abuses are unreal or unimportant or that animals don't have rights.

Suppose it's true that some animal rights groups have behaved violently, even hatefully, to researchers. Again, that doesn't show their reasons for moral outrage are mistaken. Suppose — as is certainly not true of Singer — animal rights advocates are often motivated by "Disneyish anthropomorphism." As long as such feelings are not their sole or most important reasons for advocating animal rights, such activists still have not been proven wrong. Indeed, if Singer is right, any anthropomorphism along the lines of sensitivity to pain and its relevance to morality would be justified.

Animal rights advocates are very concerned about the treatment of farm animals. Singer discusses it in his paper and devotes portions of three chapters to it in *Animal Liberation*. He opposes using animals as pets and specifically mentions the immorality of experimenting on *mice*, not just cats, dogs, rabbits, and monkeys. ("A mouse, on the other hand, does have an interest in not being tormented, because it will suffer if it is.") And why shouldn't an animal rights activist use medicines developed through animal experimentation? If the goal is to prevent suffering, using the medicine will do that, whereas nothing will prevent the suffering that has already occurred as the medicine was being developed.

We're now in a position to see why the replies to Singer we've been looking at may not be successful. The problem is, instead of critically examining Singer's reasons and arguments, his critics have often replied in ways not directly relevant to the morality of "speciesism." If we are to find rational ways to justify continued animal research, animal husbandry, pet ownership, and the like, we will need to address that question directly. That is, we will need to think carefully about whether Singer's reasons are rationally justified and whether his arguments are sound. We will begin to do this in the next section. But we can only begin here; much will be left for you to work out for yourself.

Before leaving this section, however, it is worthwhile to remember some points on which Singer and Krasney may agree. Although he doesn't emphasize this, Singer may acknowledge that some animal research is very important to both human and animal welfare. And, for that matter, there may be other negative consequences of animal rights that should be counted in the moral balance. If we can isolate exactly what are the points of dispute, there may be a sufficient shared basis of agreement to launch another effort to justify at least some animal experimentation, animal husbandry, and/or pet ownership. Searching out areas of agreement and disagreement is an essential part of resolving cases in which there are good arguments on more than one side of an issue.

ANIMAL RIGHTS ARGUMENTS RECONSIDERED

In this section, we will explore how one might go about arguing against Singer that it may be morally justifiable to use animals for medical experimentation, food, and pets. We will not resolve these questions conclusively, not because this is a question of value but because there are good reasons on both sides. Still, it's worth looking at how we might begin to work toward a reasonable position on this issue that respects both what is persuasive about Singer's article and what is important about the positions of Krasney and McCabe. We need to begin by carefully analyzing the arguments.

First, neither side is interested in defending "animal research that is not clearly for biomedical benefits, such as military, cosmetic, or behavioral studies" (Krasney). This is a worthwhile area of agreement. Although we need not be dogmatic about this, perhaps we should agree too that we can get along very well without new animal experiments along these lines. At the least, we might use this agreement to narrow the discussion to biomedical experiments; we'll return to the topics of food and pets in the exercises at the end of this chapter.

As we noted earlier, there can be no doubt about the importance of some animal research to biomedical progress. And there is no dispute about the need to treat animals as humanely as possible; neither Singer nor Krasney wants animals to suffer unnecessarily. But they disagree about whether all animal-research suffering is necessary. Singer is surely guilty of overstatement when he suggests that much experimentation goes on "testing various compounds just to see if something turns up." (To verify this, we might note how expensive animal experiments are, how difficult it is to get approval to conduct them, etc.) Krasney is surely wrong in suggesting that review by interested parties will necessarily screen out illegitimate experiments. (To verify this, we might find references to some especially useless and painful animal experiments.)

So perhaps the truth lies in the middle; probably some experiments — but not most — inflict pointless suffering. And if so, perhaps a reasonable position would be one McCabe mentions:

> All but lost in the shrill exchange between anti-vivisectionists and scientists called upon to justify animal research are the voices of moderation, advocates of the "three R's" of animal welfare — replacement of animals where feasible alternatives exist, reduction in numbers where possible, and refinement of techniques to minimize pain.

Perhaps these "three R's" are also something all sides could agree to.

Now, what does each side mean by "pointless" experimental suffering? Singer thinks a morally objectionable experiment is one that we would not be willing to do on a human being but would be willing to do on an animal with a similar level of consciousness. Krasney thinks worthwhile experiments include those that yield new biomedical knowledge or train physicians. Granted that each side should be prepared to substitute alternatives, reduce numbers, and minimize pain, the question between them is, how many (and what kinds of) animal experiments are left over? Perhaps not many. (To verify this, we would need to investigate responsible medical opinion, because only experts in experimentation can give us a reasonable account of what can and what cannot be done with alternatives such as computer models and cadavers.) In any case, both sides would probably agree it is important to minimize animal experiments.

Still, what of Singer's claim that refusing to use an orphaned human infant with severe and irreversible brain damage in experiments is mere speciesism? Earlier, we noted that Singer's argument depends on showing that speciesism is just like racism and sexism and that a preference for the interests of one's own species is necessarily irrational. To test this analogy, we need to consider whether there are relevant differences that outweigh the similarities. Might there be any good reasons why it might not be irrational to extend the protection of rights to such infants but deny it to some animals?

One approach would be to raise the question of concept "What is a right?" It might turn out that a moral right would be a kind of protection people (or beings) have not only by virtue of their actual or potential capacity to suffer, as Singer thinks, but also by virtue of something else or something more. Perhaps beings have rights in proportion to their actual or potential capacity to claim what is due them and respect what is due others as part of the human community. Then the decision to extend rights to borderline-case persons— such as brain dead or severely retarded infants and perhaps, some animals—who cannot claim what is due them or respect what is due others would be an act of kindness or charity rather than obligation.[4]

Of course, this is only one possible analysis of the concept "rights." But it would have interesting consequences if applied seriously. For example, if there are animals, such as chimpanzees, gorillas, porpoises, or whales, that do appear to claim what is due them and/or respect what is due others, they would deserve rights. But it might not be true that the severely retarded infant or comatose elderly patient would deserve rights, only that each would be granted them as a kindness. The main point, though, is that animals without rights couldn't have their rights violated by being the subjects of experiments.

---

4. This approach to rights seems similar to that taken by Joel Feinberg in "The Nature and Value of Rights" and to the ideas of a number of other philosophers. See David Lyons, *Rights* (Belmont, Calif.: Wadsworth, 1979).

Another approach might be to accept Singer's claim that the capacity to enjoy and suffer is what confers rights, and then to argue that it's only when the probable results of medical experiments are very important that we are morally justified in overriding the right not to be harmed in the interests of others. Then we could go on to argue that animals but not people could be experimental subjects because people, but not (most) animals, feel anxiety and fear on top of the suffering caused by experiments. Of course, this claim would need some proof. (How would you go about trying to prove it?) Besides, this approach wouldn't protect comatose orphans from being experimental subjects. And it would mean that if there are animals that appear to feel anxiety or fear over the suffering of others, they would also have a right not to be experimental subjects. But that might be an acceptable result.

Perhaps at this point we have enough possibilities to suggest how we might rationally reach a tentative conclusion different from Singer's. Of course, these possibilities have to be worked out in detail to be sure. Still, it begins to be possible to make a strong argument for this conclusion: It may be morally acceptable to experiment on animals, but only (1) when the animal does not appear to fear or grieve and/or has some concept of what is due itself and/or others, (2) when the prospective results of the experiment are very important, (3) when there is no feasible alternative to animal experimentation, (4) when the fewest animals are used, and (5) when the pain and other suffering of the animals are minimized.

Now, there remains a good deal of work to be done. How do we know whether an animal has a sense of self? What does "very important" mean, regarding the results of justifiable experiments? Until such questions as this are answered, we have only the beginning of a thorough analysis of these issues. It is included here to get you thinking and using the techniques of argument analysis we've developed during this course. Also, the point is not whether you agree with Singer, McCabe, Krasney, or one of the lines of argument we've just been discussing. The point is, you should now be getting a sense for how a complicated issue like this one might be tentatively resolved, so that we can go on and act responsibly. We may have to change our current behavior in some respects (perhaps not doing pointless experiments), and we may need to remain open to new arguments and information. But meanwhile, we can act, even as we remain open to new ideas and arguments.

Summary

In this chapter we examined two interesting lines of argument concerning animal rights. Peter Singer argued that because animals have interests like those of people, among them their interest in not suffering, they have rights similar to those people have unless there are relevant differences between people and animals that justify us in treating them differently. If there are no such relevant differences, then using animals for research rather than using humans with similar awareness is immoral speciesism. Many replies to Singer's arguments involve fallacies — attacks against the motives and character of animal rights activists or morally irrelevant claims of medical progress, for example. But there may be other, more logically appealing lines of argument. Perhaps people — and animals — have rights only if they can make claims of what is due them and if they respect others' similar claims. If so, few if any animals would have the rights Singer thinks they do. Or perhaps people's interests do sometimes outweigh animal interests, because people add fear and anxiety to the actual suffering that would otherwise result from experiments; that might explain why it's more wrong to use people than animals in experiments. Neither of these arguments is conclusive, though, so the issue is still open to new ideas.

Exercise I

Discuss the arguments in this chapter thoroughly, making sure you understand them clearly. Then decide which arguments you find most convincing. Why? Can you carry the discussion further by anticipating a reply from the animal rights side? Can you think of additional persuasive arguments on the other side?

Exercise II

As a capable thinker, you have the opportunity to join in this conversation about uses of animals. Use the information in the text as well as the information that follows and your own ideas to argue for one of the following thesis statements:

1. There is nothing necessarily immoral about eating meat.

2. Using animals for food is necessarily immoral; people ought to become vegetarians.

Here are some things to think about; remember, although there are good reasons to support each of these claims, some *might* still questioned.

- The best scientific evidence suggests that suffering requires a spinal cord, so animals lacking that kind of central nervous system, as well as plants, probably don't suffer. (What animals commonly used for food don't have spinal cords?)

- Some farm animals (e.g., veal calves) cannot be raised without causing them to suffer greatly. Other farm animals (e.g., lambs) are not normally raised in conditions that cause them much discomfort. And still others (e.g., chickens, beef cattle) can be raised in either relatively comfortable or uncomfortable conditions.

- Animals being prepared for market are now often confined in cramped pens and slaughtered without anesthetic.

- If Americans reduced their intake of meat by 10 percent, the grains and soybeans saved could adequately feed 60 million people, which is the number of people who starve to death each year. There is no human nutritional need that cannot be satisfied by vegetables and vitamins.

- Much human starvation may be due to overpopulation, unwise economic arrangements, political strife, inadequate transportation and other facilities, and bad farming and land-use practices.

- If farm animals were not raised for food, most existing farm animals might die out quickly, and there would be few such animals left.

- Although the lives of animals in the wild are subject to diseases and predators that farm animals are not, wild animals seldom accept domestication without a struggle (voluntarily).

- Raising farm animals provides a deeply satisfying way of life for many people while contributing to the enjoyment of many others.

- Although 40 percent of the world's oxygen is produced by the Amazon rain forest, and nearly half of the world's species of wild plants, animals, and insects live in rain forests, about 40 percent of rain forests have been cut down for beef production.

- There are serious practical problems about raising food and distributing it to the world's needy populations. (What are some of these? Could they be overcome?)

Glossary

Numbers within parentheses following definitions refer to the chapters in which terms are defined.

Aesthetic (value) Having to do with how satisfying, fulfilling, appealing, attractive, or beautiful something is. (3)

Ambiguity (ambiguous) An expression is ambiguous if its meaning in the context cannot be clearly determined because there is more than one possibility and neither can be ruled out. (5)

Analogues The things being compared in an argument from analogy. (12)

Analogy An argument in which two things are compared, and it is argued that because they are similar in some respects, they are probably similar in some further respect. (12)

Anticipated replies Trying to imagine how a member of one's audience who is not initially persuaded by an argument might respond or reply to it. (10)

Appeal to anger A fallacy of relevance that substitutes arousing anger for giving reasons. (6)

Appeal to excitement A fallacy of relevance that uses the fact or possibility of people being excited or enthusiastic about something as a reason to believe it. (6)

Appeal to fear A fallacy of relevance that substitutes a threat for good reasons. (6)

Appeal to hope A fallacy of relevance that plays on people's strong optimistic desires as a substitute for giving reasons. (6)

Appeal to improper authority A fallacy of improper authority in which a person's genuine expertise in one area is used to support an opinion in an unrelated area. (11)

Appeal to pity A fallacy of relevance that substitutes feeling sorry for someone for good reasons. (6)

Appeal to sex A fallacy of relevance that substitutes an associated or suggested linkage between a sexually attractive image and a belief otherwise not related to it. (6)

Appeal to the authority of ordinary folks A fallacy of improper authority that assigns expert status to people who are not distinguished in any way. (11)

Appeal to the authority of the many A fallacy of improper authority that assigns expertise to the opinions of a group merely because a number of people believe something. (11)

Appeal to the authority of the select few A fallacy of improper authority that assigns expert status to people who are distinguished in some way unrelated to the issue. (11)

Appeal to the authority of unreal experts A fallacy of improper authority that assigns expert status to imaginary characters or performing actors. (11)

Appeal to tradition A fallacy of improper authority which assumes that if something is of long standing, or has always been done in some way, it must be true. (11)

Argument At least one reason offered to influence a person's belief about something. (2)

Argument from ignorance An argument which assumes that since something has not been proved to be false it must be true, or since something has not been proved to be true it must be false. (6)

Argument of simple irrelevance A fallacy of relevance in which information with some topical association with something else is treated as if it had an evidential connection with it. (6)

Association Our tendency to identify ourselves in all respects with people who are like us in some respects; often used in advertising. (2)

Attacking the motive A critical fallacy in which one criticizes a person's possible motivation for saying something rather than criticizing what he or she actually said. (13)

Audience Those to whom an argument is directed or offered. (2)

Background information Unstated assumptions on which an argument depends. (2)

Begging the question A fallacy of assumption in which a form of the conclusion is given as a reason, or in which the reason depends on the conclusion. (7)

Belief An opinion based on some kind of support, such as evidence or reasons. (1)

Chain argument A valid deductive argument form in which a series of claims is related in the following way: If A is true, then B is, and if B is true, then C is, so (conclusion) if A is true, then C is. (4)

Coercion (in place of argument) Using force or pressure to induce people to believe or do something. (1)

Complex question A fallacy of assumption in which an unjustified assumption is concealed in the form of a question; for example, "When did you stop beating your spouse?" (7)

Conclusions Beliefs that reasons are offered to support. (2)

Connotation Emotional responses associated with a term in context. (5)

Counterexample A case or instance that tends to disprove a claim, especially regarding definitions or inductive arguments. (5)

Counterproposal A suggestion made after having rejected an earlier idea. (14)

Critical fallacies Arguments criticizing other positions unfairly through personal attacks, attacks against false or biased versions of other ideas, or trivial objections. (13)

Critical paper An essay in which the main purpose is to criticize another's position. (14)

Deductive (argument) A form of argument in which relations among the ideas presented in the reasons (premises) are offered to provide conclusive proof of a conclusion. (4)

Denotation What a term literally means or refers to. (5)

Denying the consequent A valid deductive argument form in which the truth of one claim is said to depend on another ("If A . . . then B"), the dependent claim is denied ("not B"), and the antecedent claim is denied as the conclusion ("therefore not A"). (4)

Differentia Features that make
something different from
other, similar objects especially in the same genus. (5)

Dilemma A valid deductive argument form in which two
or more alternatives are
presented, all but one is
ruled out, and the conclusion is the alternative that
remains. (4)

Directive (language use) Language is used directively
when it is used to tell people
to do things, give commands
or instructions, order, guide
actions, and so on. (3)

Equivocation A fallacy of confusion in which an argument
depends on using a single
idea in more than one way,
to mean more than one
thing. (8)

Ethics (ethical) Having to do
with matters of right and
wrong, good and bad, duty,
and obligation, especially
within a given profession or
field of activity; often used
interchangeably with
"moral." (3)

Evidence Factual support or
justification for belief. (1)

Expressive (language use) Language is used expressively
when it directly vents (not
reports) feelings, as in cheering, booing, cursing, reassuring, and the like. (3)

Extensive definition Gives a
complete list of things referred to by a term or an expression. (5)

Fact True information or evidence. (3)

Fallacies of assumption Arguments which depend on
background information
that is rationally unjustified
on the basis of the best available information or which
depend on strained or in-
valid ways of understanding
and applying that information. (7)

Fallacies of confusion Arguments that make use of
unclearly defined or inconsistent terms, obscure structure, or unfair interpretations to convince people. (8)

Fallacies of improper authority
Arguments which depend on
expert or other sources that
are not rationally trust-
worthy. (11)

Fallacies of insufficiency Arguments in which not enough
evidence is given to support
a conclusion. (9)

Fallacies of relevance Arguments which offer reasons
that have no connection of
evidential support to the
conclusions they're used to
persuade people of. (6)

Fallacy An argument (or supposed argument) that should
not persuade a rational person. (4)

Fallacy of false context A fallacy of confusion which

occurs when passages or excerpts that are used as reasons are taken out of the surroundings that point to one interpretation so they can be used to mean something else. (8)

Fallacy of misreading A fallacy of confusion which involves using a passage taken from some other source in a way that would not have been consistent with its author's intentions or its usual interpretation. (8)

Fallacy of obscurity A fallacy of confusion which occurs when reasons are given with such an air of authority that people accept them even though they don't understand them. (8)

Fallacy of unreasonable definition A fallacy of confusion that consists in reasoning by means of biased or questionable terms. (8)

False analogies Fallacies which make use of analogues that depend on false or questionable similarities, where the similarities are not relevant, or where there are differences between the analogues that outweigh their similarities. (12)

False dilemma An argument in the form of a dilemma in which one or more alternatives has been overlooked. (4, 7)

Form (in arguments) Relations among parts of an argument, each of which has an independent truth value; the grammar, as opposed to the content, of an argument. (4)

Formal logic The study and practice of reasoning in arguments symbolized so as to reveal truth-functional relationships among argument components.

Genus A general category to which something belongs. (5)

Hasty generalization A fallacy of insufficiency that occurs when a small, inappropriate, or unrepresentative sample is used as the basis for a broad rule or claim. (9)

Hedging A fallacy of confusion which occurs when an argument's key terms are so vague that one can change one's position to avoid criticism. (8)

Ignoring the facts A fallacy of assumption in which information that reasonably should have been taken into account is disregarded. (7)

Implication A valid deductive argument form in which the truth of one claim is said to depend on another ("If A . . . then B"), the supporting claim is said to be true ("A"), and the dependent claim is the conclusion ("B"). (4)

Inductive (argument) A form of argument in which evidence is offered to increase the probability that a conclusion is true. (4)

Informal logic The study and practice of reasoning in the form of ordinary language arguments.

Informative (language use) Language is used informatively when it is used to say something that could be either true or false: stating, commenting, explaining, answering questions, and so on. (3)

Intensive definition Gives the common features shared by everything correctly referred to by a term or an expression. (5)

Interrogative (language use) Language is used interrogatively when it is used to ask questions, find out information, inquire, and so on, and the desired response is an informative reply. (3)

Invalidity (invalid) An invalid deductive argument can have true reasons and a false conclusion; an invalid inductive argument is one in which the truth of the reasons does not increase the probability that the conclusion is true. (2)

Irrelevant association The willingness of people to see things as connected when they aren't. (6)

Lexical (or reportive) definition A list of the ways in which most people who speak the same language use a term. (5)

Logic The study and practice of reasoning and of judging how rationally persuasive arguments are. (1)

Logically relevant A sentence is logically relevant to a given conclusion if the truth of that sentence affects the probabliity that the conclusion is also true. (6)

Logical reasoning Offering good reasons and evidence to support a belief.

Manipulation (in place of argument) Using psychological tricks on yourself or others to induce belief. (1)

Moral (value) Having to do with matters of right and wrong, good and bad, duty, and obligation; often used interchangeably with "ethical." (3)

Necessary conditions Features required for something to count as an example of a given kind; for example, it is necessary for the president of the United States to be over thirty-five years old, but not sufficient. (5)

Objective Truth is independent of feelings, attitudes, opinions, or beliefs. (6)

Operational assumptions Background information needed to understand an argument. (7)

Opinion A personal feeling or attitude about a subject. (1)

Ostensive definition Gives one or more examples of things referred to by a term or an expression. (5)

Paradigm case An ideal example used to help define a term. (5)

Paraphrase Putting someone else's ideas into one's own words. (14)

Personally relevant A sentence is personally relevant for someone if it would tend to influence that person's beliefs, feelings, or attitudes. (6)

Personal attack A critical fallacy in which one tries to discredit the person giving an argument rather than questioning the argument itself. (13)

Persuasion Attempting to influence someone's opinions or beliefs. (2)

Persuasive (language use) Language is used persuasively when it is used to induce people to believe things by giving reasons, exerting emotional influence, using connotations to influence attitudes, and so forth. (3)

Persuasive paper An essay in which the main purpose is to influence someone to agree with your point of view. (10)

Pragmatic (value) Having to do with how well something fulfills its function(s) or lives up to criteria for things of its kind. (3)

Premise A stated assumption used as a reason. (2)

Projection Our tendency to adopt all of the feelings and attitudes required by roles we play in imagined situations; often used in advertising. (2)

Qualify (a conclusion) To make a less broad, universal, or certain claim than one might otherwise do. (9)

Question-begging accusations A fallacy of assumption in which efforts are made to discredit a position by making unproved criticisms that assume the position is already discredited. (7)

Question of concept An issue that depends on how one or more key terms is used. (3)

Question of fact An issue that can be settled completely by finding out the right information, from either direct observation or reliable sources. (3)

Question of interpretation An issue that involves making judgments or offering a theory about how best to organize, understand, or explain data. (3)

Question of value An issue that can be resolved only by reference to what people consider important (their values). (3)

Rational Deciding what to believe and how strongly to believe it on the basis of the best available evidence and reasoning. (1)

Reasoning The experience of seeing supporting or evidential connection between ideas and adjusting one's beliefs on the basis of those connections (2); more specifically, reasoning involves weighing evidence and reasons for beliefs; it also involves showing how shared beliefs can lead to, justify, or support further beliefs (also called "conclusions"). (1)

Reasons Support or justification for beliefs including evidence, value judgments, principles, and definitions. (1, 2)

Relevance, logical A sentence is logically relevant to a given conclusion if the truth of that sentence affects the probability that the conclusion is true. (6)

Relevance, personal A sentence is personally relevant for someone if it would tend to influence that person's beliefs, feelings, or attitudes. (6)

Rhetorical question (language use) A statement in the form of a question that can function informatively, directively, expressively, or persuasively. (3)

Soundness (sound) A sound argument is a valid argument with only true reasons; the conclusion of a sound deductive argument cannot be false. (2, 4)

Stipulative definition Specifies a particular meaning for a term within a given context or for special purposes. (5)

Straw man A critical fallacy in which one misrepresents an argument in order to make it easier to criticize. (13)

Subjective (claim) Depends on feelings, attitudes, opinions or beliefs. (6)

Substantive assumptions Background information on which an argument depends for its persuasive force. (7)

Sufficient conditions Features that are adequate to count something as an example of a given kind; for example, being George Bush is sufficient to be president of the United States, but not necessary. (5)

Sweeping generalization A fallacy of insufficiency that occurs when a rule or general claim is applied inappropriately to a nonstandard or unrepresentative particular case. (9)

Thesis The main idea of an essay. (10, 14)

Topic The general area someone writes about. (10)

Trivial objections A critical fallacy in which the aspects of the position one criticizes make little difference to whether or not the position is acceptable. (13)

True A sentence is true when what it expresses corresponds with the facts; what can be verified through interpersonally acceptable decision procedures. (2)

Vagueness (vague) An expression is vague if its meaning in the context cannot be clearly determined because it is not sufficiently specific. (5)

Validity (valid) A valid deductive argument cannot have true reasons and a false conclusion; a valid (or strong) inductive argument is one in which the truth of the reasons increases the probability that the conclusion is true. (2)

Value What someone considers important. (3)

You're just as bad A critical fallacy in which one tries to show that the person one argues with is not in a position to criticize because he's also guilty of a similar or worse error. (13)

Index

ACKNOWLEDGMENTS

P. 20 advertisement is used with permission of Prudential-Blackhurst, Realtors. P. 25 advertisement is reprinted with permission from Revlon, Inc. P. 62 excerpt is reprinted by permission of Oxford University Press. P. 64 excerpt Copyright © 1985 by Houghton Mifflin Company. Adapted and reprinted by permission from *The American Heritage Dictionary, Second College Edition.* P. 81 advertisement is reprinted with permission from United Way of Southeastern Michigan. P. 83 advertisement Copyright © 1987 Ms. Magazine. Reprinted by permission. P. 90 advertisement is reprinted by permission of the U.S. Council for Energy Awareness. P. 123 advertisement is reprinted by permission of Euphonic Technology. P. 163 article is reprinted by permission of *Weekly World News* and National Enquirer, Inc. P. 165 article appears courtesy of *Vogue.* Copyright © 1987 by the Conde Nast Publications, Inc. P. 168 advertisement is reprinted by permission of Tourneau, Inc. P. 172 advertisement is reprinted by permission of Rolex Watch USA, Inc. Pp. 180–181; 187 excerpt is reprinted by permission of Princeton University Press. Pp. 229–232 excerpts are reprinted by permission of Peter Singer. Pp. 233, 236 excerpts are reprinted by permission from John A. Krasney, Ph.D., and "Buffalo Physician," a periodical of the State University of New York at Buffalo School of Medicine. Pp. 236, 240 excerpts are reprinted by permission of *The Washingtonian.*